COMPASS
Your Guide for Leadership Development and Coaching

COMPASS

Your Guide for Leadership Development and Coaching

Peter Scisco
Elaine Biech
George Hallenbeck

CCL No. 00360
Copyright © 2017 Center for Creative Leadership.

978-1-60491-651-5 – Print
978-1-60491-652-2 – eBook (ePDF)
978-1-60491-654-6 – eBook (EPUB)

Cataloging in publication data on file with the Library of Congress.

Cover photo by Getty Images.

Published by CCL Press

Manager, Publication Development: Peter Scisco

Associate Editor: Shaun Martin

Design and Layout: Joanne Ferguson

Rights and Permissions: Kelly Lombardino

CONTENTS

Chapters 53–100 aren't included in this book because those numbers are reserved for future additions.

ABOUT THE AUTHORS

Peter Scisco

Peter (Pete) leads CCL's publishing program, which consists of CCL Press and publishing partnerships with commercial publishing houses. He is coauthor of *Change Now! 5 Steps to Better Leadership* and coeditor of the *CCL Handbook of Coaching: A Guide for the Leader Coach*. He holds a PhD in rhetoric from the University of North Carolina at Greensboro.

Elaine Biech

Elaine currently serves on CCL's Board of Governors. She's been the recipient of numerous Association of Talent Development (ATD) awards, including the Torch Award and the Gordon Bliss Memorial Award, and in 2012 she received the first CPLP Fellow Award from ASTD. She was also honored with the Wisconsin Women Entrepreneur's Mentor Award. She is the author or editor of more than 75 books, including *The Art and Science of Training* and the *ASTD Leadership Handbook*.

George Hallenbeck

George is director, commercialization, in CCL's Commercialization and Innovation Group. He is the author or coauthor of seven books, including *Learning Agility: Unlock the Lessons of Experience*. He holds a PhD in industrial-organizational psychology from Colorado State University.

ACKNOWLEDGMENTS

The authors are sincerely grateful to all of the CCL faculty who have participated in the work of CCL since its founding in 1970. Out of that work, CCL's understanding of leadership development has emerged in its assessments, its coaching practices, its publishing activities, and in many other ways.

Special thanks to Cynthia D. McCauley and Craig Chappelow, two CCL faculty members who reviewed earlier versions of this work and improved it. Also thank you to CCL's Sara Howard, the artist who assisted in designing the iconography that illustrates the book, and to Joanne Ferguson for her design and layout of the book. We also owe a debt to Felecia Corbett, senior librarian in CCL's special library, for her dogged research into the leader examples throughout this book. And sincere thanks to Taylor Scisco, who brought that research to life in stories of leadership in action.

To all of the CCL contributors whose work was foundational to this book and to all of the colleagues and thought partners outside CCL who joined with us in its development, thank you. And most importantly, thank you to the leaders and managers who have engaged with CCL over the years—they are the teachers from whom we all learn.

INTRODUCTION

You know this much about yourself at least—you're strong in some areas and weak in others. Who isn't? Because you're reading this, you might have received feedback about your leadership strengths and weaknesses from a trusted source or learned from a formal feedback program at work. Do you know when to rely on your strengths to carry you through? Are you aware of weaknesses you want to improve? And do you know how to round out your abilities so you don't count on the same remedy in every situation? This book can help you answer those questions and spur your development as a leader—at your pace and according to your priorities. And if you're a coach or a manager responsible for developing others, you can use this book to support developmental conversations and for devising developmental activities.

Through research and practice, CCL has confirmed the actions that contribute to effective leadership—the kind of leadership that generates an inclusive process among managers, peers, employees, and senior leaders and is marked by direction, alignment, and commitment. CCL calls these outcomes *DAC*, and when they are present, effective leadership is at play. Conversely, underdeveloped or overused competencies can act as a detriment to leadership, and their absence or willful avoidance can derail careers and even entire companies.

What's in This Book and Why It's Important

Leading often requires that you bring to bear a generous range of abilities on any given situation. Some of these situations, such as strategic planning or resource management, are predictable. Other situations, such as an unexpected competitor entering the scene or a radical turn in the marketplace, arise from unforeseen circumstances. Expected or not, when you confidently address those situations you ensure the sustainability of your organization. Given the consequences of globalization, the

1

Direction, alignment, and commitment are group outcomes of effective leadership.

contemporary sea change in demographics, continuing technological, economic, and market disruptions, and other markers of a world in flux, leaders well versed in a broad set of abilities can help ensure that their organizations and the people in them and associated with them thrive in uncertain times.

Who This Book Is For

This book is for leaders and managers looking to develop themselves and others. It is also for training and development professionals, either inside companies or working as independent consultants, who can use the book as a coaching tool, a blueprint for leader development plans, and in other ways. For leaders concerned with their development, dedicated to developing their people for more responsibility, and committed to organizational sustainability, this book will help in those efforts.

It's the goal of every leader at every level of an organization to create sustainability, whether for a business, a community service, or a government agency. H. Smith Richardson, whose ideas formed the foundation of CCL, was most concerned with the questions of why some organizations thrive while others wither. He sensed that organizational sustainability depended on creative leadership—a leadership capable of adapting, inventing, and renewing itself with changing times. The competencies at the core of this book are a distillation of the characteristics, actions, and perspectives at the heart of creative leadership—always becoming what is needed in any circumstance to galvanize organizations and help people move toward a thriving future.

How You Can Use This Book

Use *Compass* as a guide to figure out what skills you need to improve or what skills you need to develop in others. It makes an excellent companion to CCL's suite of 360-degree assessments*, from which many of the competencies are drawn. The book can also be used with assessments from other vendors. Browsing the table of contents or thumbing through the chapters will likely spark a response about one or more leadership competencies in areas that haven't received enough attention. A list of those competencies is the first step to building a framework for setting and achieving development goals. Dive into the relevant chapters to learn what kinds of results can be achieved with the addition or improvement of a competency. See what kinds of activities and tactics are especially suited for developing specific skill sets and knowledge. Consult the developmental opportunities in each chapter for ideas about how to practice those competencies or how to create those experiences for others.

There are many other uses for this book, depending on the role you play in your organization. Team leaders might address a competency area from a group perspective, for example. A manager can use the book as a guide and resource for developing direct reports. HR leaders and training consultants can use the book

- to support a mentoring program
- to create classes for early-career managers
- to pair with an executive coach
- as a focal point in coaching conversations
- to design a development path for high-potential employees

---

* CCL's 360-degree assessments include *Benchmarks for Executives, Benchmarks for Managers, Benchmarks for Learning Agility, Benchmarks by Design* (collectively known as the Benchmarks 360 Assessment Suite), and *Skillscope*. More information can be found at https://www.ccl.org/lead-it-yourself-solutions/assessments/

It should be noted that this book can work equally well outside of corporations and industry, as many of the same competencies are essential for community organizations, nonprofit groups, and government, even though the settings and challenges differ from commercial enterprises.

How This Book Is Organized

The book is divided into four sections. Part One concentrates on the four essential competencies every leader needs to develop: communication, influence, learning agility, and self-awareness. Part Two contains 48 additional competencies, derived from CCL research and practice, and Part Three deals with five career derailers and what you can do about them to avoid that fate. Part Four is a guide to goal setting, using an approach that CCL's research and practice have shown to be effective.

Each of the book's competency chapters opens with a simple description of the skill and a brief overview to provide some context—why it's important to leaders, what effects its mastery can produce, and the consequences of not developing the competency. Following the overview, Leadership in Action tells a story drawn from real-life accounts of leaders displaying their skill in the competency area. You can look to those stories for examples to emulate, for inspiration, and for understanding the effect of that competency on other people and on organizations.

What High Performance Looks Like lists descriptive words and phrases for how leaders appear to others when performing the competency well. What's in Your Way? presents common obstacles to development. The Coach Yourself section poses reflective questions designed to spur thinking about the areas of focus in which the competency can be developed. The sections Improve Now and Developmental Opportunities provide tactics and suggestions for developing skills. Improve Now items are quick changes, and Developmental Opportunities are longer in duration and might require buy-in and support from a boss, team, or someone else.

The Activity Center contains links to worksheets and exercises that help to develop skill and competency. Activities can be accessed and downloaded from the book's resource site at www.ccl.org/compassbook. A list of Related Competencies follows. Building your skill in those areas (or some of them) will support development of other competencies. And finally, Resources suggests additional places to look for help and advice.

Take special note of Part Three, which deals with common career *derailers* that CCL research identifies as damaging to careers. A derailed leader is one who, after having reached a level of success in the organization, is fired, demoted, or involuntarily reaches a career plateau. Before these managers derailed, their organizations saw them as having high potential for advancement, having an impressive track record of results, and holding an established leadership position. But then something happened. CCL research shows that the most common causes of career derailment are predictable. The chapters in this section show what kinds of skills and knowledge need to be developed to keep a career on track and reduce the risk of derailing.

Finally, in Part Four, *Compass* covers how to set development goals as you make the personal changes necessary to gain the skills you need. This section talks about the essential ingredients for development and how to best go about it. It also discusses how to make yourself ready for development, actions to consider for getting others to notice the changes you are making, and information on goal-setting that will increase the chances of your success, according to CCL research and practice (hint: don't start with a goal). Finally, *Compass* looks ahead, beyond the competencies we're familiar with. Diverse fields such as neuroscience, network analysis, mindfulness practice, and others may generate competencies that become significant, even critical, to leaders' success in the future.

Part One
THE FUNDAMENTAL FOUR

Of all the competencies leaders bring to bear on challenges and use to create results, CCL highlights four that are crucial to generating direction, alignment, and commitment. These are communication, influence, learning agility, and self-awareness. The fundamental nature of these four is backed by CCL's research and its experiences training thousands of leaders. These competencies are relevant to leadership at any stage in your career and at any level of an organization, no matter its size or status (commercial, educational, nonprofit, or community).

As described in this book's Introduction, CCL believes leadership involves more than the person identified as the leader. It is a social process that enables individuals to work together to produce results they could never achieve working as individuals. Central to the process are the interactions and exchanges between leaders and group members and among group members themselves.

It's not hard to see, then, why communication, influence, learning agility, and self-awareness are such critical competencies. Plainly, a leader cannot inspire commitment, encourage alignment, or guide others in a common direction without communicating with them. And leadership cannot emerge if leaders don't remove obstacles to communication so that organizational members can interact freely to establish trust and collaboration. Influence operates similarly—without the skill to influence others and the willingness to be influenced, leaders are hard pressed to move people toward a common goal.

Self-awareness is somewhat more subtle but no less critical. To interact with others and contribute to direction, alignment, and commitment, leaders need a sound idea of how others see them. Self-awareness isn't navel-gazing. On the contrary, the *self* in self-awareness is

7

the self that others identify as you. Your attention to how you affect others influences how others respond to you and helps others know what to expect from you.

Rounding out the core four, learning agility accompanies leaders throughout their careers. Leaders who embrace new experiences and who can learn quickly from them and apply those lessons to new situations and challenges will face fewer career roadblocks. No matter how insightful a strategy, unforeseen challenges always occur to potentially disrupt the leadership process. The ability to take what is learned in one situation and use it in a similar situation keeps leadership on track toward results that matter.

1

Communication

Speak, write, and listen clearly and consistently.

The greatest opportunity and greatest challenge for any leader is to communicate effectively. Listen, convey your ideas and emotions with clarity and authenticity, and adapt your personal speaking as needed for the situation and audience to foster an environment of trust. Inspire others not only with your speech but also with your written communications. Write clearly, succinctly, and logically. Avoid jargon, obscure terms, and other distractions that interfere with your readers' understanding.

Consistently articulate your vision, goals, and objectives for your team and the organization. Demystify your organization's priorities. Speak and write clearly and with passion. Acknowledge challenges in realistic terms that others readily understand. Connect with others by listening attentively, probing when necessary to get below the surface of conversations. You will find your way to leadership less difficult, because other people want to work with effective communicators and the trust and commitment they inspire. See the effect of skillful communication amid the confusion of a natural disaster in the story that follows.

Leadership in Action

In late October of 2012, Hurricane Sandy made landfall in the northeastern United States, causing billions of dollars in damage and costing dozens of lives. In the aftermath of the storm, neighborhoods and businesses were left without electricity and streets were blocked with snow and debris. As the mayor of Newark, New Jersey, Cory Booker faced an impossible task: returning his city to working order and normalcy after an unprecedented disaster.

In such a situation, public morale is as critical a factor as logistical preparation. To manage the public feeling in his city, Booker led from the front, personally touring snowed-in neighborhoods and tweeting round-the-clock updates. Twitter is a public forum, so all affected citizens (indeed, anyone with a computer or cell phone) could access, repeat, and reply to Booker's tweets. This created an open network of communication that served two important purposes: keeping Booker informed of trouble spots in the city and keeping the populace informed about the recovery effort. Tweets are necessarily brief, so Booker's strategy was comparatively low-effort and high-yield. Quoted in an online story by Everett Merrill, Booker says: "The reality is, it doesn't take as much time as people think it does. For me, [Twitter is] a very powerful tool to connect with hundreds of thousands of New Jerseyans."

Although the damage left by the storm created an overwhelming strain on resources and staff, Booker was able to supplement recovery efforts with open communication. By maintaining an earnest connection with his constituents, he was able to reduce uncertainty and stress for the citizens of Newark. Although tweets couldn't make the plows move any faster, Booker's constituents knew they were heard, understood, and cared for, according to Krissah Thompson of *The Washington Post* and Gabrielle Levy of UPI. It was the communication citizens needed during and after Sandy.

What High Performance Looks Like

Leaders who communicate well

- are crisp, clear, articulate
- tailor their communications based on others' needs, motivations, and agendas
- listen carefully to others' ideas and suggestions
- show a command of nonverbal communication—smile, show confidence, and project calm or enthusiasm as appropriate
- communicate equally well in speech and in writing
- use multiple modes of communication, such as speeches, email, and video
- make organizational goals and plans clear
- motivate others with their speaking and writing
- are forthright in expressing themselves
- practice active listening
- command attention when speaking
- convey ideas through lively examples, stories, and images
- keep people informed of future changes that may affect them

What's in Your Way?

Communicating is a highly visible skill. It's readily apparent when leaders can't present their ideas and intentions clearly and distinctly to others. An inability to communicate well may isolate you from the hum of conversation in your organization and cause you to miss opportunities to build strong and essential personal connections with others. If others perceive a lack of clarity or authenticity in how you communicate, their

11

beliefs can undermine commitment and trust, leading to mistakes, missed goals, and low engagement. Review the following list and note the items that you believe make it difficult for you to communicate at your best.

- ❏ You have not developed attentive listening skills.
- ❏ You don't understand the specific needs and interests of your audience.
- ❏ You pay more attention to the content of communication rather than how it connects emotionally with your audience.
- ❏ You fail to convey the big picture to your employees—they do not understand the rationale for key decisions.
- ❏ You spend more time thinking about and refining the appearance of your slide show than its content.
- ❏ You're afraid your ideas will be criticized.
- ❏ You're introverted and don't know how to use your particular way of processing and relaying information to build memorable communication.
- ❏ You overwhelm people with details that they don't need to know.
- ❏ You address the wrong audience or you don't understand what your audience's needs are.
- ❏ You focus so much attention on listening to others that you don't express your own perspective enough.
- ❏ You've received feedback that your communication style comes across as slick or manipulative.

Coach Yourself

To develop your skill as a communicator, create goals in areas that call for you to persuade groups of people, place you in the position of informing groups about organizational projects, or otherwise challenge your ability to get ideas and positions in front of others. These questions can help:

- How can you communicate your values or priorities more clearly?

- Are you empathetic toward other people? Do you show empathy?

- Do you understand what people want or need?

- What percentage of the time do you talk compared with listening?

- Have you established and honed your personal style of communication? Are you able to adapt this style to meet the different needs of your colleagues?

- Have you ever seen a recording of yourself communicating? What emotions did you see yourself convey? Does your body language match your speech?

- What training opportunities are available to help you improve your communication skills?

Improve Now

Get others' perspectives first. Before offering your own ideas and perceptions, take a moment to let others provide their point of view. This will give you more insight into your audience and allow you to tailor your communication appropriately. This is especially effective when exploring issues that are complex and when there might be a diversity of views.

Focus on "we." Leaders who use inclusive language, like "we" and "us," inspire their listeners and draw on shared effort and interests.

Tell stories. Leaders who give examples through brief, relevant stories create more engaging and effective communication. For example, a story about how a problem was solved or about someone who did something notable helps your listeners to see themselves in the story. Tie the story to the key message you are trying to convey to your audience.

Stop spinning. People have a highly developed sense of when they're being sold a bill of goods. Don't try to get around it—just be straightforward and open.

Be an active listener. People who listen are listened to. Active listening strategies—paying attention, withholding judgment, reflecting, clarifying, summarizing, sharing, and reading nonverbal cues—can be learned, practiced, and used to improve your communication skills.

Learn to speak to the hearts of people. Try talking about your vision or the needs of the audience, rather than just delivering facts and arguments. Connect with them on an emotional level, not just a logical one.

Know your audience. Know not only who is going to be in the room, but their level of understanding about what you will be communicating, likely perceptions, and potential questions and concerns. This is especially important when communicating to multiple groups on the same issue. Use what you know about your audience to adjust your message and your delivery to align with their expectations.

Learn from the best. Find mentors or role models who communicate well and watch what they do. See if they can provide you with feedback and ideas on how you can improve your communication.

Work with a voice or communication coach. If your intonation or speaking style isn't helping to hold your audience's attention, work with someone trained to develop speaking skills.

Invest in media or presentation skills training. If your delivery isn't dynamic and your audience is falling asleep on you, hire experts to train you on making more compelling performances.

Get me rewrite! Find a brief quote from a CEO in a newspaper or online. Rewrite it, removing all spin and jargon. Consider the difference between the two versions from a listener's or reader's point of view.

Do a strengths and weaknesses audit. List three of your personal communication strengths and one weakness. Try to think of what others would say about your communication skills. Remember, communication is not only about speaking or writing but also about listening. How would you go about building on your strengths? For your weakness, pick one simple step you can do to improve and commit to practicing it for the next few weeks.

Developmental Opportunities

- Take on tasks that allow you to practice communicating with different audiences.

- Make a presentation to top management.

- Serve as a subject matter expert in media interviews.

- Speak to external groups as a representative of your organization.

- Write reports for your boss.

- Write for your organization's blog and social media accounts.

- Join Toastmasters to practice public speaking and get feedback in a low-risk setting.

- Start or join a leadership book club in your organization—use the club's discussions to help you learn different ways of giving your communication greater impact.

Activity Center

Review and download these activities you can use for your development or with your team from this book's resource page at www.ccl.org/compassbook.

Communication: Listen to Everyone, Even When . . .
Communication: It's Your Reputation

Related Competencies

Coach and Develop Others
Credibility and Integrity
Influence
Interpersonal Savvy
Vision

Resources

Bolton, R. (1986). *People skills: How to assert yourself, listen to others, and resolve conflicts*. New York, NY: Touchstone.

Booher, D. (2007). *The voice of authority: 10 communication strategies every leader needs to know*. New York, NY: McGraw-Hill.

Cain, S. (2013). *Quiet: The power of introverts in a world that can't stop talking*. New York, NY: Broadway Books.

Harvard Business Review Press. (2014). *Giving effective feedback*. (HBR 20-Minute Manager Series). Boston, MA: Harvard Business School Publishing.

Hoppe, M. H. (2006). *Active listening: Improve your ability to listen and lead*. Greensboro, NC: Center for Creative Leadership.

Levy, G. (2012, Oct. 30). Super mayor Cory Booker takes on Superstorm Sandy, one crisis at a time. UPI. Retrieved from http://www.upi.com/blog/2012/10/30/Super-mayor-Cory-Booker-takes-on-Superstorm-Sandy-one-crisis-at-a-time/5291351611808/

Maxwell, J. C. (2010). *Everyone communicates, few connect: What the most effective people do differently.* Nashville, TN: Thomas Nelson.

Merrill, E. (2015, Jan. 4). Inside the twitter world of U.S. Sen. Cory Booker. *MyCentralJersey.Com*. Retrieved from http://www.mycentraljersey.com/story/news/local/new-jersey/2015/01/04/sen-cory-booker-twitter/21192545/

Patterson, K., Grenny, J., McMillan, R., & Switzler, A. (2011). *Crucial conversations: Tools for talking when stakes are high* (2nd ed.). New York, NY: McGraw-Hill.

Prince, D. W., & Hoppe, M. H. (2000). *Communicating across cultures*. Greensboro, NC: Center for Creative Leadership.

Scharlatt, H. (2008). *Selling your ideas to your organization*. Greensboro, NC: Center for Creative Leadership.

Scharlatt, H., & Smith, R. (2014). *Influence: Gaining commitment, getting results* (2nd ed.). Greensboro, NC: Center for Creative Leadership.

Thompson, K. (2010, Dec. 30). Newark mayor receiving avalanche of attention for snowstorm tweets. *The Washington Post*. Retrieved from http://www.washingtonpost.com/wp-dyn/content/article/2010/12/29/AR2010122904240.html

2

Influence

Persuade others to gain their cooperation and commitment.

Perhaps more than any other skill, the ability to influence employees, partners, suppliers, vendors, customers, and others is critical to your leadership success. You don't want to fall into the habit of barking orders rather than inspiring commitment. It's through the latter that you create high levels of engagement that lead to high productivity. Your greatest leadership asset is your ability to understand and persuade others.

Influential leaders know how to get others to work with them, whether or not formal authority exists. Build collaborative relationships and accept that influence involves some give and take. With this knowledge and ability, you will build a broad network of supporters inside and outside the organization. Leverage that network in versatile ways to confront various situations. In recent years, at least in the United States, almost no one has wielded influence like Oprah Winfrey. Let's see how she does it.

Leadership in Action

As an internationally recognizable media juggernaut, Oprah Winfrey is a great example of what an influential leader can accomplish at the highest levels. Through gradual expansion of her reach, she has attained a level of influence that can change national conversations and transform individuals into overnight success stories.

During her first season, when Oprah could hardly be considered a household name, CNN's Megan Clifford (2017) describes how Oprah filmed a show in Forsyth County, Georgia, where not a single black person had lived for 75 years. This served as a provocation and an invitation to a public conversation that had remained under wraps for generations. Now, more than 7,000 African-Americans call Forsyth County home. Oprah influenced these events by putting the uncomfortable facts on television, where they couldn't be ignored.

By framing public conversation, Oprah has brought much new thinking into the lives of her followers. Her candid and vulnerable conversations about weight loss and personal nutrition have positioned her as a relatable authority on diet and personal care. Her book club keeps her fans well-read, with selections ranging from contemporary memoirs to classic fiction. All the while she has continued to open doors on taboo subjects, including addiction, infidelity, and domestic abuse.

Oprah didn't hammer away at hard social problems every day. Some days she just talked about new movies or a new cookbook. These are things people care about in their daily lives, and by keeping herself involved in those conversations, Oprah built her influence. When she decides to cast a light on something hidden, her network of followers is already present and already looking.

What High Performance Looks Like

Influential leaders

- understand what motivates people
- can promote an idea or vision and persuade others to take the same perspective
- have an astute sense of organizational and personal politics
- can influence up, down, and across the organization
- can influence others without using formal authority
- can get things done by finding common ground when working with a group over whom they have no formal control
- possess an extensive network of contacts necessary to build support and bolster the power of their influence
- are seen as persuasive and inspirational, sparking others to join their efforts
- are connected to other influences in the organization
- are regarded as collaborative and flexible
- practice active listening
- cross boundaries to build partnerships and share resources
- are willing to listen and to be influenced

What's in Your Way?

Leaders who struggle to influence others may give the impression that they can't achieve important organizational goals. They struggle leading large, strategic projects requiring collaboration among various entities.  Leaders who cannot be influenced will find it difficult to influence others. Check the items on the list below to identify what might stand between you and the influence you need to lead.

- ❏ You aren't assertive.

- ❏ It's hard for you to empathize with others or to see things from their perspective.

- ❏ You're unwilling to be influenced or to participate in a give-and-take of opinions and positions.

- ❏ You don't invest time in other people and don't build the relationships that support your influence.

- ❏ You're inflexible and unwilling to meet the needs of other people.

- ❏ You're arrogant and don't value the input of others—and they know it.

- ❏ You approach relationships focused solely on what you can get out of them.

- ❏ You expect others to reach out to you.

- ❏ You've received feedback that others see you as selfish or pursuing your own agenda.

- ❏ You've received feedback that others see you as a distraction and unaligned with the company's current direction.

- ❏ You overlook people who could extend your influence.

- ❏ You've received feedback that people sense you are always trying to sell something.

- ❏ You push ideas that often fail.

- ❏ You grow impatient and frustrated with resistance to your ideas.

Coach Yourself

To develop your influencing skill, create goals in areas that require your cooperation, that call for a new answer to an old problem, and that require you to get someone to help you who doesn't directly report to you. These questions can help you define a focus area:

- Who are the gatekeepers in your organization? How can you earn their trust?

- Whom do you struggle to influence: peers, direct reports, or higher management? How do their needs differ? How can you vary your approach?

- Who in your organization is most experienced in influencing others to get things done? Would they be open to giving you some guidance?

- How can you cultivate new supporters? Are you willing to reach out and develop different relationships that will add to your influence?

- Whom can you engage to help you achieve your vision? What responsibilities would they be willing to take on?

Improve Now

Consider the other person's situation. What can you give them? Find a way to appeal to the common good or common interests.

Highlight the benefits. Explain how carrying out a request or supporting a proposal will benefit other people or help them advance in their careers.

Identify how you can help. Consider all of the people you are trying to influence. What does each person need? What resources are at your disposal that you can use to fill these needs?

Depart from the comfortable. Your default methods of influence may come naturally to you, but they might not be the most effective. Leave your comfort zone to explore other methods. For example, if you tend to use data to influence people or if you tend to rely on email, meet with people in person and focus more on your vision or the needs of the person you're trying to influence.

Align yourself with other influencers. Whom do you know who has a gift for crafting a business case? Telling a story? Applying pressure? Imagine that you are building a diverse team of influencers made up of the best and brightest—who makes the team?

Create a coalition. Enlist the support of others to help you influence or use their endorsement of your request or proposal in your efforts to influence others.

Vary your influencing tactics. Make appeals based on logic, emotion, or a sense of cooperation. The most effective influencers know how to use all three approaches.

Explore what's negotiable. What is possible given current constraints? In what ways can other people be flexible?

Get creative. Coming up with solutions that are attractive to many different people can be your toughest challenge. Relaxing and stepping back from the problem allows creative solutions to surface. Give yourself time to reflect on how you might positively influence the situation.

Developmental Opportunities

- Seek experiences in which you have to collaborate across organizational boundaries with groups that have competing or different priorities than yours.

- Ask your group to generate a new idea to implement; work to move that idea through the organization and get the necessary support from others.

- Manage an annual organizational event with high visibility.

- Take a negotiations class.

- Regain a lost customer.

- Play a key role in a community fund-raising event.

- Work with a colleague in another function on a project proposal.

Activity Center

Review and download these activities you can use for your development or with your team from this book's resource page at www.ccl.org/compassbook.

Influence: Influence Up
Influence: Planning to Influence

Related Competencies

Boundary Spanning
Communication
Interpersonal Savvy
Organizational Savvy
Relationship Management

Resources

Carnegie, D. (1937/2009). *How to win friends and influence people*. New York, NY: Simon & Schuster.

Clifford, M. (2011, May 20). How Oprah has changed the way we live. *CNN.* Retrieved from http://www.cnn.com/2011/SHOWBIZ/TV/05/13/oprah.influence/

Center for Creative Leadership. (2013). *Interpersonal savvy: Building and maintaining solid working relationships.* Greensboro, NC: Author.

Gentry, W. A., & Leslie, J. B. (2013). *Developing political savvy.* Greensboro, NC: Center for Creative Leadership.

Scharlatt, H., & Smith, R. (2011). *Influence: Gaining commitment, getting results* (2nd ed.). Greensboro, NC: Center for Creative Leadership.

Zack, D. (2010). *Networking for people who hate networking: A field guide for introverts, the overwhelmed, and the underconnected*. San Francisco, CA: Berrett-Koehler.

3
Learning Agility

Seek out diverse experiences and apply lessons learned to new challenges.

Learning agility is a constellation of behaviors that support curiosity, insight, resourcefulness, adaptability, and resilience. Beneath all these behaviors stands a single principle that has held up through years of research from CCL and others and untold generations of everyday routines and practice: experience is the best teacher.

Learning-agile leaders have a talent for knowing what to do when they don't know what to do. They are committed to broadening their skills, and seeking new challenges makes them versatile and adaptive, capable of succeeding in a variety of situations. They often develop a reputation for leading the organization through changing, ambiguous times. Further, learning-agile leaders quickly grasp the lessons of experience. They can rapidly size up a new situation, compare it with previous experiences, and apply what they have learned previously that is analogous to the current circumstances.

Learning agility doesn't draw only from successful experiences. Leaders who become learning agile also take lessons from setbacks, hardships, and failures. Every experience is fodder for development in the eyes of the learning-agile leader. And, as we see when we visit the lab of James Lovelock, the benefits of learning agility aren't confined to corporations.

Leadership in Action

Thirty years after their initial publication, the ideas presented in James Lovelock's *Gaia: A New Look at Life on Earth* finally percolated into the mainstream of environmental science. In his book, Lovelock explores the idea of the planet Earth as a kind of "super-organism,"

a unified system of interdependent cycles. The idea is that the super-organism is resilient and ever-changing, but too rapid a change can break down enough smaller systems that the major system itself is thrown into collapse. This interpretation of ecology is now so widely accepted that it's a part of popular culture. What gave Lovelock the idea?

In brief, it was the sum of Lovelock's desire to learn new things. Fantasy and eco-thriller author Ian Irvine describes how Lovelock began his scientific career directly out of secondary school with an apprenticeship program at a firm of consulting chemists (2005). He was able to earn a scholarship with his work and then studied at the University of Manchester, where his work was so exact (a credit to his apprenticeship) that he was initially suspected of cheating. His dedication to exact measurement led him to invent the electron capture detector, a device that can detect tiny particles in the atmosphere. But it was his observations about the atmosphere of Mars that led to his theory about Earth as a super-organism.

When asked by NASA how scientists could go about testing whether life existed on Mars, he suggested measuring the chemistry of the Martian atmosphere. Because living ecologies create a broad, dynamic mix of gases, the relative nothingness of the Martian atmosphere suggested that no life existed there.

Lovelock applied that idea to Earth's ecology and developed his Gaia theory. Initially published for a layman audience, the theory was scoffed at by scientists. But decades later, in the face of rapidly expanding ecological change on Earth, the Gaia theory commands much more respect.

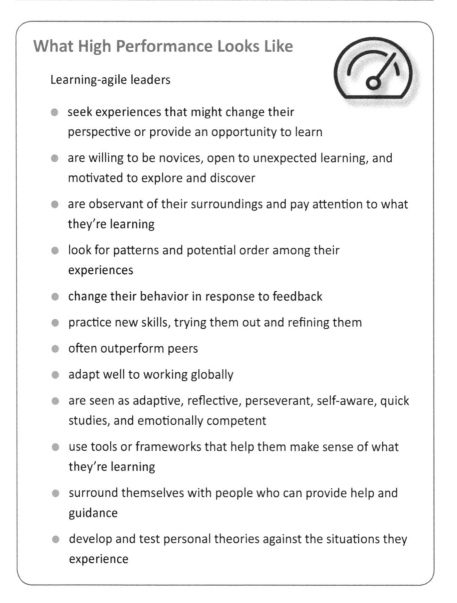

What High Performance Looks Like

Learning-agile leaders

- seek experiences that might change their perspective or provide an opportunity to learn
- are willing to be novices, open to unexpected learning, and motivated to explore and discover
- are observant of their surroundings and pay attention to what they're learning
- look for patterns and potential order among their experiences
- change their behavior in response to feedback
- practice new skills, trying them out and refining them
- often outperform peers
- adapt well to working globally
- are seen as adaptive, reflective, perseverant, self-aware, quick studies, and emotionally competent
- use tools or frameworks that help them make sense of what they're learning
- surround themselves with people who can provide help and guidance
- develop and test personal theories against the situations they experience

What's in Your Way?

Many organizations see learning agility as a sign of potential in a leader. If you struggle to adopt learning-agile habits, you can hurt your chances of advancing in your career and miss opportunities that often go to people identified as capable of taking on roles with important responsibilities. A reputation for not adapting quickly and easily to new challenges and having a limited comfort zone might keep you in narrowly defined roles. Take a look at the following list and mark what you think might prevent you from honing your learning agility.

- ❑ You avoid challenges to your knowledge or skills.
- ❑ You're not willing to make the effort to learn.
- ❑ You're in a later stage of your career and don't feel a pressing need to learn.
- ❑ You have yet to experience failure and the learning that can come from it.
- ❑ You're overconfident or complacent.
- ❑ You prefer stability and comfort.
- ❑ You take on learning assignments that relate only to your core career path.
- ❑ You draw the wrong conclusions from your experiences.
- ❑ You apply lessons from one situation to a new situation that don't fit.
- ❑ You spend too much time learning and not doing.
- ❑ You respond defensively or dismissively to feedback.

Coach Yourself

Developing learning agility requires a willingness to immerse yourself in new and challenging situations that broaden and expand your experiences. Create goals in areas that are unfamiliar to you and then work hard at learning the lessons those experiences offer. These questions can help you focus on such areas:

- ● What are your most significant learning experiences and what lessons did you learn from them? How can you apply them?

- How could a mentor help you learn and grow? To whom can you turn for assistance and advice?

- Reflect on past struggles in your life and ask yourself what you need to learn to meet similar difficulties in the future. What were you missing in the past?

- What new experiences would help you to learn and develop what you need to thrive in the future? How can you challenge yourself to get that experience?

- Do you have a support network? Who will tell you the truth even if it's unpleasant to hear? Who values you for who you are and wants to help you become who you want to be?

- Do you set aside time to reflect? Is reflection part of your daily or weekly routine? How can you plan for it and make it a habit?

- What is your greatest achievement, and what skills did you use to accomplish it? How can you leverage these skills in other areas?

Improve Now

Break up your routine. Doing things the same way repeatedly, even if it works, is a detriment to learning and growth. Intentionally experiment with new ways of doing things. Observe what happens and monitor your results, including what doesn't work. Once new habits start to form, continue to push yourself to reinvent.

Commit to reflecting on and monitoring your progress and learning. Make it a part of your work—put it on your calendar so you can make sure it happens.

Seek feedback. Get observations from others on your behavior to identify strengths and weaknesses. Listen openly and ask questions to deepen your understanding. Accept what others perceive as their reality and show your appreciation for their input and guidance.

Learn your preference for how you accept, understand, and use information. Do you talk your ideas out with others, or do you prefer to reflect on them until you feel ready to communicate them to others? Do you rely on pro-and-con lists to make decisions, or do you contemplate the potential reactions from others to your decision? Being aware of your learning preferences will help you decode the reactions others have toward you. If you prefer to reflect before acting, for example, some people may perceive you as indecisive. But you aren't—you just prefer to fine-tune your decisions before publicizing them. Let people who consider you indecisive know your preference so they can adapt their perspective.

Challenge yourself. Identify your growth needs, and then intentionally immerse yourself in situations that will push you to your limits in these areas. This may be uncomfortable and frightening at first, but it is important for you to reframe these threats as opportunities if you hope to gain the most learning from them.

Take risks. Some leaders are content to accept the status quo and remain safe within their comfort zones. In order to become a learning-agile leader, you must be willing to accept new roles, pursue new opportunities, advocate for the unusual, and risk the possibility of failure.

Challenge the status quo. Move beyond business-as-usual to discover new and unique ways of doing things. Innovating new practices requires considerable bravery and ingenuity but is essential to become a high-performing, learning-agile leader.

Seek developmental relationships. Search for members of your organization who exemplify expertise in the areas you wish to develop. Ask them about their experiences in those areas, what they learned, and how they used those lessons in other areas. Use what they say to form your own path toward learning agility.

Pursue lifelong development. Identify your personal and professional goals, and regularly assess whether you are making progress toward achieving them. Stagnation can derail even the most promising leaders from achieving their full potential.

Keep a leadership journal. Opportunities for learning and practice can reveal themselves through journaling, and recording your experiences is an excellent way to capture your feelings and thoughts as you are learning. Take time to jot down your thoughts and feelings in a journal when you meet a new situation so you can review it later—much like looking at an old picture.

Developmental Opportunities

- Ask your manager for a special assignment for which he or she feels you are qualified but that also challenges your skills and knowledge. Make a list of the skills the assignment requires and candidly measure yourself on each one.

- Seek an additional job assignment that adds diversity to your work or requires you to work in a completely different context from what you're used to.

- Start a new group, club, or team at work based on a common interest in exploring a new topic or practice.

- Take over a project that is in trouble or failing.

- Lead a benchmarking team that visits and learns from other organizations.

- Work in a short-term assignment at another office, in another region, or in another country.

Activity Center

Review and download these activities you can use for your development or with your team from this book's resource page at www.ccl.org/compassbook.

Learning Agility: Find a Mentor
Learning Agility: Create a Mind Map

Related Competencies

Flexibility

Problem Solving

Resilience

Resourcefulness

Self-Awareness

Self-Development

Tolerating Ambiguity

Resources

Hallenbeck, G. (2016). *Learning agility: Unlock the lessons of experience.* Greensboro, NC: Center for Creative Leadership.

Irvine, I. (2005, Dec. 2). James Lovelock: The green man. *The Independent.* Retrieved from http://www.independent.co.uk/news/people/profiles/james-lovelock-the-green-man-517953.html

McCauley, C. D. (2006). *Developmental assignments: Creating learning experiences without changing jobs.* Greensboro, NC: Center for Creative Leadership.

McCauley, C. D., DeRue, D. S., Yost, P. R., & Taylor, S. (Eds.). *Experience-driven leader development: Models, tools, best practices, and advice for on-the-job development.* San Francisco, CA: John Wiley & Sons.

McCauley, C. D., & McCall, M. W., Jr. (Eds.). (2014). *Using experience to develop leadership talent: How organizations leverage on-the-job development.* San Francisco, CA: Jossey-Bass.

Meyer, P. (2015). *The agility shift: Creating agile and effective leaders, teams, and organizations.* New York, NY: Taylor & Francis Group.

Morgan, A., & Barden, M. (2015). *A beautiful constraint: How to transform your limitations into advantages, and why it's everyone's business.* Hoboken, NJ: John Wiley & Sons.

Ruderman, M. N., & Ohlott, P. J. (2001). *Learning from life: Turning life's lessons into leadership experience.* Greensboro, NC: Center for Creative Leadership.

Scisco, P., McCauley, C. D., Leslie, J. B., & Elsey, R. (2014). *Change now! Five steps to better leadership.* Greensboro, NC: Center for Creative Leadership.

Wilson, M. S., & Chandrasekar, N. A. (2014). *Experience explorer facilitator's guide set.* Greensboro, NC: Center for Creative Leadership.

Yip, J. (2009). *Return on experience: Learning leadership at work.* Greensboro, NC: Center for Creative Leadership.

4

Self-Awareness

Use reflection and feedback to gain insight into your strengths and address your development needs.

We all have a mental picture of ourselves—what we believe, how we treat others, what talents and skills we carry. But do you have an accurate picture of yourself as others see you? If you asked one of your peers to rate you on a specific skill, could you accurately predict what that person would say? Self-awareness is your understanding of your strengths and development needs. Your awareness of the positive qualities you want to demonstrate, when matched to your expectation of how others perceive those qualities, will help you create positive results from your interactions with others. Can you think of another example of self-awareness so keenly developed as that of the Dalai Lama?

Leadership in Action

As the spiritual head of Tibetan Buddhism, the Dalai Lama knows a thing or two about self-awareness. Understanding and sharing knowledge of the inner life of the human being is his mission, and indeed, it's his job. However, not everyone can claim unlimited time to plumb the depths of their own souls, so the Dalai Lama has commissioned a tool to help the rest of us.

He calls it "The Atlas of Emotion," and it's a fusion of meditative self-reflection, psychological science, and infographics. In *The New York Times*, Kevin Randall writes that the Dalai Lama commissioned psychologist Paul Ekman to construct the project, envisioning a fun and enjoyable tool that can help any person get a better grip on their internal life. The purpose of all this self-reflection, according to the Dalai Lama, is to learn how to take constructive action from that calm state. Describing the project to Dr. Ekman, the Dalai Lama said, "When we wanted to get to the New World, we needed a map. So make a map of emotions so we can get to a calm state" (2016).

The result is a kind of super-Venn diagram, illustrating a person's emotional topography by dividing the material into five core emotions: Enjoyment, Sadness, Anger, Fear, and Disgust. Within these groups and between them lie the uncountable facets of a person's overall emotional state.

Dr. Ekman stresses that the map is not a scientific publication for peer review but is "built around knowledge and wisdom, not data." The Dalai Lama is equally eager to keep religion out of the picture. This gives the map a universal application, intended for use by everybody seeking self-awareness (Design, n.d.).

What High Performance Looks Like

Self-aware leaders

- understand their impact on situations and people

- adjust their behavior to suit circumstances

- have an accurate picture of their strengths and weaknesses and are willing to improve

- are aware of their feelings

- reflect on and learn from experience

- seek feedback to improve

- are open to criticism and can hear negative feedback without getting defensive

- embrace what they need to learn

- respond well to new situations that require them to stretch and grow

- compensate for weaknesses

- capitalize on strengths

- hold fast to personal values while considering the values that other people hold

- are seen as authentic, attentive, thoughtful, responsive, reflective, and observant

What's in Your Way?

A lack of self-awareness distorts your perceptions of how others perceive your actions. That distortion limits your ability to calibrate your behavior to the people and situations you encounter—a key piece to influencing others and to building and maintaining working relationships that

35

produce results. If you fail to recognize the positive and negative impact that your words and deeds are having on others, you might be shocked to learn what people really think about your performance and how they feel about you. The result is confusion and frustration for you and others, leading to mistakes and missed opportunities. Review the following list and note the items that might give you trouble developing self-awareness.

- ❏ You don't reflect on what you learn from your interactions with others.
- ❏ You have punished people for giving you feedback in the past.
- ❏ You don't believe you have any room for improvement.
- ❏ Your organization or its culture doesn't support continuous learning or open feedback.
- ❏ You avoid situations in which you are vulnerable to criticism.
- ❏ You have limited experience receiving feedback.
- ❏ People in your organization are encouraged to hide their flaws to maintain an image of perfection.
- ❏ You become more focused on yourself rather than on your team.
- ❏ You respond defensively to feedback.
- ❏ People hesitate to tell you something because they don't want to hurt or offend you.
- ❏ You act as someone you are not.
- ❏ You follow advice that doesn't fit you or the situation you're in.
- ❏ You downplay positive feedback.
- ❏ You doubt people will trust the "new you."

Coach Yourself

To become more self-aware, create goals in areas that accentuate the accuracy of your perceptions of how others see you and respond to your actions. These questions can help you refine that focus:

- Do you react to feedback defensively? If you do, ask yourself why.

- Do you have a trusted confidant you can ask for honest feedback? Whose advice or guidance would be most helpful?

- To what extent do you over-rely on certain strengths, missing opportunities for growth and turning your strengths into weaknesses?

- When have you been affected by someone who was not self-aware? How did you react? What was the person's impact on the organization? What could he or she have done differently?

- Is there anything about yourself that you're unwilling to admit to others? How might you come to terms with that characteristic so you can acknowledge it but not dwell on it? How might things be different for you if you could?

Improve Now

Participate in a 360-degree feedback survey. A confidential measurement can show you how you appear to superiors, peers, and direct reports.

Notice how others respond to your actions. If they respond to you in unexpected ways, use that information to review where your self-awareness may be lacking—what are you doing or not doing that provokes unexpected responses? Ask a trusted colleague for feedback.

Do an honest inventory of your personal values. What are you willing to do to reach your goals? Where you are willing to compromise? Some of your values will be more important to you than others. Think about how your values compare to the values supported in your organization.

Accept feedback as a gift. What others observe about you provides opportunities for self-growth and a sharper self-awareness. Listen without becoming defensive or justifying your actions. Thank the people who give you feedback.

See change as an opportunity. The beliefs that others hold about you signal the changes you can make. To change the expectations of others, you must first change yourself—your actions, your approach to different situations, and your sense of what others need.

Consider your values in relationship to the values that others hold. Pay attention to the interplay between and among your values and those of others. Observe and note how your values coexist or don't with the values that others hold. Many people share the same values but may display them differently. For example, one person who values family may work long hours to provide what his or her family needs, while another person may seek a limited or flexible schedule that gives him or her more time with family.

Note how you respond in times of stress. When the pressure is on, can you maintain your emotional equilibrium or do you lash out, retreat, or adopt a benign neglect of the situation? Reflect on your experiences. Every challenge is an opportunity when you reflect on your experience and grow from it. Take the time to think back on the activities of your day, the actions you took, and the choices you made, and decide what changes you ought to make in the future.

Get comfortable with discomfort. Like physical strength, self-awareness requires that you do some work and feel some pain. Gradually increase your tolerance for discomfort and learn to appreciate it as a signal of improved self-awareness.

Seek training. After you've identified your development needs, identify programs designed to help leaders grow in these skills. Training can be effective in accelerating improvement.

Find an accountability partner. Self-awareness and self-development require an ongoing commitment to a process that will often feel difficult. Just as you can benefit from a workout partner, you may also benefit from a partner who is willing to support, guide, and walk with you on the path toward leadership excellence.

Developmental Opportunities

- Form a developmental relationship. Search for members of your organization who exemplify expertise in the areas where you wish to develop. Approach them for guidance that will help you hone your self-awareness and convey your commitment to self-development and learning.

- Ask your manager to delegate one of his or her responsibilities to you and give you regular feedback on how well you are doing.

- Participate in a job rotation program, seeking feedback from each department or unit in which you work.

- Improve your relationship with a difficult colleague.

- Take on an assignment that no one else wants to do.

Activity Center

Review and download these activities you can use for your development or with your team from this book's resource page at www.ccl.org/compassbook.

Self-Awareness: Johari Window

Self-Awareness: Your Social Identity

Related Competencies

Communication

Credibility and Integrity

Interpersonal Savvy

Learning Agility

Relationship Management

Self-Development

Resources

Bradberry, T., & Greaves, J. (2009). *Emotional Intelligence 2.0.* San Diego, CA: TalentSmart.

Cartwright, T. (2009). *Changing yourself and your reputation.* Greensboro, NC: Center for Creative Leadership.

Center for Creative Leadership. (2013). *Interpersonal savvy: Building and maintaining solid working relationships.* Greensboro, NC: Author.

Design, S. (n.d.). *The Ekmans' Atlas of Emotion.* Retrieved February 15, 2017, from http://atlasofemotions.org/

Goldsmith, M., & Reiter, M. (2015). *Triggers: Creating behavior that lasts— becoming the person you want to be.* New York, NY: Crown Business.

Goleman, D. *Emotional intelligence: Why it can matter more than IQ.* (2005). New York, NY: Random House.

Hannum, K. M. (2007). *Social identity: Knowing yourself, leading others.* Greensboro, NC: Center for Creative Leadership.

Kaplan, R. E., & Kaiser, R. B. (2013). *Fear your strengths: What you are best at could be your biggest problem.* San Francisco, CA: Berrett-Koehler.

King, S. N., & Altman, D. G. (2011). *Discovering the leader in you.* (Workbook). San Francisco, CA: Jossey-Bass.

King, S. N., Altman, D. G., & Lee, R. J. (2011). *Discovering the leader in you: How to realize your leadership potential* (New and Rev. ed.). San Francisco, CA: Jossey-Bass.

Kirkland, K., & Manoogian, S. (1998). *Ongoing feedback: How to get it, how to use it.* Greensboro, NC: Center for Creative Leadership.

Mount, P., & Tardanico, S. (2014). *Beating the impostor syndrome.* Greensboro, NC: Center for Creative Leadership.

Randall, K. (2016, May 6). Inner peace? The Dalai Lama made a website for that. *The New York Times.* Retrieved from http://www.nytimes.com/2016/05/07/world/dalai-lama-website-atlas-of-emotions.html

Sternbergh, B., & Weitzel, S. R. (2001). *Setting your development goals: Start with your values.* Greensboro, NC: Center for Creative Leadership.

Part Two
COMPETENCIES FOR IMPACT AND ACHIEVEMENT

Think of a competency as an interrelated set of knowledge, skills, and perspectives. For example, think about what it takes to delegate well: the knowledge of who is capable of doing what work and who can be counted on; the skill to give clear direction to people with differing knowledge and abilities to process information; and the perspective that you don't need to do everything yourself.

The key idea here is that a competency goes beyond an isolated behavior. A competency serves leaders in broad areas such as strategic thinking, delegation, personal resilience, resolving conflict, leading upward, and others. Developing a competency takes time. And some of what you develop isn't visible to others, at least in the beginning. Other people might not notice right away the changes you've made—but as you expose yourself to more and various situations, your grasp of how to exploit your knowledge, skills, and aptitude becomes apparent. Other people will take notice and respond to your actions, and through that process of recognition, action, and response, leadership takes hold.

Most of the competencies covered in this section are drawn from several of CCL's assessments, which have been used with more than half a million leaders. A few additional competencies, based on the fact that CCL research has highlighted their importance to effective leadership performance, were added for readers who want to develop in an important area not measured in a CCL assessment (feedback, for example). Whether represented in a CCL assessment or revealed in CCL research, all of the competencies in this section are important for your leadership development and affect your ability to lead.

5

Balance

Make thoughtful decisions about how to invest your time.

You can't control time, but you can control how you spend it. Unfortunately, in today's helter-skelter business environment, that's not easy to do. For example, a recent CCL study discovered that managers, executives, and other business people who carry smartphones for work report interacting with the office up to 13.5 hours every workday (Deal, 2015).

To attain a meaningful sense of balance, focus on looking within rather than measuring yourself against others or copying their tactics. It's your personal solution that will result in the rejuvenating and invigorating results of a balanced life. Though balance is difficult to attain and hard to sustain, make it a goal and reap the benefits of a life (including a career) lived in harmony with your personal values and aspirations. Take a look at Jeff Stibel, CEO of Dun and Bradstreet Credibility Corp. His story exemplifies the fact that finding and maintaining balance in life isn't a prescriptive, one-size-fits-all proposition. It's a habit that changes over time.

Leadership in Action

Stibel's 2013 article, "Entrepreneurs Don't Need Work-Life Balance," argues that inventive, ambitious people have to surrender "trivial pursuits" in order to realize their dreams. However, later in the article, Stibel suggests something different: "I may be an entrepreneur, but in my  family our kids come first." He mentions that he has left board meetings in progress in order to return home and care for his children. A more accurate title for his article might have been, "At This Time in My Life, My Children and My Work Are My Top Priorities."

Only three years later, Joe Robinson's article in *Entrepreneur* showed how Stibel's attitude had changed further. Under the headline "The Secret to Increased Productivity: Taking Time Off," he is quoted as saying, "If you overtax your heart, the next thing you need to do is relax, or you'll die. The same thing is true of the brain." During the time between Stibel's article and Robinson's interview, Stibel's personal priorities had shifted. He recalibrated his work habits to find a new balance. That is the real nature of balance as a habit: You don't settle on one routine and depend on it forever. You recreate balance over and over again.

What High Performance Looks Like

Leaders skilled at maintaining balance in their lives

- set priorities well and periodically reevaluate them
- set clear expectations with others regarding their priorities
- periodically evaluate how successfully priorities are met
- make the most of their available time
- are wary of the signs of burnout
- are flexible in responding to near-term demands on their time
- have a clear understanding of what their career means to them
- maintain activities and interests outside their career
- consider the trade-offs associated with their decisions about how to spend their time

What's in Your Way?

Achieving and maintaining balance comes down to having control over how you choose to spend your time and having those choices align with your values. Common reasons that people struggle with balance are listed below. Note which of the items on the list are keeping you from realizing a fully balanced life.

- ❏ You don't feel that you control how you spend your time.
- ❏ You don't feel empowered to renegotiate your responsibilities to work and/or family.
- ❏ You feel an overinflated sense of obligation to either work or family ("I must . . . ").
- ❏ You are undisciplined in managing your time.

- ❏ You refuse to compromise or make trade-offs.
- ❏ You try to do it all.
- ❏ You hold yourself to unreasonable standards.
- ❏ You're following the example of your parents or other influential role models.
- ❏ You take on more than you are capable of doing.
- ❏ You refuse to say "no."
- ❏ You underestimate the time it takes to complete work.
- ❏ You don't manage others' expectations of what you can/should do.
- ❏ You have difficulty switching between diverse responsibilities.
- ❏ You're unsure how your values align with what you do.
- ❏ You try to do everything yourself instead of partnering with others or delegating.

Coach Yourself

To develop your ability to achieve and sustain balance, create goals in areas that prompt you to gain more understanding and control over how you manage your time. These questions can help you define areas on which to focus your development:

- Start by establishing a baseline. Ask yourself "How am I currently spending my time?" Literally map it out over the course of a week. Look for patterns and themes. What surprises you?

- Identify the gaps. Pinpoint the differences between how you currently spend your time and how you would ideally like to. How many gaps are there? Which are the largest? Which could be closed the most easily?

- Consider why the gaps exist in the first place. What choices have led you to this point? How do those choices align with your values? Why haven't you addressed these gaps up to now?

- Imagine a different reality. How might life be different for you and others if you found ways to exercise greater control over your time and live in greater accordance with your values?

- Identify sources of support and inspiration. Who can understand your challenges and provide you with the needed encouragement and feedback to help you on your path to achieving greater balance?

Improve Now

Establish control over your boundaries. Individuals who exercise high boundary control actively choose how they divide their time and attention between work and family. They feel that they have the authority or ability to make these decisions and to manage any resulting trade-offs. Be deliberate. Say to yourself, "I now choose to…" when making decisions about how to allocate your time.

Break a routine. In order to commit to a change in how you choose to spend your time, you also need to acknowledge what you have to give up along with what you have to gain. Making a change may require you to let go of routines or ways of thinking to which you have grown accustomed. Breaking a routine can, of course, be difficult. It's best to come to terms with this early on.

Save your energy. Reduce draining activities as much as possible. If you can, hire someone to run errands, cook, or clean if that feels like a burden to you. Do you really need to do all the things you are doing? Perhaps you can trade time with someone who likes to do the things you do not and vice versa.

Conduct a values inventory. Knowing your current values and their priorities can help you attain more consistency between your values and your behavior. Take a valid values assessment or, alternatively, brainstorm and rank-order a list of your own personal values. Do you see your values reflected in the way you spend your time? What's congruent? What's in conflict? What's missing?

Use technology to manage boundaries. Used thoughtfully, technology can be used to either blur boundaries (staying in touch with home from work or vice-versa) or keep them separate (different emails for personal and business use).

Create or manage physical boundaries. You can use physical objects to symbolize the degree to which you integrate boundaries or keep them separate. Do you have personal photos in your office? Do you have a stack of work papers on your desk at home?

Be the boss of your calendar. Block time for critical activities like planning, writing, exercising, and keeping personal appointments. Set aside time each day, week, or month for specific tasks.

Set and manage expectations. Indicate your preferences about how you manage your time to your boss, coworkers, family, etc. Communicate your various obligations to significant people in your life so that others have an adequate understanding of your situation.

Smooth out role transitions. Identify rituals that help you go from one role to another; for example, listening to music, having a cup of coffee or glass of wine, or clearing your desk. Even changing clothes can help signify to yourself and others that you have changed roles.

Developmental Assignments

- Secure a mentor or coach to provide support. Achieving a sense of balance that fulfills you can be difficult. You will require emotional, cognitive and possibly even physical support along the way.

- Agree with others that you will take a respite from family or work obligations to clear your head, get perspective, and recharge your batteries. Keep your word.

- Pursue a fresh assignment, which will provide you with an opportunity to start fresh in setting and maintaining expectations about managing your time.

- Delegate a time-consuming responsibility. Consider assigning it to someone who would appreciate the opportunity to expand his or her responsibilities and develop new skills.

- Switch responsibilities with someone where you will both feel like you are making more valuable use of your time.

Activity Center

Review and download these activities you can use for your development or with your team from this book's resource page at www.ccl.org/compassbook.

Balance: Balancing Challenge
Balance: Balance for You, Too
Balance: Balancing Goals for Life

Related Competencies

Flexibility
Leading with Purpose
Resilience
Resourcefulness
Self-Awareness
Tolerating Ambiguity

Resources

Connolly, C., Ruderman, M. N., & Leslie, J. B. (2014). Sleep well, lead well: How better sleep can improve leadership, boost productivity, and spark innovation. (White paper). Greensboro, NC: Center for Creative Leadership.

Deal, J. J. (2015). *Always on, never done? Don't blame the smartphone.* (White paper). Greensboro, NC: Center for Creative Leadership.

Gurvis, J., & Patterson, G. (2004). *Finding your balance.* Greensboro, NC: Center for Creative Leadership.

Kossek, E. E., & Lautsch, B. A. (2007). *CEO of me: Creating a life that works in the flexible job age.* Upper Saddle River, NJ: Wharton School Publishing.

Kossek, E. E., Ruderman, M. N., Braddy, P. W., & Hannum, K. M. (2011). *WorkLife indicator: Increasing your effectiveness on and off the job.* (Feedback report and development planning guide). Greensboro, NC: Center for Creative Leadership.

Robinson, J. (2016, May 30). The secret to increased productivity: Taking time off. *Entrepreneur.* Retrieved from https://www.entrepreneur.com/article/237446

Ruderman, M. N., Braddy, P. W., Hannum, K. M., & Kossek, E. E. (2013). *Managing your whole life.* Greensboro, NC: Center for Creative Leadership.

Stibel, J. (2013, April 2). Entrepreneurs don't need work-life balance. *Harvard Business Review.*

6

Boundary Spanning

Collaborate across formal and informal boundaries to drive results.

Organizational boundaries of all kinds magnify the challenges of leadership. Borders separate functional areas and leader levels, and they divide clients, stakeholders, and employees. Outside of organizations, there are stark differences between genders, ethnicities, and ideologies. Geographical distance separates team members, cultures, and markets. While leaders were once called to operate within the confines of organizational structures, that isn't the case anymore. Too often, leaders are constrained by their inability to see past the superficial boundaries within their organizations. While 86 percent of senior executives believe spanning boundaries is critical to business, according to Chris Ernst and Donna Chrobot-Mason, only 7 percent say they are very good at it.

Solving complicated organizational challenges requires collaboration across the organization, from top to bottom, and across time zones and geography. High-level collaboration includes all of the organization's diverse voices, including those outside the organization, such as customers, vendors, and other external stakeholders. Your skill as a boundary spanner can make a direct, visible, and measurable contribution to your organization and to your career. And while your boundary-spanning efforts might not be as dramatic as those of Kobi Tzafrir, his story shows how crossing lines opens the door to positive results—even if on a small scale.

Leadership in Action

Sometimes it seems like the boundaries we make between one another are insurmountable. But it doesn't always require a lofty approach to chip away at the walls between human beings. In Tel Aviv, local chef Kobi Tzafrir tries to heal decades of political strife with a simple promotion at his restaurant: he will take 50 percent off the price of any meal shared by Jews and Arabs. The premise behind his idea is straightforward, explains multimedia journalist Daniella Cheslow (2015). In Tzafrir's words, "If you eat good hummus, you will feel love for the person who made it. You don't want to stab him."

The list of grievances between the two peoples is too long to detail here. At the time of Tzafrir's promotion, the death toll on both sides from recent violence was in the dozens. These are not differences to be made light of, and yet there's something refreshing about the offer of cheap food. It's earnest, it's charming, and it smells good.

Perhaps Tzafrir's hummus promotion won't be the key to a wide-reaching solution to Israeli-Palestinian conflict. But gathering people around a meal has a long history of fostering common feeling. Instead of throwing up his hands and leaving people to their discord, Tzafrir is doing what he can, where he is, with what he has: hummus. At the very least, he hopes to send a signal: "Maybe the idea will reach politicians that we're fed up."

What High Performance Looks Like

Leaders skilled at spanning boundaries

- see beyond their function or department
- build buffers to separate groups in conflict and allow them to interact safely to build trust and cooperation
- break down barriers between groups by representing all sides and facilitating information exchanges between them
- suspend boundaries by encouraging person-to-person engagements that establish collaborative relationships and alliances throughout the organization
- reframe boundaries to create a common purpose among different groups
- integrate different groups to share resources and contributions in service of a common good
- understand the politics of the organization and work accordingly
- balance what is good for their unit with the organization's needs
- view problems or opportunities from various perspectives
- work with other leaders to develop a common vision or strategy
- consider the impact of their actions on the group, function, unit, and organization
- deal appropriately with contradictory requirements or organizational inconsistencies
- collaborate and listen well
- are open-minded toward differences and inclusive of others

What Gets in Your Way?

You will make a substantial impact as a leader by facilitating collaboration across dividing lines. If you aren't a skilled boundary spanner, you might struggle to create organizational benefits, have difficulty earning organizational support for your projects, and isolate yourself from key players or groups. You may miss opportunities to broaden your organizational perspective and be perceived as too narrowly focused on a specific function or group (a common *career derailer*). As a result, others may regard you as inefficient, ineffective, or interested only in pursuing an individual agenda. Those perceptions create conflicts that aren't easily resolved and limit your career potential. Which of the following might interfere with your developing skill in spanning boundaries?

- ❏ You see people in other functions as competition.
- ❏ You haven't established relationships with key people from other functions.
- ❏ Your organizational culture encourages competition between groups.
- ❏ Your functional experience is too narrow.
- ❏ Your organization rewards individual over collaborative achievement.
- ❏ Your organization's structure does not lend itself to cross-functional collaboration.
- ❏ You overlook opportunities to collaborate.
- ❏ You fear reigniting historical tensions or conflict.
- ❏ You worry that other people might refuse to reciprocate.
- ❏ You're concerned that other leaders will question your motives.
- ❏ You worry that you might be seen as intruding on other areas of the company.
- ❏ You don't want your team to think you're disloyal.

Coach Yourself

To develop your boundary-spanning ability, create goals in areas that require broad organizational participation, put you in a different leadership role with a different unit, or place you in other areas in which you have to reach across boundaries to achieve your goal. These questions can help you define such focus areas:

- What are your fears about working across boundaries? What is the worst that could happen if you reach out across or break down barriers?

- What are your organization's unwritten rules about collaborating across boundaries? Are you making incorrect assumptions about who you can or cannot engage to seek new solutions?

- What are the barriers to collaboration between groups?

- Who in your organization spans boundaries well and what can you learn from them?

- Which senior managers are apt to encourage more cross-functional or cross-department collaboration?

Improve Now

Start small. Begin with a tactic or two that feels easy to introduce and execute. Don't launch a boundary-spanning campaign. Begin where you can, find some allies, build on success, and learn from failure.

Wear the other shoe. During team meetings, make time to think and learn about other perspectives. Ask team members how other departments or divisions might think about the team's work.

Hold skip-level meetings. Meet with people who report to your direct reports. Not only will you get to hear their perspectives and ideas, but you will communicate strategic information that will help them align their work with team and organizational goals. Make sure to inform your direct reports of your plan and its purpose.

Make time to connect. Reserve time in meetings, especially when conducted virtually, to build relationships and for personal updates.

Accept and extend invitations. Eat and drink with colleagues when you visit; be the host when they visit.

State your rules of engagement. Specify how your group and other groups will interact. Set realistic expectations with other groups about what your group can and can't do.

Be a translator. Help groups uncover their work language—unique jargon, acronyms, and processes. Then translate for other groups.

Champion communities of practice. Provide time, space, and support for people with shared expertise or technical domains to share their knowledge and practices. Do likewise for affinity groups based on shared interests or demographics.

Access other groups. Invite other groups or leaders to join your team meeting, weigh in, and share their knowledge. Extend the practice to clients or suppliers.

Span to expand understanding. Choose one of your department's customers or suppliers, identify a problem or concern they have, and agree to bring different teams together to solve it.

Developmental Opportunities

- Launch or serve on a cross-functional team or manage a virtual team whose members are distributed in different geographical regions.

- Bring together members of two groups to work on a single project and commit to delivering a specific result.

- Take a team assignment located in part of the organization with which you are unfamiliar.

- Join your organization to another from a different industry sector (for example, pharmaceutical and aerospace) to tackle a shared problem.

- Serve simultaneously on multiple projects.

- Seek highly visible experiences in which you work across organizational boundaries or must influence without authority.

- Take on a boundary-spanning responsibility previously handled by your boss.

- Ask your group to generate a new idea to implement. Move that idea through the organization and get the necessary support from others outside your group.

Activity Center

Review and download these short activities you can use for your development from the *Compass* resource page at www.compassbook.com.

Boundary Spanning: A Plan to Span
Boundary Spanning: Powerful Questions

Related Competencies

Conflict Resolution
Difference, Diversity, Inclusion
Influence
Organizational Savvy
Relationship Management
Systems Thinking

Resources

Cheslow, D. (2015, Oct. 23). "Hummus diplomacy: Israeli cafe discounts meals shared by Jews and Arabs. *NPR*. Retrieved from http://www.npr.org/sections/ thesalt/2015/10/23/450905869/israeli-cafe-offers -discounts-for-jews-and-arabs-to-share-a-meal

Ernst, C., & Chrobot-Mason, D. (2010). *Boundary spanning leadership: Six practices for solving problems, driving innovation, and transforming organizations.* New York, NY: McGraw-Hill.

Ernst, C., & Martin, A. (2006). *Critical reflections: How groups can learn from success and failure.* Greensboro, NC: Center for Creative Leadership.

Gentry, W. A., & Leslie, J. B. (2013). *Developing political savvy*. Greensboro, NC: Center for Creative Leadership.

Johansen, B. (2012). *Leaders make the future: Ten new leadership skills for an uncertain world* (2nd ed.). San Francisco, CA: Berrett-Koehler.

Scharlatt, H. (2016). *Resolving conflict: Ten steps for turning negatives to positives*. Greensboro, NC: Center for Creative Leadership.

Van Velsor, E. (2013). *Broadening your organizational perspective*. Greensboro, NC: Center for Creative Leadership.

7

Business Development

Guide the organization toward profitable new ventures.

Despite overwhelming evidence that entrepreneurial leadership leads to positive business outcomes, only 19 percent of leaders would describe themselves as courageous risk-takers, an essential ingredient to entrepreneurialism, according to the auditing firm Grant Thornton. Given such a meager showing, it stands to reason that you can help your organization gain competitive advantage by being bold, thoughtful, and determined in your efforts to lead it into new frontiers. If you hone your ability to identify and pursue opportunities for your organization, others will notice, and you will be able to identify and pursue career opportunities as well. Perhaps there is no contemporary leader that exhibits these qualities in quite the way the founder of Virgin Airlines does.

Leadership in Action

Under the influence of founder Sir Richard Branson, the Virgin Group has had its hands in just about everything. That is, just about everything that Branson finds interesting, enjoyable, profitable, or challenging. From music and records to health spas, cruise ships, and cutting-edge aerospace engineering, Branson sees opportunities everywhere and seizes them.

Numerous personal qualities contribute to Branson's facility with entrepreneurship. He likes to test his own limits. He likes the idea of contributing to society, building a legacy, and working in big, luxurious lifestyle industries. Although he makes a lot of money, that doesn't seem to be the source of his passion. Rather, he seems to simply love running the business. After all, once his ventures hit a certain pitch of success, he has a habit of selling them off.

How does Branson decide where to put his efforts next? He seems to have a proclivity for selecting industries where his company could shake things up. Not exactly doing something brand new, but satisfying a proven demand in a unique way, creating a disruption and then taking advantage of it. With this tactic, Branson creates new opportunities where none may appear to exist at first. Quoted in *Business & Economy* (2013), in reference to the day-to-day work of running business this way, he says: "An entrepreneur is expected to keep tabs on the daily occurrences and changes in the industry where he functions. This is, so that it allows him to minimize risks involved in a future course of action, make higher profits than otherwise and make his company a tough competitor to beat."

What High Performance Looks Like

Leaders skilled at business development

- spend time with potential clients and ask them about their needs in order to see the world from their perspective

- keep an eye on customers and what drives their purchases

- spend time with frontline employees, such as salespeople, to better understand their perspectives and experiences

- spend time with employees throughout the organization to gather input on what they see as potential opportunity and to see the business through their eyes

- constantly scan the internal and external environments for factors, trends, and patterns that may affect the organization's business

- understand the competitive landscape, including the products or services offered by competitors

- form novel associations and ideas that create new and different ways of solving problems

- are entrepreneurial, knowledgeable, curious, intuitive, imaginative, and opportunistic

- depart from traditional approaches to products or services

- explore new concepts before knowing if they are viable

- have vision

- often bring up ideas about future possibilities

- look beyond existing data about what has worked before and what is working now

- see beyond current resources or technology and aren't wedded to what has been done in the past

What's in Your Way?

Your difficulties with identifying new business opportunities could cause your organization to stagnate, becoming less profitable or competitive, or see its market position erode. You will likely lose the support of your boss, peers, subordinates, and others for your projects and vision. Ultimately, you will lose access to resources, and the best and brightest people will look elsewhere for opportunities for challenge and growth—whether at your organization or another. If you have trouble seeing new business opportunities, mark any of the following descriptions that you think work against your entrepreneurial potential.

- ❏ When you interact with customers, you spend too much time talking or advocating and not enough time listening or learning.
- ❏ You need a broader business network—people who expose you to new ideas and keep you informed about the industry.
- ❏ You're overly proud or committed to what you have produced in the past.
- ❏ You are overly cautious.
- ❏ Your functional experience is too narrow—you can't see the many possibilities beyond your current role.
- ❏ You are too stressed in meeting your objectives to think about the broader needs of the organization.
- ❏ You fear that you'll fall off your career track if you were to branch out from your current role.
- ❏ Your organization has lost money on some of your past decisions.
- ❏ You pursue exciting ideas without fully understanding the risks and drawbacks.
- ❏ You struggle to develop a practical plan for implementing your ideas.
- ❏ You spread your resources too thin.
- ❏ You neglect the organization's core business.

- [ ] Your boss loses faith in you.
- [ ] Your direct reports become unsure of your ability to pick a winning opportunity.

Coach Yourself

To develop your business development abilities, create goals in the areas of cross-functional work, unfamiliar assignments, or in areas of direct customer contact (if that is not part of your current role). These questions can help you focus on such areas:

- Have you ever identified a unique opportunity and pursued it successfully in another aspect of life (outside of your current position)? What did you do? Did you know if it would work before you tried it?

- Are there people in your organization or life who are highly skilled at finding new business opportunities? What do they do? How did they develop the skill?

- What are the potential costs of avoiding risks associated with new business ventures (for example, lost opportunity)?

- Does your personality, or do your beliefs and assumptions, hinder your experimentation, exploration, or risk taking?

- Do you have a deep understanding of your organization's competitive challenges and opportunities?

Improve Now

See things anew. Training and experience often teach us to analyze problems in a prescribed manner, sometimes to our detriment. Look at each issue from multiple perspectives to gain a more complete insight into all its elements and possible solutions.

Ask powerful questions. Predictable questions result in predictable answers. Instead, try asking something unexpected. This may be as simple as What's missing? or What are the patterns? You could try oddball what-if scenarios, or challenge long-held beliefs. New possibilities emerge by asking questions that no one has asked before.

Brainstorm. Give your team members time to develop their own ideas, and then bring the team together to present and build upon each other's ideas in a judgment-free environment.

Change it up. Take your team out of its usual environment, whether that means a literal change of scenery or just a simple change of pace. Have a conversation with a group member while taking a walk, or hold a meeting over lunch. Have your team read a new book, or discuss a relevant film or news piece together. These activities often inspire new thinking.

Repeat business. The best business is repeat business. The second best is word-of-mouth business. Identify how showing a personal interest in the interests and ideas of customers can ensure that your organization will be shoulder deep in repeat and word-of-mouth business. If you were the senior leader in your organization, how would you create an atmosphere that would encourage the groundwork for that to take place?

Consider the customer's perspective. Pay attention to the choices your customers make and their responses to what your organization offers. Feedback from your customers is invaluable.

Change your level of analysis. If your group typically focuses on the tasks in its area, try reexamining opportunities with the big picture in mind. Conversely, if you typically are responsible for large-scale decisions, consider how your actions affect the smaller details of organizational life. Shifting between an expansive and a focused view can bring new insights onto your team's actions.

Stay attuned to the business environment. Constantly scan the external climate for patterns and trends that may have an effect on your organization. What is your competition doing? Attend and contribute to industry conferences to take the pulse of the industry.

Foster learning. Encourage those you work with to tackle new experiences and find opportunities for growth. This will broaden your group's skill set, improve member performance, and position team members to see beyond the organization to new opportunities.

Bring talent together across boundaries. Facilitate an interaction among the most talented and imaginative people from different groups to generate possible opportunities.

Hire creative geniuses. If your group doesn't have the horsepower to generate industry-leading innovation, look around the industry for smart and creative people who can point the organization in new directions.

See me, hear me. When working to develop the business, you need to watch for what you don't want to see and listen for what you don't want to hear. Make a list of items that you have heard and seen recently that you know need to be addressed in order to grow the business—everything from newspaper articles to blog posts to research reports to poll numbers.

Develop your network. Business development depends on the strength of its supporting network. Leaders successful at business development have honed their ability to look beyond the organizational chart to see, understand, and engage the informal structure and how it affects new business opportunities.

Keep up with your reading. Read your industry journals. Encourage your employees to do the same. Bring them together and ask them to lead discussions at staff meetings about what they learn and how it can affect business development.

Developmental Opportunities

- Go on sales calls with a sales rep.

- Tour a client's facilities.

- Ask to serve on a team that is working to improve customer satisfaction.

- Take a strategy assignment that forces you to scan the environment.

- Review competitors and report on their product lines.

- Take an assignment that forces you to critically examine your organization's product lines and find where it might create new product ideas.

- Take an assignment that brings you into contact with customers and frontline employees.

Activity Center

Review and download these short activities you can use for your development on the *Compass* resource page at www.ccl.org/compassbook.

Business Development: Organizational Drivers

Business Development: Can You Identify a New Idea?

Related Competencies

Boundary Spanning

Innovation

Problem Solving

Risk Taking

Vision

Resources

Branson, R. *Losing my virginity: How I survived, had fun, and made a fortune doing business my way.* (2011). New York, NY: Crown Business.

Business & Economy. (2013). The outrageous man who never lost his virginity. Author. *8*(7), 74–76. Retrieved from http://www.businessandeconomy .org/30082013/storyd.asp?sid=7349&pageno=2

Elkington, J., & Hartigan, P. (2008). *The power of unreasonable people: How social entrepreneurs create markets that change the world.* Boston, MA: Harvard Business School Press.

Grant, T. (2005). What makes a good leader? Grant Thornton's leadership survey suggests that today's leaders may have lost their risk taking bottle. London, UK: Author. Retrieved from http://docplayer.net/8690591-What -makes-a-good-leader-grant-thornton-s-leadership-survey-suggests-that -today-s-leaders-may-have-lost-their-risk-taking-bottle.html

Gryskiewicz, S. S. (1999). *Positive turbulence: Developing climates for creativity, innovation, and renewal.* San Francisco, CA: Jossey-Bass.

Horth, D. M. (2010, Jan. 27). How to be an innovative, not just business, leader. *Forbes.* Retrieved from http://www.forbes.com/2010/01/27/innovation -change-strategy-leadership-managing-ccl.html

Horth, D. M., & Vehar, J. R. (2016). From innovation graveyard to innovation hotbed. *Developing Leaders*, (23), 10–16.

Johansen, B., & Ronn, K. (2014). *The Reciprocity advantage: A new way to partner for innovation and growth*. Oakland, CA: Berrett-Koehler.

Palus, C. J., Asif, V., & Cullen, K. (2016). *Network-savvy executives: Five advantages for leaders in a networked world.* (White paper). Center for Creative Leadership. Retrieved from https://www.ccl.org/wp-content/uploads/2015/04/NetworkSavvy.pdf

Rampton, J. (2014, Oct. 6). How to find and recognize good business opportunities. *Inc*. Retrieved Aug. 24, 2016, from http://www.inc.com/john-rampton/how-to-find-and-recognize-good-business-opportunities.html

Scharlatt, H. (2008). *Selling your ideas to your organization*. Greensboro, NC: Center for Creative Leadership.

Sobel, A., & Panas, J. (2012). *Power questions: Build relationships, win new business, and influence others*. Hoboken, NJ: Jossey-Bass.

Zack, D. (2010). *Networking for people who hate networking: A field guide for introverts, the overwhelmed, and the underconnected*. Oakland, CA: Berrett-Koehler.

8

Business and Professional Knowledge

Master professional skills and proficiency in understanding your industry.

A chief component to developing yourself as a leader is to gain mastery over the specific function for which you're responsible. You'll need to quickly grasp the purpose and processes of the function, understand the mechanics of achieving results within that function, know how those results integrate with the rest of the organization's operations, and be able to comfortably analyze data—specifically financial results—that benchmark performance.

Knowledge of the business includes practical knowledge of global markets and trends and the way they affect your organization and its competitors. That entails knowledge and comfort with marketing—from research to planning to strategy. Concepts and metrics pertaining to budgeting, forecasting, and reporting play a role in that leaders with mastery over their job function and an overall understanding of the business can manage costs and resources and work toward greater efficiency.

Once competent in this area, you'll be recognized as capable of stepping into the highest levels of organizational leadership—from the top rungs of management to the C-suite of strategic and operational activities that set the organization's agenda and propel it toward sustained relevance and performance. High-level stuff—and critical to leading a successful enterprise. Listen to Karen Kaplan's rise from entry level to senior-most level in her organization to see what a sharp and superior grasp of business and professional knowledge can do.

Leadership in Action

When she first became a receptionist at the Hill Holliday advertising agency, Karen Kaplan didn't even know how to type. So how did a barely-qualified employee climb from the bottom of the ladder to the position of CEO? Simple: she learned the function of her position in the company and set herself to maximizing that function. According to *Forbes's* The Muse, as a receptionist, her task was to facilitate communication, and that job put her in contact with every one of her coworkers, at every level of the company (2013). So she started that task and seized every opportunity it provided, going beyond the expectations of her position in a way that benefited the firm and herself.

Next, she moved to a secretarial position. Although she was underqualified for that job as well, she set to learning its essential function and mastering it. She "kept every business card she ever received," writes journalist Laura Stampler (2013). She pulled hours on the weekend to keep up with duties that went beyond her experience. And once she'd mastered the task, she was able to exceed the boundaries of expectation and prove she could handle the next step. And the next. And the next. As she puts it, "I had the same 12 jobs that everyone has, I've just had them all at Hill Holliday."

Eventually, Kaplan's relentless pursuit of mastery put her at the top. She is now the CEO of Hill Holliday, and her experience with the entire organization lends her a unique strategic acumen. It's a story so tidy it sounds like a bootstraps fable, but Kaplan wasn't carried from the receptionist's desk to the CEO's office by vague "determination" or "grit." The practical pursuit of competence, followed by the daily effort to exceed her role, brought her an astounding success.

What High Performance Looks Like

Leaders with an exceptionally professional grasp of their work and knowledge of their organization's purpose within the industry it operates

- excel at their functions or specialties
- are strong generalists, and are good general managers in particular
- work well in a job with a big scope
- pick up knowledge and expertise quickly and easily
- understand and are comfortable using graphs, charts, statistics, and budgets
- understand cash flows, financial reports, and corporate annual reports
- are comfortable discussing market research, planning, and strategy
- are seen as strategic, competent, engaging, tactical, and good problem solvers
- communicate in ways that show their credibility and expertise
- are regarded as subject matter experts and thought leaders
- are good negotiators
- can juggle competing priorities
- can see across functions and grasp the entire business

What's in Your Way?

Knowledge of your profession and of your business and high competence in your work make you visible to others in the organization. If you are unable to develop a sound understanding of your job and apply that to the business in general, you are unlikely to be selected to lead a division, function, or some other significant part of your organization, which might impede your career. Review the following descriptions and mark those that get in the way of achieving mastery of your job and a comprehensive knowledge of your organization and the industry in which it operates.

❑ You're insecure in your current level of knowledge and can't admit and learn from mistakes.

❑ You're so invested in your current understanding that you resist change and have difficulty adapting to shifting circumstances.

❑ You have difficulty listening to others because you're sure that you already know what they are trying to tell you.

❑ You don't account for different perspectives.

❑ You haven't experienced failure nor gained the lessons that come from it.

❑ You're overconfident or, on the other extreme, complacent.

❑ You use your specialty knowledge as power over direct reports and peers, and you have received feedback that they perceive you as abrasive and domineering.

❑ Your well-honed knowledge gives you the impression that you are at the center of your network, rather than in a relationship with others in your network.

❑ Your knowledge gives you a track record of success that convinces you that you can't fail.

❑ You try to apply what you know in your specialty area to another area without adapting it to the situation.

Coach Yourself

To develop your knowledge of job and business, create goals in areas that require broad organizational participation, give you a sense of leadership at a different organizational level, and broaden and deepen the scope of your work. These questions can help you define such focus areas:

- Put yourself in the shoes of someone two levels above you. What does that person need to be successful in that role?

- Think of a leader in your organization who you believe possesses high learning agility. Think of a leader in your organization who you believe lacks learning agility. Where do you fall between those two positions?

- What books, journals, magazines, or other media do you need to pay attention to for building a broader understanding of your organization's field?

- Who might be a role model for you as you seek to develop a broader understanding of your organization's business?

- How would you describe your response to change? Are you entrenched in your habits, do unfamiliar situations overwhelm you, does change encourage you to learn, or do you treat new circumstances as business as usual?

Improve Now

Share. Share the knowledge you have about your work with others across the organization to establish general understanding of the relationship among workgroups and functions.

Seek new experiences. Take on assignments that are outside your area of expertise. Figure out what you need to learn, challenge yourself to learn it, and support yourself with a coach or trusted peer while you're learning. Reflect on your experiences and apply the lessons you've learned to other situations.

Chart the flow. Create a flowchart of how the business operates. Start with a long sheet of paper on the wall (you can get newsprint in office-supply stores) and use sticky notes so you can easily move steps in your organization's business processes around. Invite some of your employees to learn with you.

Know your financial indicators. Brush up on your financial comprehension. A deep understanding of how the business operates means that you understand and can translate its financial indicators. For example, what do these mean: gross profit margin, ROI, net profit margin, return on total assets, and return on shareholder equity? Why are they important?

Show some love. Show your passion for your work and its importance to the organization's strategic goals through your actions. This will engage your team to perform better, and the resulting outcomes will encourage other groups to learn from you (and at the same time you can learn about their work).

Share the paper of record. Share your copy of *The Wall Street Journal* (you do read it, right?) with some of your employees and show them what is in the paper that pertains to their jobs and to the business in general. Encourage that employee to take the paper home and read it. Recommend an article that you can discuss. In the future, when you have completed reading a copy, pass it on to other team members who you believe have leadership potential and who contribute to driving the business.

Humble yourself. Don't mistake your expertise in your given area as expertise in every area. Ask questions to learn, at least at a general level, the work of other groups, how they do that work, and the results they seek.

Know what you don't know. Make an honest assessment of your capabilities and set goals for supplementing those with knowledge you can use to step into work with higher stakes and more uncertainty.

Developmental Opportunities

■ To broaden your strategic view, get beyond the role your team plays and ask for an assignment to the company's strategy team. Seek out opportunities to contribute to the organization's strategic planning to gain a holistic view of all the company's functions.

■ Take on assignments that connect you with different perspectives: operational, cultural, geographical, and so on. Use that opportunity to strengthen the diversity of your professional network.

■ Take an assignment that is larger in scale and scope than your current work.

■ Spend time in an internal customer or supplier's department. Learn their technology and how it interfaces with your department's technology.

■ Design and deliver a workshop to help colleagues learn more about a "hot" topic in the industry or one affecting another function in the organization.

■ Seek an assignment to geographical areas with which you're unfamiliar and in which your organization operates. Use such opportunities to learn which of the organization's functions are necessary for success in specific areas and how the functions come together to achieve a successful global outcome.

Activity Center

Review and download these activities you can use for your development or with your team from the *Compass* resource page at www.ccl.org/compassbook.

Business and Professional Knowledge: To Achieve Results

Business and Professional Knowledge: Help Managers Excel

Related Competencies

Influence

Learning Agility

Organizational Savvy

Problem Solving

Systems Thinking

Resources

Calarco, A., & Gurvis, J. (2006). *Adaptability: Responding effectively to change*. Greensboro, NC: Center for Creative Leadership.

Chappelow, C., & Leslie, J. B. (2004). *Keeping your career on track: Twenty success strategies*. Greensboro, NC: Center for Creative Leadership.

Charan, R. (2001). *What the CEO wants you to know: How your company really works*. New York, NY: Crown Business.

Cullen-Lester, K., Ruderman, M., & Gentry, B. (2016). Motivating your managers: What's the right strategy? *Leading Effectively*. Retrieved from https://www.ccl.org/articles/white-papers/motivating-your-managers-whats-the-right-strategy/

McCall, M. W., Jr., & Hollenbeck, G. P. (2001). *Developing global executives: The lessons of international experience*. Boston, MA: Harvard Business School Press.

McCauley, C. D. (2002). Developing individuals for leadership roles. In M. Pearn (Ed.), *Individual differences and development in organizations* (pp. 321–339). West Sussex, England: John Wiley & Sons.

Stampler, L. (2013, May 29). The incredible story of Karen Kaplan's meteoric rise from receptionist to CEO. *Business Insider*.

The Muse. (2013, Sept. 9). From intern to CEO: How 3 execs climbed to the top. *Forbes*.

Van Velsor, E. (2013). *Broadening your organizational perspective*. Greensboro, NC: Center for Creative Leadership.

9

Champion Change

Inspire, champion, and drive change.

Does your organization find itself playing catch-up to more nimble competitors? Are you looking to "light a fire" to motivate your organization to change and adapt? Despite the widespread belief among executives that driving change is of critical importance, 43 percent say they are ineffective at it, according to a 2011 DDI study (Boatman & Wellins).

Change champions—*change leaders*—offer novel ideas and perspectives on organizational issues and help their peers overcome resistance to change. Change leaders prepare their organization for its next challenge and the challenges that are sure to follow. They succeed in future-proofing their organizations and their own careers. Even changes to well-entrenched organizations, as evident in the story of Pope Francis, can take root with the right champion.

Leadership in Action

Pope Francis came into his role as the leader of the Catholic Church known for his humility, service to the poor, and unpretentious manners. And he has been the catalyst for changes to Catholic perspectives and teachings, moving the church toward adopting a role of compassion toward  its believers as well as fulfilling its traditional role of defining the moral life under Catholic doctrine.

Changing one of the world's biggest Christian sects is slow, will take a long time, and is bound to stir resistance. There are thousands of years of tradition, and different degrees of belief and values at work among church followers. A profile in *Fortune* describes Pope Francis's strategy: not to make change from the top with decrees but to make change by giving voice to the millions of people who share Catholic beliefs. A shift from top-down authority to an authority derived from the faith of its followers is a profound change, and Pope Francis has embraced the role of leading it.

What High Performance Looks Like

Leaders who champion change

- draw attention to a threat that requires urgent action

- position change as a long-term undertaking that requires persistence

- explain how change benefits the organization and its people

- effectively promote an idea or vision and inspire action and commitment toward it

- engage others, especially those who resist change

- are open and authentic in addressing fears about change

- serve as role models in enacting proposed organization changes

- are seen as strong-willed

- have vision and can inspire others to it

- portray a realistic optimism

- influence superiors and are capable of selling their ideas to the organization

- listen to understand other points of view

- help people see the role they can play in transforming the organization

- go where the energy for change is highest, leveraging people and resources already aligned toward change

- celebrate incremental success in creating change

- are willing to drive out people who resist change

What's in Your Way?

Leaders unable to inspire, champion, and drive change hurt their reputation when others see them as inflexible. They face the prospect of change leading them instead of them leading change. They may lose political clout and see their organization's products and services overtaken by competitors. Look at the list below and mark those items that you believe are interfering with your ability to champion change.

- ❏ You have good ideas but your communication style is uninspiring.
- ❏ You don't have the patience, tolerance, or emotional energy to drive change.
- ❏ You simply don't know how your organization should change.
- ❏ You struggle to incorporate others' ideas into the change process.
- ❏ The people you need to influence are resistant to change.
- ❏ The organization has grown confident in its complacency.
- ❏ The organization has been burned by change initiatives in the past.
- ❏ You spend too much time getting people to endorse your ideas, failing to provide strong leadership when it's needed.
- ❏ You invest in many new ideas that fail.
- ❏ Your changes don't meet the customer's needs.
- ❏ You create commitment to change but fail to execute.
- ❏ Your proposed changes are seen as a fad.
- ❏ You overlook key forces aligned against you.
- ❏ People see your change as a threat to the informal or formal power structure.

Coach Yourself

To develop yourself as a change champion, create goals in the areas of promoting ideas, influencing a course of action, or solving an intractable problem. These questions can help you define such focus areas:

- What is the most burning problem confronting you or your organization? How does it necessitate change? How is the problem a threat and an opportunity?

- What do people in your organization fear most about change? Why? How might you address their fears?

- Who are the most effective change agents in your organization? Why are they effective? How do others perceive and respond to them? How might you emulate their actions?

- Who is most likely to fight your change? Where can you find the allies you need to sustain change against resistance?

- Do you have the sustained energy and patience to drive change? What sources can you tap into to support your effort?

Improve Now

Draw a stakeholder wheel. Understand the forces aligned against and for change. Your wheel should identify everyone and every group affected by the change. Study the incentives those stakeholders have for changing or resisting. You can also use your wheel to illustrate the distribution of power in the organization. Look for allies.

Frame the threat and the opportunity that necessitate change. Look at change as an opportunity to avoid a viable threat. Communicate what will happen if nothing changes. Create positive attitudes by pointing to the benefits to people and to the organization if changes are adopted.

Find your passion. What about the intended change makes you excited? You will convey more energy and enthusiasm if you first communicate aspects of the change about which you care the most.

Stay authentic. Allow yourself to still be human. That is, allow yourself to be vulnerable about the change. Admit that you don't know all the answers. Be open to how the change will affect others and you.

Establish a sense of urgency. To spark the need for urgency, do two things simultaneously: One, raise energy and motivation about the need to change. Two, reduce any fear, anger, or complacency that you spot.

Act as a role model for change. Everyone will be watching you and how you lead the change effort. List all the things you think you are doing well and those you think you could do better. Ask a trusted colleague for additional feedback.

Foster change-ready employees. This is something you need to address all year round—not just during times of change. Ensure your employees are ready for the barrage of change that will constantly come at them.

Look beyond. Explore the field outside your organization for examples of successful change. Select what in those stories you can transfer to the change in your organization.

Change quotes. Ask your team members to bring a quote that represents their attitude about change. Open your next meeting with each person stating their quote and why they chose it. Share your own quote. Explain it to your team members. Help your team members see that everyone responds to change differently.

Developmental Opportunities

- Join the board of a struggling nonprofit.

- Lead a project team opening business in a new market.

- Represent your group on a task force making changes in organizational policies.

- Lead a task force to fix a major problem (for example, to correct a quality problem, redesign a flawed system, or streamline a critical process).

- Work with your direct reports as a group to reorganize their work responsibilities to fit proposed organizational changes.

- Develop processes for tracking progress toward the long-term goals that a change initiative is designed to achieve.

Activity Center

Review and download these activities you can use for your development or with your team from the *Compass* resource page at www.ccl.org/compassbook.

Champion Change: Communicate Change
Champion Change: Roles for Everyone

Related Competencies

Change Acceptance
Change Implementation
Credibility and Integrity
Flexibility
Risk Taking
Vision

Resources

Boatman, J., & Wellins, R. S. (2011). *Global leadership forecast 2011: Time for a leadership revolution*. Bridgeville, PA: Development Dimensions International.

Bunker, K. (2008). *Responses to change: Helping people manage transition*. Greensboro, NC: Center for Creative Leadership.

Dinwoodie, D. (2014). *Transformational change: An ecosystem approach*. (White paper). Center for Creative Leadership. http://insights.ccl.org/articles/white-papers/transformational-change-an-ecosystem-approach/

Fortune. (n.d.). Pope Francis, 79. Retrieved from http://fortune.com/worlds-greatest-leaders/pope-francis-4/

Kotter, J. P. (2012). *Leading change*. Boston, MA: Harvard Business Review Press.

McGuire, J. B., & Rhodes, G. (2009). *Transforming your leadership culture*. San Francisco, CA: Jossey-Bass.

Muhly, S. (2016) *Change-capable leadership: The real power propelling successful change*. (White paper.) Center for Creative Leadership. Retrieved from http://insights.ccl.org/articles/white-papers/change-capable-leadership-the-real-power-propelling-successful-change/

Pasmore, B. (2015). It's a new game: Leading complex, continuous change. (White paper). Center for Creative Leadership. Retrieved from https://www .ccl.org/wp-content/uploads/2015/08/continuous-change-white-paper.pdf

Pasmore, B. (2015). *Leading continuous change: Navigating churn in the real world*. Oakland, CA: Berrett-Koehler.

10

Change Acceptance

Adjust to, learn from, and embrace change as necessary for future success.

Francis Bacon once said, "He that will not apply new remedies must expect new evils; for time is the greatest innovator" (2008). Change seems to be the only constant in today's organizational life, driven by shifts in external conditions and the response to those conditions. Because of the magnitude of the changes occurring within organizations and the frequency with which these changes happen, leaders who readily accept change are greatly valued over those who can't.

Even if you do not lead a change initiative, you are bound to be affected by change from time to time. It is much better to accept it than to resist. Otherwise you might fall behind in advancing your career. Want to know how radical change can get? Stop by the Nevada desert in the United States at a certain time of year. Let this story take you there.

Leadership in Action

The annual Burning Man festival draws tens of thousands of celebrants to Nevada's Black Rock Desert. They come for music, art, self-expression, spectacle, and community. Obviously, the Black Rock Desert isn't exactly a bustling population center for most of the year, so participants take it upon themselves to erect Black Rock City to accommodate the massive event.

Black Rock City is not just a funny name for a big collection of tents. It's a literal description. The city boasts a complete electrical grid and numerous municipal necessities, such as a post office, in addition to the more traditional arts and entertainment, including dance clubs, restaurants, and even beauty salons. The city springs up in a matter of days as the festival gets under way, but as impressive as that may sound, it's overshadowed by the incredible disappearing act that follows. As described by writer Gregory Dicum, within weeks of the festival's end, all trace of the city's existence is erased, leaving the landscape pristine (2005).

This is accomplished through massive communal effort on the part of every "citizen" of Black Rock City, each acting as an individual leader with a one-person team. The cleanup effort begins not as a well-oiled hierarchical machine, but a community of individual leaders at every level. These people are able to embrace the temporary aspect of their surroundings and participate in the ephemeral, without abandoning their personal responsibilities.

Nonstop change is part and parcel of the Burning Man festival. Instead of attempting to impose control over their surroundings, individual participants remain flexible, doing whatever they can, wherever they happen to be, to keep the city running.

What High Performance Looks Like

Leaders who accept and embrace change

- adjust easily to organizational changes
- aren't intimidated by change or challenge
- extract lessons from change or turmoil
- use optimistic language in describing change
- see challenges as opportunities, not problems
- see the need to change in order to stay relevant
- remain resilient in the face of challenges, rebounding quickly from setbacks
- are adventurous
- are realistic about change
- are willing to take risks
- are eager to learn and grow
- seek out new and diverse work experiences
- believe most problems can be solved
- focus on skills and resources that will be needed in the future

What's in Your Way?

Resistance to change creates negative energy in your team and the organization, will cause you to miss opportunities to grow as a leader, and will hold direct reports and the organization back in their responses to changing circumstances. Others may see your resistance as stubbornness or fear, perhaps even as weakness and ineffectiveness. You may ultimately be replaced because change will happen with or without your resistance—it's just easier for others to respond if resistance is muted. Take a look at the descriptions that follow and mark any that you suspect are getting in the way of your developing comfort with embracing change.

- ❑ You feel little control over how change is implemented.
- ❑ You fear failure.
- ❑ You're afraid of losing your job.
- ❑ You give up when you encounter challenges that frustrate you.
- ❑ You have struggled to learn from past changes or experiences.
- ❑ You disagree with proposed changes.
- ❑ You lack the resources (time, people, money) to implement changes.
- ❑ People see you as a chameleon, changing to meet the needs of every situation.
- ❑ Your team or organization loses momentum as it constantly shifts direction in response to change.
- ❑ You become impatient with the rate of change and give up too quickly.
- ❑ You try to do too much too soon.
- ❑ You underestimate the scope or complexity of the change required.

Coach Yourself

To develop your skill at accepting change, create goals in areas that allow you to take controlled risks, that put you into unfamiliar situations or roles, that ask you to bounce back from failures, or that otherwise force you to not rely only on your traditional strengths. These questions can help you focus on such areas:

- ● Can you think of a time when you made a change and it worked out for you? What was the change and what happened?

- What are your personal strategies for coping with change? Which ones are healthy? Unhealthy?

- Do you have colleagues who cope well with change? What are their strategies? How does their view of change differ from yours?

- What changes in your organization have you disagreed with? Rather than resistance, are there more constructive ways to voice your disagreement?

- What are the risks of resisting change when that change is inevitable?

- What resources or support would make change more acceptable to you?

Improve Now

Pay attention to your emotions. When you encounter change, how do you feel and react? What might be causing you to react this way? How might you address those emotions in the future?

Avoid knee-jerk reactions. Delay your response to change until you can calm down and assess the situation.

Avoid complainers. Surrounding yourself with people who are negative or unhappy with change will take a toll on you. Plan how you will react when people begin to complain.

Anticipate change. Always keep one eye on the horizon, looking for the next big opportunity or the coming storm. This will prevent events from catching you unaware and help to give you a competitive advantage.

Be a change advocate. If you have a vision for the future, voice it, and work toward achieving it. A core element of leadership lies in paving new ground and forging into uncharted territory.

Influence the change process. If changes are occurring within your organization, don't be a bystander. Contribute your thoughts and energy to the implementation. This will increase your visibility, provide you with experience, and highlight your stance as a change leader.

Get to know people who embrace change. Ask them about how they view or approach change. What are their fears about change, and how do they overcome them?

Learn cautious optimism. When confronted with change, try to stay optimistic as you gather information about the change and plan your response.

Be prepared to work. Change requires learning, and learning is work. There's no way around it.

Be prepared to learn. If this is a relatively new role for you, read "Change-Capable Leadership: The Real Power of Propelling Successful Change," a CCL White Paper. See the Resource section at the end of this chapter for download options.

Get up and go. Read Dr. Seuss's book, *Oh the Places You'll Go!* We mean it. The book's characters react and respond to doing things differently and challenging the status quo. It delivers several powerful messages: (1) Change is either difficult or fun; (2) The road to change may be a scary experience or a confusing one; (3) The experience can be one that you hope will go away or one that evokes responsibility to get it done; (4) Change can be an exciting open road or a speed bump to avoid. Share the book with employees.

Developmental Opportunities

- Work with a team that is unfamiliar with you and has perspectives different from your own.

- Lead a team responsible for creating new directions for the organization or fixing problems.

- Take on part of a colleague's job while he or she is on temporary leave.

- Represent your group on a task force making changes in organizational policies.

- Volunteer your work group as a test site for a new organizational system or process.

Activity Center

Review and download these activities you can use for your development or with your team from the *Compass* resource page at www.ccl.org/compassbook.

Change Acceptance: Your View of Change

Change Acceptance: You and Change

Related Competencies

Change Implementation

Flexibility

Learning Agility

Resilience

Risk Taking

Tolerating Ambiguity

Resources

Adams, M. G. (2016). *Change your questions, change your life: 12 powerful tools for leadership, coaching, and life* (3rd ed.). Oakland, CA: Berrett-Koehler.

Bacon, F. (2008). *Francis Bacon: The major works.* (B. Vickers, Ed.). New York, NY: Oxford University Press.

Bendixen, S. M., Campbell, M., Criswell, C., & Smith, R. (2016). *Change-capable leadership: The real power of propelling successful change.* (White paper). Center for Creative Leadership. Retrieved from https://www.ccl.org/wp-content/uploads/2016/04/Change-Capable-Leadership.pdf

Bunker, K. A. (2008). *Responses to change: Helping people manage transition.* Greensboro, NC: Center for Creative Leadership.

Bunker, K. A., & Wakefield, M. (2005). *Leading with authenticity in times of transition.* Greensboro, NC: Center for Creative Leadership.

Bunker, K. A., & Wakefield, M. (2010). *Leading through transitions: Facilitator's guide set.* San Francisco, CA: Pfeiffer.

Dicum, G. (2005, Sept. 14). GREEN burning man leaves no trace. *SF Gate.* Retrieved from http://www.sfgate.com/homeandgarden/article/GREEN-Burning-Man-Leaves-No-Trace-3238869.php

Gryskiewicz, S. S. (1999). *Positive turbulence: Developing climates for creativity, innovation, and renewal*. San Francisco, CA: Jossey-Bass.

Heath, C., & Heath, D. (2010). *Switch: How to change things when change is hard*. New York, NY: Crown Business.

McGuire, J. B., & Rhodes, G. (2009). *Transforming your leadership culture*. San Francisco, CA: Jossey-Bass.

Pasmore, B. (2015). *Leading continuous change: Navigating churn in the real world*. Oakland, CA: Berrett-Koehler.

Rush, S. (Ed.) (2012). *On leading in times of change*. Greensboro, NC: Center for Creative Leadership.

Seuss, D. (1990). *Oh, the places you'll go!* New York, NY: Random House.

11

Change Implementation

Lead, organize, and execute organizational change efforts, taking employee concerns into consideration.

Amid the challenges of technological advancements, globalization, and economic volatility, your ability as a leader to implement change is increasingly crucial to your organization's survival (and your career). Yet 70 percent of all organizational change initiatives fail (Balogun & Hope Hailey, 2004), underscoring an acute need for leadership in planning strategic change, inspiring commitment to change, and executing change initiatives.

Because of the magnitude of the changes occurring within organizations and the frequency with which these changes happen, the leaders who develop the skills needed to implement change in organizations will be greatly valued over their counterparts. Implementing change initiatives is no longer a skill that's nice to have but one you must have. Let's look in on the story of a young girl from Pakistan who pressed for change and succeeded.

Leadership in Action

Sheikh Hasina Wazed could not attend school as
a young child living in Pakistan. She wasn't prevented by
the conservative culture of her birthplace, but by practical
barriers that made attendance impossible. "I was not allowed
to go to the school. Because I had to cross the canal by a
wooden bridge, [my grandmother] was very much afraid that if I fall from
this wooden bridge I will fall in the river." Decades later, as prime minister of
Bangladesh, Sheikh Hasina has made it her goal to change the opportunities
for women in her country.

Implementing this change requires careful maneuvering between
cultural demands (Bangladesh has a strong Islamic tradition, with the
world's fourth-largest Muslim population) and policy goals. Rather than
attempt a fundamental cultural shift, Sheikh Hasina has accomplished her
mission by removing the practical barriers between girls and the education
they seek. Her interventions include exemption of tuition fees for girls in
rural areas and a stipend scheme for girls at the secondary level.

The effect of these interventions is clear: since 1990, primary school
enrollment increased from 12 million (with 6.6 million boys and 5.4 million
girls) to over 19 million, with an even split between boys and girls. In 2000,
enrollment of female students in secondary education actually exceeded
that of male students (Rahman, 2014).

To effect these changes, Sheikh Hasina had to face the entrenched
traditions of her society and deal with them realistically. She couldn't simply
wave her hand and shift the entire culture in which she worked. By creating
a series of incentives and opportunities, she was able to achieve her goal
cooperatively, which allowed the changes she sought to become permanent.

What High Performance Looks Like

Leaders adept at implementing change

- genuinely try to understand the impact of change on others
- keep people in the organization informed of future changes that may affect them
- involve key people in the design and implementation of change
- encourage people to generate and take responsibility for their ideas about implementing change
- modify and refine implementation plans based on input from others during the change and make adjustments along the way
- ensure that internal sponsors of the change remain aligned and committed to it
- manage resistance to change
- are seen as flexible
- possess courage and credibility
- are good listeners and interpersonally sensitive to concerns and ideas about change
- are seen as direct and proactive
- determine what people are fearful of and why they resist change
- thank people and affirm their efforts for their help in creating change
- seek counsel from people who are not directly involved or encumbered by proposed changes
- lead change by example

What's in Your Way?

If you've been ineffective at implementing change, you already know that the change you're working for doesn't stick. Consequently, your organization may lose competitive advantage, the results of its work can be negatively impacted, and people in the organization can fall into conflict. Any one of these outcomes would clearly signal to others you are not suited to lead significant organizational initiatives, leading to fewer opportunities and stalling your career. In more extreme cases, where the magnitude of failure is great or more than one negative outcome results from your leadership, your career in the organization might end. From the list below, choose those items that you suspect are making you ineffective at implementing change.

❏ You have limited experience implementing large-scale change.

❏ You fail to convey the big picture to your employees—they do not understand the rationale for key decisions.

❏ You don't fully understand the rationale for change communicated from more senior leadership levels.

❏ You try to control when instead you need to engage others.

❏ You have limited insight into the people in and outside your organization who will be affected by the change.

❏ You have limited relationship and collaboration skills.

❏ You don't know how to influence others.

❏ You become associated with a proposed change that has not been thoroughly planned and causes unnecessary disruption.

❏ You don't have the energy to drive change during its long and involved process.

❏ You cut corners in the interest of time.

❏ You try to implement change too quickly, causing others to feel confused or overwhelmed.

❏ You get frustrated and give up.

❏ You focus on consensus at the expense of quality or excellence.

Coach Yourself

To develop your skill at implementing change, create goals in areas where you must start new operations or a new business and that put your team in the lead for implementing a change, for example. These questions can help you focus on these skills:

- What changes in the organization threaten you? What changes in the organization excite you? What change would you be willing to sacrifice for?

- Do you understand the rationale for proposed changes? Can you explain and defend these changes to your team?

- How much of the work of implementing change have you delegated? How are you involving other people and allowing for ownership?

- What kinds of change does your team find most unsettling? Why?

- What will it take to get needed support for the change? Who do you go to for help or guidance when you run into resistance?

- How often do you communicate with the people affected by change? What is your message to them?

Improve Now

Meet in person. Make an effort to periodically meet with people and spend time with them discussing the change, its impact, and their feelings about it. Email and phone contact is insufficient.

Provide options. People want a sense of control, so give them viable options within the boundaries of the change initiative.

Maintain FAQs. Create an easily accessed and used mechanism for people to learn about changes and find answers to their questions. Ask your employees to write the answers to keep them involved in the implementation and to increase their buy-in.

Make a clear case for change. Boil the argument for change down to a well-honed series of compelling talking points.

Do your homework. Provide clear, compelling evidence for the need to change.

Communicate a vision. Engage others in imagining a changed organization. How does it feel? How is it different or better?

Engage a team in planning change. Recruit employees to work on an implementation team. Define the parameters of the team so its members know where they can or cannot add their own ideas.

Keep stakeholders involved. Hold regular check-ins with your stakeholders to discuss progress, make adjustments, and maintain their support.

Focus energy on those who have the most to lose. Identify people or functions that may have a legitimate reason to feel threatened. Create a plan for getting their support and for addressing their concerns early in the process.

Define outcome measures. How will you measure the success of a change? What will people say? What metrics will change? What else will happen?

Developmental Opportunities

- Join a project team opening a new market.

- Join a project team installing new systems into the organization.

- Lead a task force to fix a problem (for example, correct a quality procedure, redesign a flawed system, or simplify a process).

- Work with your direct reports to reorganize individual work responsibilities to better fit with organizational priorities.

- With your employees, analyze a past change initiative and look at what was done well and what could have been done differently.

- Observe and participate in a change effort that you don't lead—watch how the leaders act and how other people respond.

Activity Center

Review and download these activities you can use for your development or with your team from the *Compass* resource page at www.ccl.org/compassbook.

Change Implementation: Read Two Change Classics
Change Implementation: Four Questions of Change
Change Implementation: Force Field Analysis

Related Competencies

Communication
Conflict Resolution
Credibility and Integrity
Influence
Organizational Savvy
Relationship Management

Resources

Balogun, J., & Hope Hailey, V. (2004). *Exploring strategic change* (2nd ed.). London, UK: Prentice Hall.

Bunker, K. A. (2008). *Responses to change: Helping people manage transition*. Greensboro, NC: Center for Creative Leadership.

Calarco, A., & Gurvis, J. (2006). *Adaptability: Responding effectively to change*. Greensboro, NC: Center for Creative Leadership.

Johnson, S. (1998). *Who moved my cheese? An amazing way to deal with change in your work and in your life.* New York, NY: Putnam.

Kotter, J. P. (2008). *A sense of urgency*. Boston, MA: Harvard Business School Publishing.

McGuire, J. B., & Rhodes, G. (2009). *Transforming your leadership culture*. San Francisco, CA: Jossey-Bass.

Pasmore, B. (2015). *Leading continuous change: navigating churn in the real world*. Oakland, CA: Berrett-Koehler.

Rahman, M. (2014, Sept. 8). Unesco honours Hasina for promotion of girls' education. *Gulf Times*.

12

Coach and Develop Others

Provide guidance and support to help others learn and grow.

The Center for Creative Leadership (CCL) has coached leaders since its beginning, and it recognizes that coaching is vital to learning and development. CCL also thinks coaching is a key skill for leaders who want to make a difference. Leader-coaches create safe and challenging environments for their direct reports and for others. Within those environments, people can develop their talents and make a bigger impact on their work and in their relationships with others. By harnessing that cycle of learning and development, organizations reap huge rewards in terms of profitability, service, and sustainability.

Boatman and Wellins's 2011 research indicates that most leaders aren't seen as highly effective at developing others. If you're among that group, you are losing out. The ability (or inability) to develop others is associated with career and leadership advancement, derailment, relationships with direct reports, employee engagement, measures of your performance, and, in the final analysis, your organization's sustainability (Zenger & Folkman, 2007). So ask yourself: Are you doing all you can to contribute to and develop your organization's leadership pipeline? What if you compare yourself to the leader in the following story?

Leadership in Action

From his humble beginnings as the son of slaves, Benjamin Mays devoted himself to learning and to teaching others. His focus on self-reliance, rooted in his deep religious convictions, brought an entire generation of African-American men to prominence during the struggle for civil rights in the United States. As described by the late civil rights leader, author, and professor Roger Wilkins (2003), Coretta Scott King attributes Mays with providing the example of social justice that inspired her husband, Martin Luther King Jr. Julian Bond, who served as head of the NAACP for 12 years, once said that Mays embodied all that he and his compatriots worked so hard to be.

In 1940, Mays became the president of Morehouse University. He sought out students by travelling the back roads through small Southern towns to find smart kids without much hope of a high school education, much less a university degree. Mays created a special program to bring those young boys into Morehouse so they could realize their potential. Martin Luther King Jr., for example, was only 15 years old when he entered Morehouse. It's impossible to overstate Mays's importance as a coach, mentor, and champion to the men who led the civil rights struggle and who have served in various leadership roles in government, education, and private business. His example shows that coaching and developing others isn't a skill that a leader masters only to fill a leadership pipeline. Coaching and developing others creates a leadership legacy.

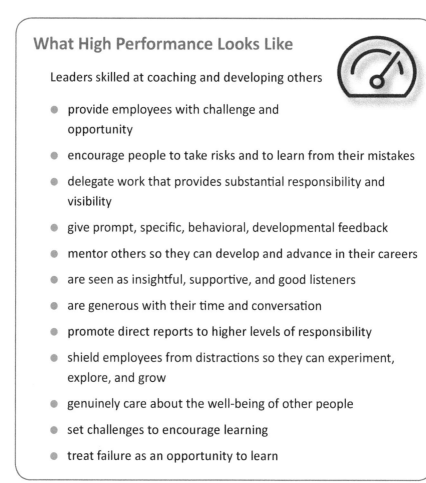

What High Performance Looks Like

Leaders skilled at coaching and developing others

- provide employees with challenge and opportunity
- encourage people to take risks and to learn from their mistakes
- delegate work that provides substantial responsibility and visibility
- give prompt, specific, behavioral, developmental feedback
- mentor others so they can develop and advance in their careers
- are seen as insightful, supportive, and good listeners
- are generous with their time and conversation
- promote direct reports to higher levels of responsibility
- shield employees from distractions so they can experiment, explore, and grow
- genuinely care about the well-being of other people
- set challenges to encourage learning
- treat failure as an opportunity to learn

What's in Your Way?

If you're ineffective at developing the talents of others, you'll end up with employees who don't improve their skills and perform. They might not feel challenged, can lose their motivation, and may disengage from meaningfully contributing to the organization. In the short term, employees might display performance problems because they can't respond positively to changes and new challenges. Over the long term, they will lose faith in their leaders and their organizations because they believe they have more to offer but don't have the opportunity to show what they can do. Without the skill to coach and develop the talent others have to offer, leaders can miss opportunities to guide and support employees in their work and to share in their successes. Such leaders might also lose the opportunity to create a high-performing team. Mark items on the list below that you think are affecting your developing skill at coaching and developing others.

- ❏ You don't invest time in your people.
- ❏ You don't know how to handle performance problems.
- ❏ You prefer to talk rather than listen.
- ❏ You struggle to understand the perspective or intentions of others.
- ❏ You don't see coaching as your job.
- ❏ You drive people too hard and they leave the organization.
- ❏ You press people toward a specific development path rather than helping them travel the path they choose for themselves.
- ❏ People take your feedback as overly critical, not developmental.
- ❏ You are seen as favoring certain employees, devoting an inordinate amount of time or attention to them.
- ❏ You stretch people too far and with too little support.
- ❏ You overload employees with information.

Coach Yourself

To develop skill at coaching and developing others, create goals that position you to guide work to be achieved rather than simply ordering work to be done. Look for areas in which you can delegate responsibility and create developmental assignments. Those areas might include setting a new direction for a team, situations in which you must deal with a problem employee, or circumstances in which you are involved with an uncommonly diverse group. These questions can help you define such focus areas:

- What skills do your direct reports believe they need to develop?

- Does your organization offer a formal mentoring program? If so, how can you use that program to develop your direct reports?

- What are your concerns or fears about developing others?

- What do you do now to coach or develop other people? What challenges have you given them?

- Who helped you in the past when you were learning your role? How did they help you? What actions did they take that you can apply to your coaching?

- Do you spend time observing your direct reports at work? Do you have enough information to know how to help them?

Improve Now

Give people challenging assignments. Set stretch goals that you believe they can attain with some support from you. Measure progress, celebrate milestones, and capitalize on teachable moments during their developmental experiences.

Meet with employees at least once a month. Discuss how they are doing with their development and how you can help them. Be a sounding board and provide support. Keep notes on each employee's development.

Commit to giving feedback. Provide prompt feedback, both positive and developmental, to employees. Be specific. Clarify the situation, the behaviors you observed, and their impact.

Avoid phrases like "always" or "never" in your feedback. That puts your people on the defensive and distracts from your message, because they start to think about exceptions and extenuating circumstances rather than listening to what you have to say.

Watch how other leaders coach and develop their people. What do they say, and how do they say it? What are they doing right, and what do you think they are doing wrong? What impact do they have on the attitude and behavior of the people they are trying to develop?

Learn to listen. Learn and practice active listening—pay attention, withhold judgment, reflect, clarify, summarize, share, and read nonverbal cues.

Watch the example you set. People often respond more to what you do than to what you say.

Keep clear of interpretations and problem solving. Keep your message simple, direct, and honest during developmental conversations, whether as feedback, in performance interviews, or in other situations. Stick to observations about people's behavior. Don't analyze or guess about their motives, and don't tell them how to fix it. Instead, reach a mutual understanding of the situation and let them decide the best way to approach it.

Delegate for development, not for convenience. Don't hover. Don't micromanage. Allow your people to do the work themselves and to make mistakes from which they can learn. Reward progress and emphasize what they are learning from their experiences.

Treat setbacks and mistakes as learning opportunities. Don't ignore consequences but treat inevitable mistakes as an opportunity for the person you are coaching to gain insight, learn different approaches, and emerge wiser.

Developmental Opportunities

■ Turn around a low-performing team by creating experiences that will motivate team members to be successful.

■ Lead the start-up of a team.

■ Delegate one of your job responsibilities to a direct report and provide support without micromanaging.

■ Coach one of your solid performers through a stretch assignment.

■ Work with an employee who shows promise but doesn't have the needed experience for the job.

■ Mentor the newest person in your group.

Activity Center

Review and download these activities you can use for your development or with your team from this book's resource page at www.ccl.org/compassbook.

Coach and Develop Others: 4Cs for Developing Others
Coach and Develop Others: One-on-One Coaching
Coach and Develop Others: Reflect on Your Talent Conversations
Coach and Develop Others: Six Questions

Related Competencies

Communication

Delegating

Engagement

Relationship Management

Talent Recruitment and Retention

Resources

Blanchard, K., & Johnson, S. (2015). *The new one minute manager*. New York, NY: HarperCollins Publishers.

Boatman, J., & Wellins, R. S. (2011). *Global leadership forecast 2011: Time for a leadership revolution*. Bridgeville, PA: Development Dimensions International.

Browning, H., & Van Velsor, E. (1999). *Three keys to development: Defining and meeting your leadership challenges*. Greensboro, NC: Center for Creative Leadership.

Harvard Business School. (2004). *Coaching and mentoring: How to develop top talent and achieve stronger performance.* Boston, MA: Harvard Business Essentials.

Kouzes, J., Posner, B., & Biech, E. (2010). *A coach's guide to developing exemplary leaders.* San Francisco, CA: Pfeiffer.

Merrill, A. R., Davis, C. T., Simpson, M. K., & Moon, S. D. (2017). *Talent unleashed: 3 leadership conversations to ignite the unlimited potential in people*. Franklin, TN: Post Hill Press.

Naudé, J., & Plessier, F. (2014). *Becoming a leader-coach: A step-by-step guide to developing your people*. Greensboro, NC: Center for Creative Leadership.

Nelson, B. (2012). *1501 ways to reward employees*. New York, NY: Workman Publishing.

Smith, R., & Campbell, M. (2011). *Talent conversations: What they are, why they're crucial, and how to do them right*. Greensboro, NC: Center for Creative Leadership.

Stanier, M. B. (2016). *The coaching habit: Say less, ask more, and change the way you lead forever*. Toronto, Canada: Box of Crayons Press.

Ting, S., & Scisco, P. (Eds.). (2006). *The CCL handbook of coaching: A guide for the leader coach*. San Francisco, CA: Jossey-Bass.

Turregano, C. (2013). *Delegating effectively: A leader's guide to getting things done*. Greensboro, NC: Center for Creative Leadership.

Wilkins, R. (2003, July 21). Benjamin Mays. *The Nation*. Retrieved from https://www.thenation.com/article/benjamin-mays/

Zenger, J. H., & Folkman, J. (2007). *The handbook for leaders: 24 lessons for extraordinary leadership*. New York, NY: McGraw-Hill.

13

Compassion and Sensitivity

Show genuine interest in others and sensitivity to employees' needs.

It has been estimated that two-thirds of currently employed Americans are looking for new jobs or opportunities (Jobvite, 2010). Many of these job seekers would remain with their organizations if they felt supported by their boss and their organization. A leader's genuine compassion and sensitivity play an important role in employees' decisions to leave a company and can go a long way toward keeping talent in an organization. Further, CCL research finds that leaders who exhibit compassion and sensitivity toward their employees are considered less likely to derail. It works both ways— compassion and sensitivity keep workers engaged and productive and limit a leader's chances of failing. To get a realistic understanding of the business results compassionate leaders create, let's peek into the work of the Ford Foundation.

Leadership in Action

As president of the Ford Foundation, Darren Walker faces a massively broad task every day. It's his job to lead a team of grant-makers, with a multibillion-dollar endowment, in the task of "advancing human welfare." The history of the foundation shows that it has never pursued a single mission, but actively seeks to find pressing issues in different cultures and countries—with the fundamental purpose of social justice and giving voice to underrepresented members of society. And the foundation relies on the conscience of its director to guide its efforts.

In Walker's case, compassion and sensitivity aren't merely pleasant personality traits, but form a critical competency he practices every day. After all, without these skills, how is he to recognize urgent inequalities for his foundation to address? To achieve this mindset, Walker has deliberately flattened the hierarchy within his organization. Instead of maintaining an emotional distance from the foundation's mission, he is known for his pep talks and self-effacing sense of humor. This allows his team a sense of comfort and safety that nurtures conversation and self-examination.

It was that habit of self-examination that prompted Walker's essay, "Ignorance Is the Enemy Within," which he published to the foundation's website in September of 2016. In it, he relates a story of coming to grips with his own privilege, which he describes as an "enemy of justice." In the essay, Walker tells of being confronted by his colleagues after failing to consider people with disabilities in a recent initiative by the Ford Foundation. Instead of resenting the challenge, Walker listened and looked inward, arriving at a realization that will ultimately benefit the foundation's mission.

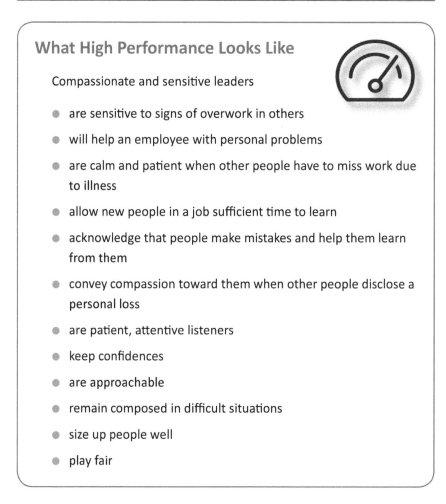

What High Performance Looks Like

Compassionate and sensitive leaders

- are sensitive to signs of overwork in others
- will help an employee with personal problems
- are calm and patient when other people have to miss work due to illness
- allow new people in a job sufficient time to learn
- acknowledge that people make mistakes and help them learn from them
- convey compassion toward them when other people disclose a personal loss
- are patient, attentive listeners
- keep confidences
- are approachable
- remain composed in difficult situations
- size up people well
- play fair

What's in Your Way?

If you're familiar with Charles Dickens' *A Christmas Carol*, then you know Ebeneezer Scrooge as the archetype of the uncaring, insensitive leader. Scrooge cares more for his power, position, and profits than for his long-suffering direct report, Bob Cratchit. Thankfully for Bob, Scrooge experiences an epiphany and changes his behavior. In real life, it doesn't work that way. Typically, toxic bosses like Scrooge don't rise far in organizations—though in some cases they can rise all the way to the top. Uncompassionate, insensitive bosses seldom develop people that the organization needs and lack the interpersonal savvy, self-awareness, and authenticity that support top leadership positions. They often leave a trail of injuries and resentment behind them in their climb to the top. Those casualties of blind ambition can be a drag on their careers and can sometimes even end them. Thankfully, healthy human beings are endowed with sympathy and empathy—that's how we maintain beneficial social order. But if you want to take your compassion and sensitivity to a higher level that inspires trust and motivates others, and you're struggling to make progress, mark any of the following descriptions that suggest areas for your development:

- ❏ You spend your time managing tasks and projects at the expense of interacting with others.
- ❏ You lack the courage to deal face-to-face with difficult personnel issues or conflict.
- ❏ You're unaware of the impact of your behavior on others.
- ❏ You're the product of a hard-driving, unsympathetic boss and have internalized that behavior as a model of leadership.
- ❏ You prefer email, text, and other electronic communication over face-to-face conversation.
- ❏ You've received feedback that you're "soft" and inattentive to the "hard skills" of management.
- ❏ People assume you're easily influenced and try to work their agenda through you.
- ❏ You're impatient with the effort it takes to change your behavior or to maintain it.
- ❏ People are skeptical of the change you are trying to make and you give up rather than giving them time to learn and trust the new relationship.
- ❏ You think that dealing with emotions interferes with your ability to do your job.
- ❏ You have such a close relationship with a direct report that you lose your objectivity.

Coach Yourself

To elevate your compassion and sensitivity, create goals in areas that require you to create close relationships and expose you to diverse personalities, backgrounds, perspectives, ethnicities, and other differences. These questions can help you define such areas:

- Think of a time when you have received compassionate treatment from someone. How did that make you feel toward that person?

- What opinions, beliefs, or stereotypes do you carry that might interfere with how you express compassion and sensitivity? For example, do you believe that avoiding conflict is a way of appearing sensitive to others?

- Does your organization's culture support or work against compassion and sensitivity? Is it a hypercompetitive and cutthroat place to work, or is it collaborative and caring?

- Think of a conflict situation you've experienced. How would you have handled that situation by showing compassion and sensitivity?

- Can you make hard calls on performance problems despite your desire to be sensitive to others?

Improve Now

Make a visit. Engage with your direct reports and others on a regular basis—walk around, don't barricade yourself in your office.

Seek first to understand. One of Stephen Covey's seven habits is to "seek first to understand, then to be understood." Covey warns that giving out advice before having empathetically understood a person and his or her situation will likely result in rejection of that advice. Thoroughly surfacing your own beliefs about the person and situation will increase the chance of establishing a working communication.

Learn the personal. Make an effort to learn something about the personal lives of your direct reports. Do they have children? What activities do they enjoy? Allow them to see you are interested in them as whole human beings, not as replaceable pieces. Don't pry—let them share what they are comfortable sharing.

Learn their differences. For those direct reports with different backgrounds, ethnicities, and geographies from yours, make an effort to learn a little about their situation. Don't use what you learn to pretend you're an expert or that you have a lot in common but to expand your awareness of difference so you can genuinely connect.

Take a stand on stereotypes. Few people have the courage to speak out against words and comments that hurt others. Demeaning remarks, stereotypes, and bias have no place in a high-performing organization. Yet they show up in the form of jokes, stories, instructions, cartoons, and other workplace expressions. These attitudes and behaviors prevent true teamwork and inclusion in your organization. It's a leader's responsibility to speak up when slurs or even subtly insulting comments arise. Simply say, "I feel uncomfortable with that comment (statement, remark, word, name)." Think about why you may not have taken a stand in the past. Make a pledge to yourself and the organization to do so in the future.

Recognize big pain. Grief over a loss or illness, concern about a wayward child, and other deep, affective events can be difficult to talk about and sometimes even to listen to. Sympathize, but don't advise unless someone asks for your counsel. Don't ever say "Get over it" or "Let it go" to someone experiencing this level of pain. Listen. Acknowledge. Let them know they have your support, whatever happens (and be ready to follow through).

Train as a volunteer mediator. There are many opportunities for you to practice compassion in a mediator's role. Whether it's representing minors in legal proceedings or working with two groups or two people to find a solution to a conflict, you'll be called to remain compassionate and sensitive to others, their circumstances, and their positions.

See how it's done. Observe the actions of someone at work who you consider compassionate and good at displaying sensitivity.

Developmental Opportunities

- Take an expat assignment to work in unfamiliar surroundings with people different from you. From that experience, note if you feel a general sense of compassion and sensitivity because you can't fall back on familiar behavior but must learn to connect across those differences.

- Serve as someone's mentor to gain deep experience in listening, empathizing, and building trust. Developmental relationships that play out over an extended time help both sides develop sensitivity toward the interests of others.

- Put on another person's shoes. For example, be a customer for your organization's products and services. Or try something more radical: in one vocational training organization for the blind, new employees don blindfolds for a day to gain sensitivity for their clients.

- During team meetings, step back from leading the meeting with your own speaking and make room for your team members to have their voices heard. Be explicit about what you're doing—it may take time for your team members to get used to the idea that you are not leading the conversation but participating in it.

- Take a role on a team that is organizing layoffs, a merger, or some other disruptive organizational change.

Activity Center

Review and download these short activities you can use for your development or with your team from this book's resource page at www.ccl.org/compassbook.

Compassion and Sensitivity: Self-Coaching for Compassion and Sensitivity

Compassion and Sensitivity: Understanding Defining Moments

Related Competencies

Difference, Diversity, Inclusion

Global Team Management

Interpersonal Savvy

Organizational Savvy

Resilience

Self-Awareness

Resources

Center for Creative Leadership. (n.d.). *Relationship skills can be learned.* [Podcast]. Greensboro, NC: Author.

Clerkin, C., Crumbacher C. A., Fernando, J., & Gentry, W. A. (2015). *How to be the boss without being the b-word (bossy).* (White paper). Center for Creative Leadership. Retrieved from https://ccl.org/wp-content/uploads/2015/02/HowToBeBoss.pdf

Gentry, W. A., Clark, M. A., Young, S. F., Cullen, K. L., & Zimmerman, L. (2015). How displaying empathic concern may differentially predict career derailment potential for women and men leaders in Australia. *The Leadership Quarterly, 26*(4), 641–653.

Grant, A. (2013). *Give and take: Why helping others drives our success.* New York, NY: Viking.

Iacoboni, M. (2008). *Mirroring people: The science of empathy and how we connect with others.* New York, NY: Farrar, Straus and Giroux.

Jobvite. (2010). *Job Seeker Nation 2010.* Author. Retrieved from http://web.jobvite.com/rs/jobvite/images/Jobvite_Survey_Jobseeker_Nation_2010_final.pdf

Klann, G. (2007). *Building character: Strengthening the heart of good leadership.* San Francisco, CA: Jossey-Bass.

Klann, G. (n.d.). *Leadership character: Five influential attributes.* [Podcast]. Center for Creative Leadership. Greensboro, NC. Retrieved from https://www.ccl.org/multimedia/podcast/leadership-character-five-influential-attributes/

Walker, D. (2016, Sept. 12). Ignorance is the enemy within: On the power of our privilege, and the privilege of our power. *Equals Change Blog.* Retrieved from https://www.fordfound.org/ideas/equals-change-blog/posts/ignorance-is-the-enemy-within-on-the-power-of-our-privilege-and-the-privilege-of-our-power/

14

Conflict Resolution

Produce positive outcomes and minimize damage by addressing conflict quickly and fairly.

Conflict can be stressful, and it's often tempting to avoid these situations whenever possible. That strategy might explain why 42 percent of employees report that their managers rarely or never resolve conflicts effectively (Weaver & Mitchell, 2012). When leaders avoid or poorly handle conflict, they waste time, money, and talent. However, when leaders reconcile conflicts, they open an opportunity to forge common ground, develop deeper relationships, and leverage divergent perspectives—all parts of achieving positive results.

Leaders who can resolve conflict are recognized in their organizations as skilled negotiators who can connect and reconnect people, contributing to more cohesive organizational cultures. Their courage to deal with conflict helps their organizations sustain themselves long term. Let's revisit one of history's most important examples of conflict resolution.

Leadership in Action

Perhaps there is no more superhuman an exemplar of conflict resolution than Mohandas Gandhi, the Indian revolutionary and statesman who led a sequence of nonviolent protests on behalf of Indian independence from Great Britain. Through patience, sacrifice, political acumen, and sheer determination, Gandhi and his people were able to secure independence for their nation without shedding a drop of British blood.

Gandhi's strategy was founded on nonviolent civil disobedience as a form of organized protest. Famously, he led tens of thousands of protesters on a 25-day march across India to the sea, as a way of protesting laws that made it illegal to gather salt within the country (creating a monopoly for the British). This massive gesture is remembered by history as an emblem of Gandhi's protests. The name of his method was "satyagraha," meaning mass civil disobedience, and it survives in the heart of nonviolent protests around the world to this day (Gandhi, Gandhi, & Vashishtha, 2012).

The principle insight in Gandhi's method—the thing that allowed the British and Indians to avoid civil war and coexist peacefully after Indian independence—was the recognition of the opposition as human. Instead of working to defeat an enemy, Gandhi struggled for a mutual recognition of justice, creating a common goal for both parties to agree upon.

What High Performance Looks Like

Leaders adept at conflict resolution

- take responsibility for their role in creating or contributing to conflict

- try to understand the challenges and obstacles other people face in their work

- try to stay unbiased and fair when addressing conflicts

- work collaboratively to create solutions to conflicts

- look for compromises that will satisfy people or groups in conflict

- focus attention on the big picture, especially common goals and overall direction

- ask questions to make sure they understand the history or causes of conflicts

- are courageous

- remain calm in tense situations

- can be assertive if the conflict demands it

- are understanding of both sides of a conflict

- remain firm in working toward a solution to conflict

- wait until they calm down before addressing conflicts

- actively listen to parties involved in conflict

- proactively address conflicts

What's in Your Way?

Leaders unable to resolve conflict may see their courage come into question. Members of their team may grow unhappy and possibly leave the organization. As conflicts fester and grow, a leader's inability to act contributes to a negative culture and climate. Review the following list and note the items that you believe block you from dealing with and resolving conflict.

- ❏ You have been hurt by conflict in the past, so you avoid it.
- ❏ You are unwilling to take the risk that comes with addressing problems.
- ❏ You never really learned how to handle conflict.
- ❏ You are more focused on tasks than on people.
- ❏ You're in competition with the people with whom you need to collaborate.
- ❏ You make a big deal out of nothing, inflating small conflicts.
- ❏ You are seen as overly confrontational.
- ❏ You don't want to divert your energy from your work to conflicts.
- ❏ You get dragged into conflicts that you can't solve.
- ❏ You make assumptions about the people with whom you're in conflict.
- ❏ You don't ask enough questions to get a full understanding of a conflict.
- ❏ You try to address conflict while you're still upset.

Coach Yourself

To develop your conflict-resolution ability, create goals in the area of change management, mediation, and in situations that require you to shift how people and groups perceive and work with one another. These questions can help you define such focus areas:

- Is your idea of successful conflict resolution about getting your way or creating a positive outcome for everyone?

- How does your organizational culture affect how conflict is addressed?

- What are your hot buttons in conflict situations? What sets you off and why? What cues do you notice before you become upset?

- When have you handled a conflict effectively? What did you do? How can you repeat this?

- Looking back on the conflicts you've experienced, do you think you have a style or tendency in handling conflict? (For example, do you tend to avoid, dominate, collaborate, compromise, or give in?) How might you need to augment or broaden that style?

Improve Now

When you encounter conflict, pause. Take a deep breath. And another. And one more.

Reflect on the conflict situation. Before acting, or reacting, consider the pros and cons of your behavior and review possible alternatives.

Listen. If you feel compelled to speak, stop to reflect on your motivations. Why do you need to talk? What is driving you to speak at this time? You're more likely to understand the causes of a conflict if you ask questions and then listen.

Summon your courage. Conflict situations can feel risky or frightening. The only way past those doubts is to bravely take on the conflict and look for a resolution.

Have someone over. Invite a department with which your department has some level of friction for a demonstration of your group's work. Create opportunities to defuse existing tensions.

Give reconciliation time. Some conflicts can ease with one or a few open conversations, but other conflicts are more difficult to resolve. If it takes weeks rather than hours to resolve the situation, remember that resolution doesn't adhere to deadlines.

Become familiar with how people respond to conflict. Common behaviors, such as the fight or flight response, occur naturally and are unavoidable in conflict situations, although they vary in degree for every person. Recognize the dangers of retaliation, a pattern of response that can increase the level of conflict until it threatens to spin out of control.

Be aware of your own reactions. What is your initial, automatic response to conflict? What is your considered response (where you have time to think and feel before reacting)? Understand your conflict triggers (hot buttons). If you know what sets you off, you can better control your response to conflict.

Craft a plan. After you've had a chance to think about the conflict you're in, make a plan for addressing the situation. What questions would you like to ask the other person or group? How can you engage respectfully and productively with them?

Replace destructive with constructive. Constructive behaviors include perspective taking, creating solutions, expressing emotions, reaching out to others, reflection, delaying your response, and adapting. Destructive behaviors include winning at all costs, displaying anger, demeaning others, retaliating, avoiding, yielding to bad judgment, hiding emotions, and self-criticizing. Which behaviors you choose will have tremendous impact on the conflict and its resolution.

Create a conflict-competent organization. Leaders who gain skill in resolving conflict can extend that competence to others in the organization. Ultimately, the organization will develop structures and processes for conflict resolution and adapt its culture so that conflicts don't fester but are treated early (Runde & Flanagan, 2013). A leader can model constructive behaviors and also support and coach others in their efforts to manage conflict competently.

Developmental Opportunities

- Work with a colleague to solve a cross-unit problem.

- Manage a project that requires coordination across the organization.

- Handle an employee performance issue you've been avoiding.

- Assemble cross-department teams to work on projects.

- Resolve a conflict between two of your employees.

- Work with the manager of a unit your group often has conflict with to create a better working partnership.

Activity Center

Review and download these activities you can use for your development or with your team from this book's resource page at www.ccl.org/compassbook.

Conflict Resolution: Resolve a Conflict
Conflict Resolution: What Influences Conflict

Related Competencies

Communication
Influence
Interpersonal Savvy
Negotiating
Relationship Management
Self-Awareness

Resources

The Arbinger Institute. (2015). *The anatomy of peace: resolving the heart of conflict* (2nd ed.). Oakland, CA: Berrett-Koehler.

Cartwright, T. (2003). *Managing conflict with peers*. Greensboro, NC: Center for Creative Leadership.

Gandhi, H., Gandhi, N. P., & Vashishtha, B. K. (2012). A Gandhian concept towards conflict resolution & peace. *Purushartha: A Journal of Management Ethics and Spirituality, 4*(1), 124–134. Retrieved from http://www.inflibnet. ac.in/ojs/index.php/PS/article/view/1059/940

Patterson, K., Grenny, J., McMillan, R., Switzler, A., & Maxfield, D. (2013). *Crucial accountability: Tools for resolving violated expectations, broken commitments, and bad behavior.* (2nd ed.). New York, NY: McGraw-Hill Education.

Popejoy, B., & McManigle, B. J. (2002). *Managing conflict with direct reports*. Greensboro, NC: Center for Creative Leadership.

Runde, C. E., & Flanagan, T. A. (2008). *Building conflict competent teams.* San Francisco, CA: Jossey-Bass.

Runde, C. E., & Flanagan, T. A. (2013). *Becoming a conflict competent leader: How you and your organization can manage conflict effectively* (2nd ed.). San Francisco, CA: Jossey-Bass.

Scharlatt, H. (2016). *Resolving conflict: Ten steps for turning negatives to positives.* Greensboro, NC: Center for Creative Leadership.

Sharpe, D., & Johnson, E. (2002). *Managing conflict with your boss.* Greensboro, NC: Center for Creative Leadership.

Weaver, P., & Mitchell, S. (2012). *Lessons for leaders from the people who matter*. DDI. Retrieved from http://www.ddiworld.com/ddi/media/ trend-research/lessonsforleadersfromthepeoplewhomatter_mis_ddi.pdf

15

Confronting Problem Employees

Act decisively, quickly, and fairly when dealing with underperforming, disruptive employees.

Dealing with difficult people is one of 15 key experiences CCL's lessons of experience research has identified as crucial to leadership success. And on CCL's Benchmarks 360-degree assessment, it's the lowest-rated competency. Leaders who are unable or unwilling to deal with problem employees can't avoid the fallout from those employees' poisonous effect on teams and others in the organization. Problem employees affect more than their own performance. They can damage entire teams by lowering morale, derailing results, and planting the seeds of disengagement. And the responsibility for maintaining team performance in many respects falls to the leader—so confronting the problem directly and quickly is essential to leadership success. To see how bad the problem can be, pay heed to this story of a CEO in trouble.

Leadership in Action

The struggle of American Apparel asks the question in a single case: Can any employee of a company have so much influence that he or she is above reproach? Dov Charney, the company's former CEO, who founded the company in 1998, would seem the perfect example of an employee who can't be confronted. After all, the company's identity is tied directly to him.

That turned out to be the problem in a nutshell. At the beginning of his enterprise, Charney had a reputation for being provocative, and that image trickled down to his brand in a beneficial way. But gradually, his behavior and reputation disintegrated. Repeated, public allegations of sexual misconduct go beyond the quirky or salacious image that can help a clothing brand and enter the territory of the disgusting. The company's reputation suffered as Charney's collapsed, and shares of American Apparel plunged from $15 in 2007 to under $1 today.

Clearly, even the boss can be a problem employee. This left the rest of Charney's management team with a difficult choice: confront Charney or allow his unchecked misconduct to drag the company into a tailspin. Between these two choices, there was only one real option: confrontation. The board of directors terminated Charney after an internal review.

The company's situation is still grim, but now seems salvageable. Despite the difficulty of losing a major player (and majority shareholder), other directors of the company are optimistic and determined about the change. Allan Mayer of the board of directors told CNN's Cristina Alesci in 2014: "Since we announced the decision, we've been contacted by mainstream, top-of-the-line institutions that have not been interested [before] in supporting us."

What High Performance Looks Like

Leaders able to confront problem employees

- deal effectively with resistant employees
- act decisively when faced with a tough decision, such as laying off workers, even if it hurts emotionally
- move quickly in confronting a problem employee
- can fire or deal firmly with loyal but incompetent people without procrastinating
- correctly identify potential performance problems early
- appropriately document employee performance problems
- can manage and resolve conflict
- possess sound judgment
- are attentive
- are fair
- confront others skillfully
- negotiate adeptly with individuals over roles and performance
- provide regular feedback

What's in Your Way?

Leaders who allow a problem employee to jeopardize those qualities above may lose credibility and influence and miss opportunities for career advancement because they may not be seen as capable of leading people toward committed performance. From the following list, mark any items you suspect are sabotaging your efforts to confront problem employees.

- ❏ You avoid conflict at any cost so you willfully blind yourself to the employee's problematic behavior.

127

❏ You don't see this as part of your role but as an "HR problem."

❏ You procrastinate on decisions.

❏ You don't listen to the employee's side to understand the situation and look for possible solutions.

❏ You don't carefully document the employee's performance.

❏ You don't set or follow through on consequences.

❏ You complain about the employee to others rather than address the problem itself.

❏ You lack the courage to do what is necessary, especially if that means firing the employee.

❏ You want to be liked by employees and are afraid to jeopardize that.

❏ You come across as weak and indecisive.

❏ You worry that people will see you as insensitive and unapproachable.

Coach Yourself

To develop your ability to deal with problem employees, create goals in areas that require you to take a position, to handle a conflict, and to hold difficult conversations. These questions can help you define such areas:

● How comfortable are you in addressing conflict?

● How would you describe your company's disciplinary procedures?

● What makes you procrastinate when assigned a task?

● Can you empathize with another person's point of view?

● Are you afraid of not being liked by others?

● How do you follow up on consequences you set?

Improve Now

Stay connected. Make sure you are giving your employees regular feedback on their performance. You might stop problem behaviors from ever arising.

Pay attention. Between feedback opportunities, observe the work of your employees and their reactions to one another. Peers might notice a problem employee before you do.

Reframe the situation. Look at a conflict with a problem employee as a development opportunity rather than as punishment or probation. If he or she doesn't respond positively, you can always fall back to disciplinary measures.

Hit the books. Read about historical figures who had to rally people from problematic behavior (like giving up) and inspire them to do more than they thought possible. Think how you might adapt their tactics to your own problem-employee situation. Take time to read up on your organization's employee manual so you know the procedures for dealing with employee problems.

Check job descriptions periodically. An employee may exhibit problem behavior if he or she is not a fit for the current job. Roles and jobs can change, and sometimes they become a mismatch for the employee. Check that he or she has the skill and knowledge to perform as you expect. Problem performance can arise from employees' defensiveness when they feel they are not prepared for the job.

Keep tabs on resources. Problem employees might be reacting to the stress of working without adequate resources. Make sure your team has what it needs and make a case for more resources if they are short.

Take care of it. Commit to handling an employee performance issue you've been avoiding. Putting off these tough issues can create unnecessary anxiety for you, and it's not fair to an employee to hit him or her with criticism about performance only at an annual review.

Reflect on your own motivation. If you know what encourages you to perform at your best, you can use that awareness to help a problem employee regain his or her heart for the work. Find out what engages him or her and help to find it.

Developmental Opportunities

- Assign tasks to problem employees to see whether the stretch of those tasks motivate them to better performance and behavior. At the very least you will observe the problem up close, which may give you other ideas.

- Engage employees in strategic decisions to give them a stake in the team's approach to its work and in its goals.

- Agree to train new employees in your group, and use the opportunity to build relationships, lay out your expectations, and hear what new employees expect from their work and from you.

- Fire an employee who has not met performance standards despite coaching and support.

- Develop a plan to support a difficult direct report who gives some indication of potential.

Activity Center

Review and download these activities you can use for your development or with your team from this book's resource page at www.ccl.org/compassbook.

Confronting Problem Employees: Confronting an Employee Work Plan
Confronting Problem Employees: Deal Directly

Related Competencies

Communication

Conflict Resolution

Courage

Delegating

Engagement

Interpersonal Savvy

Negotiating

Resources

Alesci, C. (2014, June 21). American Apparel board learned of 'disturbing misconduct' by company founder. *CNN*.

Browning, H. (2012). *Accountability: Taking ownership of your responsibility.* Greensboro, NC: Center for Creative Leadership.

Cullen-Lester, K., Ruderman, M., & Gentry, B. (n.d.). *Motivating your managers: What's the right strategy?* (White paper). Center for Creative Leadership. Retrieved from http://insights.ccl.org/articles/white-papers/motivating -your-managers-whats-the-right-strategy/

Evans, C. (2015). *Leadership trust: Build it, keep it.* Greensboro, NC: Center for Creative Leadership.

Hart, E. W. (2011). *Feedback in performance reviews.* Greensboro, NC: Center for Creative Leadership.

Patterson, K., Grenny, J., McMillan, R., & Switzler, A. (2005). *Crucial confrontations: Tools for resolving broken promises, violated expectations, and bad behavior.* New York, NY: McGraw-Hill.

Patterson, K., Grenny, J., McMillan, R., & Switzler, A. (2011). *Crucial conversations: Tools for talking when stakes are high* (2nd ed.). New York, NY: McGraw-Hill.

Popejoy, B., & McManigle, B. J. (2002). *Managing conflict with direct reports.* Greensboro, NC: Center for Creative Leadership.

Staver, M. (2012). *Leadership isn't for cowards: How to drive performance by challenging people and confronting problems.* Hoboken, NJ: Wiley.

Wilson, M. S., & Chandrasekar, N. A. (2014). *Experience explorer: Facilitator's guide set.* Greensboro, NC: Center for Creative Leadership.

16
Courage

Act decisively to tackle difficult problems and persevere in the face of adversity.

Courage takes many forms. In the special domain of organizations, leaders need courage to stand against conventional wisdom—to do things differently from "how things are done here." Leaders need courage to deal with thorny interpersonal problems, such as conflict or toxic employees. They need the courage to accept and to act on feedback. They need courage to open themselves to questions and perspectives and not stick to the position that they are right, and they need courage to alter their vision when evolving circumstances warrant change. And they need courage to let go of what has always worked for them in the past and develop new approaches to problems and to stand strong during difficult times. But most importantly, leaders need courage when stakes are high and doing the right thing in the face of threatening consequences is the only ethical choice. That's what we see in this story about Marc Edwards, who took a stand on an issue affecting people in communities far from his own and outside the walls of his organization.

Leadership in Action

What good are the rest of your skills without the courage to apply them? This was the question that faced Marc Edwards in 2015, when water samples from LeAnne Walters, a citizen of Flint, Michigan, a city in the Midwestern United States, arrived in his lab. As told by Donovan Hohn in *The New York Times Magazine* in 2016, the samples came to Edwards by way of EPA drinking-water expert Miguel Del Toral, and Edwards was able to confirm that the water was unfit for human consumption, with one sample containing so much lead it qualified as hazardous waste.

Edwards works as a professor at Virginia Tech, where he teaches and researches civil and environmental engineering. After a similar case in Washington, DC, put him in conflict with Congress and the EPA itself, he was leery of the backlash his findings might provoke. Sure enough, when Walters publicized the findings Del Toral provided, the Michigan Department of Environmental Quality made an effort to discredit the information by discrediting Del Toral. By way of rebuttal, Del Toral reached out to Edwards to conduct a more detailed analysis.

Edwards faced a choice. A direct fight with the EPA could damage his career, his reputation, and his scientific credibility. But the data was the data. He teamed up with Del Toral and helped to conduct what he calls "the most thorough independent evaluation of water in US history." The rewards were not immediate, but the data could no longer be ignored. Gradually, the wedge of the investigation pried open the shell of secrecy around the failure of oversight and quality control that led to Flint's water crisis. Although the crisis in Flint is ongoing at the time this book went to press, Edwards' courage ensured it would no longer be secret.

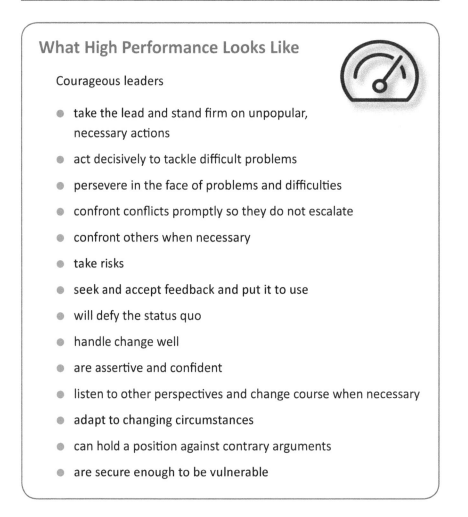

What High Performance Looks Like

Courageous leaders

- take the lead and stand firm on unpopular, necessary actions
- act decisively to tackle difficult problems
- persevere in the face of problems and difficulties
- confront conflicts promptly so they do not escalate
- confront others when necessary
- take risks
- seek and accept feedback and put it to use
- will defy the status quo
- handle change well
- are assertive and confident
- listen to other perspectives and change course when necessary
- adapt to changing circumstances
- can hold a position against contrary arguments
- are secure enough to be vulnerable

What's in Your Way?

Without courage, leaders risk being perceived as weak on handling conflict, unwilling to take necessary risks, and unable to adapt to change. Because in the minds of many courage is linked to ideas of  ethics and integrity, leaders might face doubts about their character that jeopardize developmental and promotional opportunities. In times when negative executive behavior becomes fodder for daily news and a trigger for organizational failure, organizations look harder for the fundamental qualities of ethics and integrity—and the courage it takes to stand firm in those qualities—in the people who rise to the top. Review the following list and note the items that you believe block you from developing the courage you need as a leader.

- ❑ You avoid conflict situations and allow them to fester.
- ❑ You're unwilling to accept feedback and use it to develop your leadership capability.
- ❑ You're quick to abandon your position on issues when faced with opposition.
- ❑ You find it easier to "go along" than to stand your ground.
- ❑ You revert to old behaviors when new habits prove difficult to form and maintain.
- ❑ You become uncomfortable when trying to make your case.
- ❑ You're uncomfortable with making decisions that make you more visible to the organization.
- ❑ You become frustrated with yourself when you fail to defend your position or idea against opposition.
- ❑ You feel threatened when you make yourself vulnerable to other points of view that might affect your position and actions.

Coach Yourself

To develop courage, create goals in areas that require you to take a stand, go against the status quo, or defend a strategic risk. These questions can help you define such areas:

- Does your idea of courage bring images of titanic struggle and heroic measures? How does your idea affect your developing courage?
- What projects—strategic, product, or otherwise—are happening within your organization to which you can add a different perspective?

- Reflect on stories of courage you've read. How might you fit the action in those stories with your circumstances and emulate the courage you've read about?

- Consider a leader in your organization who displays courage. How would you rank that person, from one to five, with five being the most courageous? How do you rank yourself? What can you do to close the gap?

- What ideas do you have that you suspect are too radical or different to express? How might you speak about those ideas to others, and how will you deal with their responses?

Improve Now

Start small. Define areas in which you can safely take a stand or in which the stakes are low. Use that safety zone to stake out a position. For example, you might bargain for more resources for your team, or you might turn down work that puts an undue strain on you or your team.

Consider the consequences. What specifically can the organization gain if you take a stand? What does the organization lose if you don't act?

Build a team of advisors. Seek out people who will support you through high-risk situations. Lean on their collective wisdom and emulate their actions during times when courage is called for.

Prepare for response. When you act, you generate a response in others. When you feel you need to take a stand, consider how others will react. How will you react in turn? Try to think of several scenarios so that the reactions from others don't immediately knock you off your position and force a retreat.

Who's got courage? Find engaging examples of leadership humility and courage in articles, newspapers, or books. Make copies and pass them on to members of your team. Discuss them whenever possible.

Go places. Travel to a place you've never visited, preferably outside your native country. Making your way through unfamiliar surroundings gives you the confidence and courage to try new things.

Take heart. What do you care about enough that you're willing to put yourself on the line? Choose a cause important enough to you that you're willing to make sacrifices or even fail.

Engage others. It's hard to stand at the front lines without allies. Use your powers of influence to bring people on to your side. No leader is an island, and courage doesn't require that you stand alone.

Loosen your constraints. Unless everything is at stake, and it seldom is, unshackle yourself from the limits of your position and from the expectations others have of you. Don't abandon your ethics or jeopardize your integrity, but think and act boldly.

Find the difference. Seek opportunities in areas where you can offer a different perspective to a difficult problem.

Advocate. Speak for an idea you feel strongly about but which isn't popular among your peers. If you can't find such a situation at work, consider speaking for an environmental, social, or political cause.

Developmental Opportunities

- Champion a change your group has been resisting.

- Make your voice heard. Take advantage of meetings to speak your opinion or to give your perspective. Vow to make a certain number of contributions to the conversation and keep at it while you build the courage to speak.

- Represent the concerns of frontline employees to higher management.

- Give some difficult feedback to your boss.

- Ask your boss or your team to give you one new problem to solve each year. Or work on a task force tackling a thorny business issue.

Activity Center

Review and download these short activities you can use for your development or with your team from this book's resource page at www.ccl.org/compassbook.

Courage: Dare to Be Courageous

Courage: The Marriage of Courage and Humility

Related Competencies

Conflict Resolution

Credibility and Integrity

Influence

Learning Agility

Negotiating

Risk Taking

Resources

Brown, B. (2010). *The gifts of imperfection: Let go of who you think you're supposed to be and embrace who you are.* Center City, MN: Hazelden.

Brown, B. (2012). *Daring greatly: How the courage to be vulnerable transforms the way we live, love, parent, and lead.* New York, NY: Gotham Books.

Hohn, D. (2016, Aug. 16). Flint's water crisis and the 'troublemaker' scientist. *The New York Times Magazine.*

Klann, G. (2007). *Building character: Strengthening the heart of good leadership.* San Francisco, CA: Jossey-Bass.

Palanski, M. E., Cullen, K. L., Gentry, W. A., & Nichols, C. M. (2014). Virtuous leadership: Exploring the effects of leader courage and behavioral integrity on leader performance and image. *Journal of Business Ethics*, pp. 1–14.

Riddle, D. (2016). *Truth and courage: Implementing a coaching culture.* (White paper.) Center for Creative Leadership. Retrieved from http://insights.ccl .org/articles/white-papers/truth-and-courage-implementing-a-coaching -culture/

17
Creativity

Think imaginatively and unconventionally to innovate or to develop alternative approaches to a particular task or problem.

Creativity is a skill you acquire, not a talent you're born with. Think of it as a perspective, a mindset. When you develop a capacity to embrace thinking and action that facilitate creative outcomes, you'll break free of the same old ways of doing things. Many artists never finish honing their craft, always practicing, always looking for new ways to communicate. Adopt the creative point of view of artists and bring it to bear on thorny problems, to imagine the future, and to plot the many ways to answer customer needs and expectations.

In contemporary business, creativity isn't a luxury but an increasingly important part of everyday work. Think about how artificial intelligence will affect future organizations and leadership (it already is doing so). How will leaders engage their people to generate unique value? By melding creative insight into daily tasks and connecting them to organizational goals. Machines may mimic creativity, but they can't reproduce it (not yet, anyway). Machines themselves are products of human creativity. They excel at solving problems. People excel at asking questions. As Kevin Kelly, founding executive editor of *Wired* magazine, describes (2016), the most interesting and potentially valuable space for leaders to operate in is one of uncertainty—leadership on the edge.

Leadership in Action

It's a commonly understood fact that medical technology is expensive. That common understanding is part of what makes medicine seem inaccessible, whether in the developing world or wealthier countries. Manu Prakash, a professor of bioengineering at Stanford University, has set out to challenge this understanding by engineering new tools.

Simple bloodwork is a critical medical task, essential for preventative care and diagnosis. But that work depends on an instrument called a centrifuge, which separates the components of the blood for measurement and analysis. Centrifuges are large, heavy, and expensive. Prakash asked why this had to be so. He set his team to the task of inventing one that would address those problems. It had to be small and light enough to fit in a pocket, it could not use electricity, and it had to cost less than a dollar to make.

As you can see in a 2017 video prepared by *Wired*, Prakash's solution was the paper centrifuge. The instrument is a simple disc of two paper layers, strung on a string like a bead on a necklace, with two handles on each end. The string is then twisted until it folds in on itself. The user simply tugs the handles rhythmically, sort of like playing an accordion, and the tension in the string spins the disc. Amazingly, the instrument can reach speeds up to 125,000 RPMs, which is more than enough to separate a blood sample. Prakash's creative approach didn't start with a centrifuge and apply limits to the instrument. He and his team started with the limitations (cost, materials, simplicity) and worked from there. By imposing limitations, they forced themselves to use their own creativity rather than rely on Stanford's prodigious resources.

What High Performance Looks Like

Leaders skilled at creativity

- go beyond a surface understanding of problems and probe for deeper insight
- are open to different interpretations of a problem
- ask "why?" "how?" and "what if?" questions
- reframe their understanding of problems as they gain insight
- question status quo practices and solutions
- look for and seize opportunities to do things differently
- ask "what can be done?" or "why can't it be done?"
- generate new ideas
- build off of others' ideas and insights
- experiment with new or unconventional approaches
- engage in "serious play" to spark their creativity

What's In Your Way?

Creativity combines a mindset with a skill set. Most people are capable of learning and applying various creative problem-solving techniques. It's our mindsets that often stand in the way of enacting creative behaviors. Consider the following list and note the items that you believe block you from developing your creativity as a leadership skill.

- ❏ You don't think of yourself as a creative person.
- ❏ You prefer problems that typically call for applying established methods.
- ❏ You are concerned how others might react to or judge your creative ideas.

- ❑ You tend to focus on what is (the facts) versus what could be (the imagined).

- ❑ You avoid risk.

- ❑ Your organization doesn't encourage experiments or new approaches.

- ❑ You tend to stick with "first solutions" and don't explore alternatives.

- ❑ You become quickly frustrated when new approaches don't work.

- ❑ You look to others to come up with creative solutions.

- ❑ You prefer to stick to a firm plan for getting things done and find it hard to modify the plan.

- ❑ You favor certainty and predictability over discovery and chance.

- ❑ You don't have or make time for creativity.

Coach Yourself

To develop your creativity, create goals in areas that expose you to situations where you will encounter new and challenging problems or have to address old problems with new solutions. These questions can help you define such focus areas:

- ● Name a specific instance when you felt you were at your most creative. What were the characteristics of the situation? What thoughts and behaviors spurred your creativity?

- ● Who among the people you know do you admire for their creativity? What do they do or say that makes you think of them as creative? What might you learn from them? How might you enlist them as mentors?

- ● What situations encourage your willingness to be creative? How might you seek out those situations more often? What might you do to bring elements of those situations more closely into your day-to-day work? If you tend to be more creative outside of work, how might you transfer those creative behaviors into your day-to-day work?

- What is a current work situation that would benefit from a creative solution? What do you need to do to get yourself (and others) out of conventional approaches to problem solving and approach things more creatively?

- What do you find satisfying and inspiring about doing creative work? Conversely, what about creative work makes you feel anxious or disengaged? Does this give you insight into what types of creative situations or what stages of the problem solving (for example, defining the problem versus generating solutions versus evaluating solutions versus experimenting with solutions) you might prefer?

Improve Now

Exploit ambiguity. Creativity requires freedom to find new approaches. Situations without rigid instructions—or perhaps no instruction manual at all—are the very situations that give us room to invent. Rather than feeling inhibited by the absence of a problem with a clear solution, we can actually feel liberated to define the question on our own terms and seek an answer that suits our needs.

Test a new approach. Rapid prototyping is one way to do that. Begin with a pilot project and run small-scale experiments to help you develop clarity and confidence. Test your theory in real time, and if the experiment fails, fail fast and make adjustments as you go.

Question tradition. Conventional thinking—"That's the way we've always done it"—is not always the most efficient or effective way to solve problems. It's just the most firmly entrenched. And, it's an impediment to creative solutions. There could be a better way, and it could be eminently doable. But it can only happen if someone is willing to rethink the status quo.

Dig deeper. Creative leaders are curious about new situations and express this by asking probing questions. Their questions are neither random nor superficial but designed to penetrate the surface problem and get at the root causes. When encountering a new and challenging situation, use probing questions to generate insight. One model of questions we call "The Three Ps."

- Purpose: "Why do we . . . ?"
- Practices: "How do we . . . ?"
- Possibilities: "What if we . . . ?"

The Three Ps aren't limited to one round. Keep forming and reforming these questions until you arrive at the essence of the problem and begin to generate promising solutions.

Keep searching. A solution always exists. It just hasn't been discovered yet. This keeps us in searching mode and considering "What if we . . . ?" and "How might we . . . ?" versus "We didn't" or "We can't" conclusions. This also helps us build off each other's ideas with the use of "Yes, and . . . " responses.

Compare creative stances. Write down reasons that customers might have for regarding your competition as more creative than your organization. Share your list with your manager and talk about why some of those factors will and will not work in your organization.

Carry on. In unfamiliar circumstances, first solutions rarely work. Sometimes second, third, and fourth solutions don't either. Persevere and remain resourceful to generate alternative approaches and gain insight from each attempt. Focus on the learning that occurs, not the frustration. Grit and tenacity will get you through!

Mash it up. If you are without a solution, explore unlikely combinations to stimulate new insights. Don't be afraid to be a little ridiculous or unrealistic. Do a "cocktail napkin" sketch of what this new solution might look like and see what thinking it inspires in others. Then see what new perspective you might have gained on the challenge you're facing.

Stimulate your senses. Sometimes we think about problems and solutions in overly literal terms and get fixated. Find inspiration and reinvigorate your imagination by temporarily shifting your attention to metaphorical representations of the challenge you are facing. Images, films, stories, music, even smells—all can unlock something in your awareness to give you a new perspective and the ability to generate fresh solutions.

Picture this. It helps to think of problems in different terms, especially when we find ourselves getting stuck. Use metaphors, imagery, poetry, and other analogous representations of a problem to stimulate your creativity, gain new perspective, and reframe a challenge.

Do different. Try a new road to work. Read a book that's a different genre or written by an author from another country or culture. Watch a silent movie. Cross your eyes. Watch television with the sound off. Eat an unusual fruit. Listen to a different genre of music than what you usually listen to.

Try visioning. See the task completed. See the same situation in 1850 or 2050. Imagine you are on a tropical island or in a blizzard.

Get ideas from others. Ask someone under 10 years old. Ask your child's teacher. Ask the cab driver. Ask the person next to you on the plane.

Not that crazy. Hold a "crazy idea" meeting to which everyone needs to bring one idea as admission to discuss how to improve the department. Serve popcorn and chocolate.

Have fun. Visit an arcade. Read a comic book. Color a picture. Wear a costume to work. Imagine you can spend $1,000,000 today.

Get ideas from other places. Visit a toy store. Go to an art gallery. Go to a museum. Go to the wharf. Walk in the woods. Visit an art store.

Capture ideas differently. Use a mind map. Write with crayons. Write as fast as you can. Use chalk. Doodle with your nondominant hand. Use scented markers.

Use creativity techniques. For example, use compare or combine. Compare makes use of analogy: "Fixing this problem is like _____ because _____." Combining matches the problem with some other arbitrary word or situation to generate ideas: "Our microwave units fly." Or try the What's-good-about-it technique: "What's good about this problem?"

Risk it. Risk is the heart of creativity. Without a willingness to take risks, creative ideas don't emerge and probably won't be implemented. Risk taking can turn a creative idea into a superior innovation.

Predict the future. Ask team members to think of the organization ten years from now. What do they think the organization will need to do in order to stay competitive? Decide which ideas you would like to discuss with your manager.

Developmental Opportunities

- Ask for a month-long rotation to the marketing department to learn more about their creative process.

- Create an innovation team to explore the entire organization to identify the need for innovation. Try to have representation from all parts of the organization.

- Volunteer to benchmark other organizations—in the same industry as yours or not—to determine what creative ideas can be gleaned from them. Talk to your manager about why some of those ideas will and won't work in your organization.

- Take a role on a team launching a new product.

- Join a task force exploring new business opportunities.

- Address a new or long-standing problem by a series of trials and experiments.

Activity Center

Review and download these short activities you can use for your development or with your team from this book's resource page at www.ccl.org/compassbook.

Creativity: Brainstorming
Creativity: Yes, It's a Skill

Related Competencies

Business Development
Flexibility
Learning Agility
Problem Solving
Resourcefulness
Tolerating Ambiguity

Resources

Amabile, T. M. (2010). *Keys to creativity and innovation.* User's guide. Greensboro, NC: Center for Creative Leadership.

Ernst, C., & Chrobot-Mason, D. (2011). *Boundary spanning leadership: Six practices for solving problems, driving innovation, and transforming organizations.* New York, NY: McGraw-Hill.

Gryskiewicz, S., & Taylor, S. (2003). *Making creativity practical: Innovation that gets results.* Greensboro, NC: Center for Creative Leadership.

Horth, D. M., & Vehar, J. (2014). *Becoming a leader who fosters innovation.* (White paper). Center for Creative Leadership.

Johnson, B. (1996). *Polarity management: Identifying and managing unsolvable problems.* Amherst, MA: HRD Press.

Kelly, K. (2016). *The inevitable: Understanding the 12 technological forces that will shape our future.* New York, NY: Viking.

Palus, C. J., & Horth, D. M. (2002). *The leader's edge: Six creative competencies for navigating complex challenges.* San Francisco, CA: Jossey-Bass.

Wired. (2017, Jan. 10). *This simple paper centrifuge could revolutionize global health.* (Video). Author. Retrieved from https://www.wired.com/video/2017/01/this-simple-paper-centrifuge-could-revolutionize-global-health/

18

Credibility and Integrity

Earn and maintain the trust of others by acting with integrity, honesty, and transparency.

Lack of credibility and integrity shows up in some of our most memorable folklore: remember the boy who cried "Wolf?" In the corporate world, a lack of leadership credibility and integrity has doomed many businesses to public investigation and even failure. Notorious examples include Enron, Tyco, Worldcom, and Wells Fargo. Your credibility and integrity support your reputation and your organization's image. Credibility and integrity define the level of trust you can expect from your relationships, affecting the commitment of your direct reports and your peers' willingness to collaborate. As seen in the cases mentioned above, a lack of credibility and integrity can poison an organization's culture, subjecting it to censure and perhaps spell its end. But, as we look into Uruguay's President Mujica's story, we see that some leaders press their credibility and integrity in a different direction, into much bigger realms.

Leadership in Action

When Jose Mujica talks about politics, he talks about "the problem." It's not always clear what he means, but it's clear from the way he talks that he is engaging with ideas of the human condition, human beings as a species. "The problem" is his way of contending with human short-sightedness, bickering, tribalism, and the many ways we have developed to distract ourselves from individual and collective morality. Mujica is not a man of small ideas.

As the 40th president of Uruguay, Mujica was a participant in the global government, a representative of his country at the UN, and the leader of his people at home. In this role, he consistently advocated for a guiding principle of "sobriety," a word he uses to rebuke the never-ending capitalist quest for growth. He asked rhetorically of Vladimir Hernandez of the BBC: "Does this planet have enough resources so seven or eight billion can have the same level of consumption and waste that today is seen in rich societies?" (2012). The answer is obvious, but unpopular.

But despite the unpopularity of his questions (and their obvious answers), Mujica can't be ignored or treated as a hypocrite, in part because of the credibility he has earned with a lifetime of modesty and austerity. He lives on an old farm, where he and his wife raise chrysanthemums. He gave away most of his presidential pay to charity (Arthus-Bertrand, 2015). By avoiding excess, he believes he freed himself to make the best decisions for his country, and models the behavior he believes can solve "the problem" for good.

What High Performance Looks Like

Credible leaders who act with integrity

- tell the truth
- earn the trust and respect of employees and customers
- maintain confidentiality
- place ethical behavior above personal gain
- walk the talk—consistently match actions and words to present authenticity
- admit mistakes
- are principled
- are transparent
- follow through on promises or commitments
- follow an ethical compass and not necessarily what other people want or think
- have a well-articulated set of principles

What's in Your Way?

Credible leaders act in ways that build long-term relationships and trust with others. If you struggle with credibility and integrity, you may find that team members are reluctant to work with you or lack commitment to the work at hand, leading to team conflict and underperformance. Your boss may lose faith in your ability to work effectively with others, severely limiting your potential for advancement. Take a look at the following list and mark any of the descriptions that mirror your own experience and may keep you from developing yourself as a credible leader known for integrity.

- ❑ Your previous bosses provided poor role models—either they weren't credible or they didn't behave ethically.

- ❑ You don't show who you are or talk of what you care about.

- ❑ You don't trust the people who work for you.

- ❑ You tend to focus on your own interests first.

- ❑ People know that you've broken promises in the past.

- ❑ You hold rigidly to commitments that are no longer relevant or optimal in terms of advancing your team or the organization.

- ❑ You hold back in your working relationships because you're afraid to risk them by being fully honest.

- ❑ You are overly rigid in following your principles—you don't account for people having principles different from yours and believe yours are superior.

- ❑ You sacrifice too much to uphold promises and commitments.

Coach Yourself

To develop your credibility and integrity, create goals in areas that require others to depend on you and you to depend on them. These questions can help you focus on such areas:

- ● Do you make unrealistic promises? How can you make promises that you are confident you can keep?

- ● If you have suffered a loss of credibility, what events might have led to that? What can you do to regain your credibility?

- ● What do your actions say about what you value? Are you aware of any inconsistencies?

- ● In what situations have you purposely not been direct or transparent in your communication? What was your reasoning? What were the outcomes? How might the outcomes have been different if you had been more truthful?

- How much of the "real you" do you bring to work each day? Should you show yourself more or less?

- Think of someone who is always authentic, regardless of the situation. What qualities set that person apart from others? How might you emulate some of those qualities?

- What legacy would you like to leave your organization? How would you like people to remember you?

Improve Now

Keep promises. Be clear about what you promise people and hold to your commitments. If you find yourself going back on a promise under extenuating circumstances, explain the situation and adjust your commitment.

Admit your mistakes. Denial and defensiveness undermine your ability to establish credibility, and they can damage your integrity. Quickly own up to your mistakes, try to understand what went wrong (including seeking feedback from others), and move forward.

Be yourself. Genuine leadership inspires trust and goodwill among your employees. Lead with your best attributes without exaggerating or disguising yourself. Don't present what you think others want to see.

Define norms. Help your team reach consensus on rules and procedures for how it carries out its work, and be consistent in your application of these norms. Team integrity that you help establish can prevent undesirable practices from emerging and damaging team performance.

Invest in trust. Use meetings and conversations as an opportunity to build rapport. When people get to know each other, they learn what to expect from one another. Setting and adhering to those expectations reduces the risk inherent in relationships because people can count on you to do what you've said you would do.

Bring people together. Physical proximity promotes collaboration and trust and improves communication. Create opportunities for your employees to interact face-to-face in order to bond and decrease personal distance. If you lead virtual teams, find time and budget for bringing people together or build time into virtual meetings to form personal connections beyond project goals and timelines.

Practice active listening. Credibility isn't something that you have; it's something that you build in every interaction. During conversations, pay attention to what people are saying, ask clarifying questions, withhold judgment, and summarize your understanding. People will see you as someone with integrity if you take the time to see the world as they do.

Make an authentic contribution. Bring your unique character and talents to the work at hand, not just a desire to meet others' expectations of the person you should be and the action you should take. If you start out being true to yourself, others will find it easier to connect with you and help create commitment to the work.

Invite feedback. It can be difficult to recognize when your words and actions are inconsistent. Seek others' observations and perceptions of your actions to become aware of inconsistencies before they become a fatal flaw in your credibility and integrity—and make adjustments.

Make contact. Interact daily with as many of your employees as you can.

Developmental Opportunities

- Collaborate with a team in another part of the organization with different goals from your own team. Settle on a common goal that will require a high-trust relationship to achieve.

- Resolve a conflict with a direct report, a peer, or your boss.

- Handle an employee performance issue you've been avoiding.

- Take on a role for a community or professional organization that requires you to work with several different factions.

- Create a partnership with an external organization.

- Represent concerns of employees to higher management.

Activity Center

Review and download these activities you can use for your development or with your team from this book's resource page at www.ccl.org/compassbook.

Credibility and Integrity: Do They Trust Me?
Credibility and Integrity: Three Quick Ideas to Build Credibility

Related Competencies

Communication
Conflict Resolution
Relationship Management
Self-Awareness
Self-Development

Resources

Arthus-Bertrand, Y. (Director). (2015). Human: Interview with Jose Mujica (Film). Excerpt retrieved from from https://www.youtube.com/watch?v=4GX6a2WEA1Q

Covey, S. M. R. (2006). *The speed of trust: The one thing that changes everything.* New York, NY: Free Press.

Criswell, C., & Campbell, D. (2008). *Building an authentic leadership image.* Greensboro, NC: Center for Creative Leadership.

Evans, C. *Leadership trust: Build it, keep it.* (2015). Greensboro, NC: Center for Creative Leadership.

Hernandez, V. (2012, Nov. 15). Jose Mujica: *The world's 'poorest' president.* BBC. Retrieved from http://www.bbc.com/news/magazine-20243493

Hernez-Broome, G., McLaughlin, C., & Trovas, S. (2006). *Selling yourself without selling out: A leader's guide to ethical self promotion.* Greensboro, NC: Center for Creative Leadership.

Horsager, D. (2012). *The trust edge: How top leaders gain faster results, deeper relationships, and a stronger bottom line.* New York, NY: Free Press.

Horth, D. M., Miller, L., & Mount, P. (2016). *Leadership brand: Deliver on your promise.* Greensboro, NC: Center for Creative Leadership.

Peterson, J., & Kaplan, D. A. (2016). *The 10 laws of trust: Building the bonds that make a business great.* New York, NY: AMACOM.

Sims, R. R., & Quatro, S. A. (Eds.). (2016). *Executive ethics II: Ethical dilemmas and challenges for the C suite* (2nd ed.). Charlotte, NC: Information Age Publishing.

19

Decision Making

Make sound choices in a timely way.

You don't always have complete information before you must make a decision. In those cases you depend on your own judgment to make the best choice. You increase the odds of making the right decision if you avoid stereotypes, outmoded thinking, and other faulty beliefs about how things work and what should be done. After all, decisions aren't based entirely on your knowledge of your work and your organization. They also draw from a broad range of sources, which you can cultivate with a healthy dose of curiosity, humility, a willingness to take risks, and a well-honed ability to synthesize disparate pieces of information and relate them to the problem at hand. Foresight, vision, and a capacity for long-term planning are essential tools in all leaders' decision-making repertoires. Without them, where are leaders going? They can't say for sure, and there isn't always time to figure it out. For an extreme example, we can look at the 208-second decision-making process of Captain Chesley "Sully" Sullenberger, the heroic airline pilot who famously guided the disabled US Airways Flight 1549 to an emergency landing in the Hudson River.

Leadership in Action

Minutes after takeoff, Sullenberger's aircraft was disabled when a flock of birds was sucked into both jet engines. In a 2015 *Newsweek* story of the incident that made Sullenberger a household name, he stresses the importance of knowing the exact cause of the power failure, saying "I didn't have to waste time with the 'what happened?' phase." Instead, he was left with only three possible options: two nearby airports or the surface of the Hudson River. It was immediately clear to Sullenberger that the airports were too far away. So it was the river.

It's important to note two things: Sullenberger had 42 years of experience flying airplanes, and the situation was something he had never before attempted or specifically trained for. His expertise allowed him the confidence he needed to make an unprecedented operation with great precision, even choosing a specific part of the river to make the landing, where he knew ferries would be active to assist in the rescue. Now that's foresight!

Famously, all passengers aboard Flight 1549 survived the emergency landing. Sullenberger himself double-checked the aircraft as it was sinking. His reasoning: "We had solved this huge problem of finding a way to land this huge airliner in the river—there was no way I was going to let anyone die for any other reason after that."

What High Performance Looks Like

Leaders who make their decisions using sound judgment

- see underlying concepts and patterns in complex situations
- give appropriate weight to the concerns of key stakeholders
- grasp the crux of an issue despite having ambiguous information
- accurately differentiate between important and unimportant issues
- develop solutions that address underlying problems
- seek others' advice and perspectives
- are quick learners
- have a broad range of interests
- possess quality intelligence and intellect
- can quickly set priorities
- are seen as ethical, excellent problem solvers, able to get to the root of the issue
- are self-aware
- can network and operate across the organization
- have the courage to make decisions without full information

What's in Your Way?

Leaders who don't base their decisions on sound judgment put themselves, their teams, and possibly their organizations at risk. Those negative outcomes are even more likely when a leader's judgment is compromised by a weak ethical stance or when a leader simply lacks the courage to decide and act—even without complete information. A track record of bad decisions shows itself in poor team performance, disappointing results, and an inability to innovate and address new and persistent customer problems. Others might interpret that track record as an inability to get results, which can derail a leader's career. Review the following list and note the items that you believe might be holding you back from becoming a better decision maker.

- ❏ You don't take the time to get to the root of the problem but work from faulty premises.
- ❏ You don't like to ask for input from others but prefer to go it alone.
- ❏ You fall prey to "analysis paralysis"—incessantly poring over information and approaches without making progress.
- ❏ You value complicated solutions over simple, elegant ones.
- ❏ Your intellectual heft makes you dismissive of others' perspectives.
- ❏ The pressure to produce results forces you to accept shortcuts that are not in the best interest of the organization, your team, or yourself.
- ❏ You're uncomfortable with ambiguity and anxious about making decisions without full information.
- ❏ Once you've made a decision, you insist it's the right one even in the face of contrary evidence.

Coach Yourself

To develop your decision-making abilities, create goals in areas where a situation has reached a turning point, where your decision has important consequences (start at a small scale), that involve cross-functional or organization-wide work, and in other areas where choices have to be made in the face of incomplete information and without a guarantee of positive results. These questions can help you focus on such areas:

- Who are your sources for information, and do you trust them?

- Do you make decisions quickly, or do you delay for fear of getting it wrong?

- How comfortable are you in ambiguous situations?

- How do you react in a crisis?

- Who can you help come to a decision about a vexing problem or a difficult situation?

Improve Now

Take stock of yourself. Sound judgment relies a lot on how well you know your biases, preferences, beliefs, and values. You can learn about your preferences through a 360-degree feedback survey. To learn about other traits, you will need to spend some time in serious, honest reflection. Employ a coach or solicit a mentor to help you make the most of the feedback you receive.

Look closely at the path behind. Think about the decisions you've made during your career and outside of work. Did they all turn out well? For those that didn't, can you see a pattern? Did you repeat the same mistake each time? Address those issues to develop your decision-making skill.

Question your assumptions. Though it's a key component of the critical thinking underlying sound judgment, we too often make claims or take positions without considering the assumptions we are making in coming to those positions. Good decisions rest on sound premises.

Review the past. Throughout history, leaders have made beneficial and unfortunate decisions, especially in times of crisis when time is short and information is scarce. Read their stories to see how they came to their decisions and the results.

Be smartly cautious. Often you don't have time to think about whether to support or deny an idea. When that happens, meet with a coworker and brainstorm a list of what to consider before making the call. For example, even though the situation appears to be time-sensitive, can your decision actually wait for 15 minutes while you weigh the pros and cons? How does the decision, one way or another, match with your organization's vision? How does the idea you're deciding on support balance between partnership, customer, and personal interests?

Open yourself to new approaches. An exercise in sound judgment can be an exercise in gathering and synthesizing alternative voices and approaches. If you enlist the help of others, your pool of information and your choices expand.

Ask a friend. Contact acquaintances who work at different companies (any industry) to discuss the decision-making process at their companies. Ask how people ensure that they have considered everything, what works, and what doesn't work. Ask how important balancing the impact on employees, customers, suppliers, and the community is when deciding on an action or strategy. Take this information back to your organization and figure out how you can incorporate it into your own decision making.

Google it. Really. Use Google to search for decision-making tools and watch what pops up. You may be reminded of tools you haven't used in a while. And you'll find new tools that you can try as supports to your decisions.

Enlist a partner. Ask a trusted colleague to hold you accountable and provide feedback on your judgment, based on the decisions you have made. If habits are interfering with your decisions, trusted feedback can highlight them.

Make note. In each situation you're called on to make a decision, record it in a journal or in some other way. Later, revisit the situation to see how the decision process unfolded, to observe your role in the decision, and whether your judgment was sound. Reflect on what changes in your thinking or decision-making process might have led to a different, perhaps better, result.

Build connections. Develop and maintain a network of peers and others—inside and outside your organization. Tap into your network when you are faced with situations at work that don't suggest a clear-cut answer.

Practice pros and cons. Adopt the habit of listing the pros and cons from both perspectives when facing a decision—to do or not to do.

Developmental Opportunities

- Make a presentation or proposal that addresses an organizational problem to the senior leadership team.

- Lead your team in a cost-cutting initiative.

- Serve on a hiring committee.

- Investigate and decide whether to continue a project that continues to underperform.

- Volunteer to help one of your company's most difficult customers so that you can practice grasping a problem, getting to the root of it, and deciding how to address it. Focus on their problems with the goal of reaching a mutually beneficial solution. Use your best judgment in reaching agreement about the details of the problem and in devising solutions.

- Investigate and decide whether to outsource a piece of your organization's work and present your decision to the senior leadership team.

- Lead a quality-improvement initiative.

- Investigate and make a decision about whether to continue resourcing a project that continues to underperform.

Activity Center

Review and download these activities you can use for your development or with your team from this book's resource page at www.ccl.org/compassbook.

Decision Making: Balanced Decisions
Decision Making: Teach and Learn

Related Competencies

Business and Professional Knowledge

Problem Solving

Risk Taking

Self-Awareness

Systems Thinking

Urgency

Resources

Cartwright, T. (2007). *Setting priorities: Personal values, organizational results.* Greensboro, NC: Center for Creative Leadership.

Center for Creative Leadership. (2015, Sept. 3). Hardest thing about deciding? Understanding priorities: The Warren Buffett story. (Video). Author. Retrieved from https://www.ccl.org/multimedia/video/hardest-thing-about -deciding-understanding-priorities-the-warren-buffett-story/

Gigerenzer, G. (2014). *Risk savvy: How to make good decisions.* New York, NY: Viking.

Gladwell, M. (2007). *Blink: The power of thinking without thinking.* New York, NY: Back Bay Books.

Heath, C., & Heath, D. (2013). *Decisive: How to make better choices in life and work.* New York, NY: Crown Business.

Higgins, J. M. (2005). *101 Creative problem solving techniques: The handbook of new ideas for business* (Rev. ed.). Winter Park, FL: New Management Publishing.

Kahneman, D. (2013). *Thinking, fast and slow.* New York, NY: Farrar, Straus and Giroux.

Kahneman, D., Rosenfield, A. M., Gandhi, L., & Blaser, T. (2016, Oct.). Noise: How to overcome the high, hidden cost of inconsistent decision making. *Harvard Business Review,* pp. 36–43.

Koller, G. R. (2005). *Risk assessment and decision making in business and industry: A practical guide* (2nd ed.). Boca Raton, FL: Chapman & Hall/CRC.

Maruska, D. (2004). *How great decisions get made: 10 easy steps for reaching agreement on even the toughest issues.* New York, NY: American Management Association.

Ryan, J. (2010, March 31). Four big ways leaders exercise good judgment. *Forbes* [online]. Retrieved from https://www.forbes.com/2010/03/31/ceo:judgment-ego-leadership-managing-ccl.html

'Sully' Sullenberger remembers the miracle on the Hudson. (2015, July 11). *Newsweek.* Retrieved from http://www.newsweek.com/miracle-hudson-343489

Tichy, N., & Bennis, W. (2007, Oct.). Making judgment calls. *Harvard Business Review*, pp. 94–102.

Tichy, N. M., & Bennis, W. G. (2007). *Judgment: How winning leaders make great calls*. New York, NY: Portfolio.

20
Delegating

Tap other people's talent and energy to get things done.

Delegating is key to making the transition from individual contributor to manager. There are many reasons why leaders struggle with delegation: high standards, issues with trust, a compulsion to be in control, and so on. As you master the skill of delegating, you amplify your effect on reaching organizational goals and build your reputation for getting things done.

Leaders who delegate well promote collaboration and instill a sense of trust, empowering their team's members to contribute to important tasks. Let's look inside the studios of a successful movie company to see how it all comes together.

Leadership in Action

Kathleen Kennedy took over the reins of the Lucasfilm production company in 2012, just a few months before Disney bought it out. Lucasfilm is best known for its iconic sci-fi movie series *Star Wars*, and although no new movies in the series had been produced for years, the Disney buyout signaled that the quiet period was over. This left Kennedy with a huge responsibility: not only would she now be managing Lucasfilm and its special-effects house, Industrial Light and Magic, but she also would now be heading the production of a movie that had to justify the $4 billion Disney paid for the studio.

All these responsibilities would be more than difficult for a single individual to manage alone. That's why Kennedy developed a strategy for delegation that rests upon open, practiced communication. "As she views it, her staff looks to her for guidance, but they feel more empowered to act without her explicit approval" (Lev-Ram, 2015).

Through practical delegation and a practice of open communication and trust, Kennedy has cleared the way for her real work as a leader: guiding the overall strategy of the company. She has a reputation for spotting potential problems at a distance and solving them before they can manifest, or maneuvering in such a way that the problems never arrive. That kind of strategy would be impossible if she tried to manage the entire structure of production on her own.

What High Performance Looks Like

Leaders who have learned to delegate

- assign work that provides substantial responsibility and visibility to direct reports
- involve the person or team delegated with the work in identifying the desired process for completing the task and determining its outcomes
- make sure all those involved know their own and others' roles
- explain the context of the task (challenges, resources, and prior history)
- give people the authority to make decisions and take independent action
- give the person or team a chance to work out any problems with completing the task before taking over
- provide guidance when needed and give experts the latitude they expect
- provide feedback and help people understand what they've learned from completing the assignment
- reward people when they successfully accomplish delegated tasks
- gradually increase responsibility as appropriate
- are seen as supportive, trustworthy, empowering, engaging, and self-aware
- delegate tasks to those who will most benefit and develop from the assignment
- learn what interests or excites people and delegate that kind of work if possible
- anticipate roadblocks and work to make them manageable

What's in Your Way?

Leaders who resist delegating may see their performance decrease as more and more responsibilities get added to their plate. They may also make their direct reports feel undervalued, without opportunities to grow. Take a look at the following descriptions and mark any that you believe prevent you from becoming better at delegating.

- ❏ You haven't figured out how the work should be done, which hampers your guidance and leads to your giving incomplete or erroneous instructions.

- ❏ You've been burned in the past by giving up too much control.

- ❏ You put too much responsibility and pressure on yourself.

- ❏ You underestimate the capabilities of your employees, giving them fewer responsibilities than they are able to take on.

- ❏ You overestimate the capabilities of your employees, giving them less guidance than they need.

- ❏ You hold onto work so you can receive the recognition or guidance.

- ❏ Your expectations of others aren't realistic.

- ❏ You give your direct reports more responsibility than they can handle.

- ❏ Other people just can't do the work as well as you can, so quality suffers.

- ❏ You don't want your direct reports to outshine you—to know more or to be seen as better performers than you.

- ❏ You start to delegate but don't tell the team what you're doing and why.

- ❏ You delegate but fail to take responsibility for the results.

Coach Yourself

To develop your delegating abilities, create goals in areas such as work relationships, team leadership, and accountability. These questions can help you define such focus areas:

- How do your direct reports need to develop in the future? What would give you more confidence in them?

- What responsibilities would you like to delegate in the future? How would this benefit specific individuals in your group?

- How could more delegation help free up time and energy to do more important work in the future?

- Have you clearly established your standards for quality?

- Are you afraid of losing control of the work? What do you stand to lose by shifting responsibility to other people? What might you gain?

Improve Now

Start small. If you do not have full confidence in your people, have them take on just one task and assess their performance before giving them greater responsibility.

Share the context for each assignment you delegate. What is its history? Who is invested in its satisfactory completion? Who will evaluate the work, and how will they do that? What are some likely obstacles? Tell people what you know.

Communicate your assumptions. Convey how you think the work might be done. Give people the benefit of your knowledge, but don't insist it's the way the work must be done. Invite them to suggest improvements to your approach.

Tell people how and when you'll check in. Set the expectation that you'll follow up, so when you do, it's not a surprise or misinterpreted as micromanaging.

Take stock of your team's talents. Know what skills team members bring to the job. Learn more about their experiences on this job and from previous jobs.

Know your team's passions. What do team members aspire to? What excites them? If you do not know, ask. Find the intersection of talent and passion—let people apply their best skills to work that they find most energizing.

Have a backup plan. Treat delegation as a test. You want to see whether another person can take on a challenge and handle it well. Be prepared to get personally involved or assign someone else to the work if the person assigned isn't up to the task.

Give authority but keep responsibility. Even when you delegate, you still own the responsibility to make sure the work is done well. And you're still to blame if it goes poorly. Provide oversight until the job is done, but don't meddle.

Be prepared for failure. Treat failure as an opportunity for team members to learn, not as an excuse for you to punish them.

Close the assignment. When the person assigned the task completes the work, ask what was learned, provide some feedback and affirmation, and then take the opportunity to talk about the next assignment.

Take two classes: coaching skills and delegating skills. Sound coaching skills are an important part of delegating.

Developmental Opportunities

- Delegate one of your job responsibilities to a direct report.

- Hire and develop an employee who shows promise but doesn't have the needed experience for the job. Delegate as much as you can to that employee, and maintain excellent communication.

- Use the tasks that come across your desk as developmental opportunities for others. Work with your direct reports to integrate those tasks into their development plans.

■ Take an assignment that you can't complete yourself but requires the help of your team to accomplish. Give credit to their effort—making others look good shows upper management that you can build capacity in the workforce and recognize the skills and talents of others.

Activity Center

Review and download these activities you can use for your development or with your team from this book's resource page at www.ccl.org/compassbook.

Delegating: Delegation Evaluation
Delegating: Pull Decisions Down

Related Competencies

Coach and Develop Others

Engagement

Feedback

Talent Recruitment and Retention

Team Leadership

Trust

Urgency

Resources

Genett, D. M. (2004). *If you want it done right, you don't have to do it yourself! The power of effective delegation*. Fresno, CA: Quill Driver Books.

Krohe, J., Jr. (2010). If you love your people, set them free. *Conference Board Review, 47*(5), 28–37.

Lev-Ram, M. (2015, Sept. 15). Spielberg, Lucas, and Abrams on the producer behind the new Star Wars. *Fortune*. Retrieved from http://fortune.com/2015/09/15/star-wars-spielberg-lucas-abrams-kennedy/

Tracy, B. (2013). *Delegation & supervision.* New York, NY: American Management Association.

Turregano, C. (2013). *Delegating effectively: A leader's guide to getting things done.* Greensboro, NC: Center for Creative Leadership.

21

Difference, Diversity, Inclusion

Recognize and respond positively to individual and group differences in the workplace and beyond.

Corporate culture often presents itself as unified, and it's easy to forget that you're surrounded by peers, direct reports, and bosses with diverse interests and backgrounds. They differ from you in work experience, culture, gender, age, race, technical skills, interpersonal skills, and so on. Workplace differences won't abate any time soon, if at all, because of the globalized economy within which organizations operate. We all bring our whole selves to work—differences and all. The question for you as a leader is whether you ignore these differences or leverage them to improve your organization's performance. Depending on your answer, you will establish your leadership standing as someone who can master the mindset, skill set, and toolset needed to leverage the benefits of those differences, or as someone who can manage diversity but can't exploit the power of difference to produce the results that matter for your organization. Bernard Tyson's story offers a front-row seat to how one leader embraces diversity and makes the most of the differences among his team.

Leadership in Action

Bernard J. Tyson has worked for healthcare provider
Kaiser Permanente for over three decades. In that time, he's
held many leadership roles, including president and chief
operating officer, executive vice president of health plan
and hospital operations, and senior vice president and chief
operating officer for the organization's regions outside of California. Now,
as CEO, he has made it a part of his mission to foster diversity among his
leadership staff.

According to a profile in DiversityInc., Tyson personally signs off on
executive compensation tied to diversity, diversity metrics, and progress,
goals, and achievements for supplier diversity. His personal oversight and
commitment are what make the initiative work. His work in this area is
not a mere gesture but a fully vested expression of his belief that a more
diverse company is healthier and better able to provide exemplary service.

This commitment to diversity at the top has long-term effects on the
entire organization and its mission. The social effects of good health care
can serve as a foundation for social justice, something Tyson cares deeply
about. Beyond that, the industry as a whole increasingly understands that
health care must be applied differently to different populations. Tyson's
team understands that better than many other leadership teams.

What High Performance Looks Like

Leaders skilled at leveraging differences, welcoming diversity, and including other perspectives and practices in their team

- move beyond stereotypes and treat each person as uniquely gifted
- remain aware of their own biases and cultural influences
- see and believe in the business case for diversity
- understand how individual differences add up to an organizational good
- adapt their management style to address the unique needs of different people
- strive to see problems and seek solutions from many different perspectives
- encourage people to work together to develop common solutions
- are seen as interested in other people, respectful, perceptive, curious, open-minded, adaptive, and good listeners
- can quickly change behavior to fit with a new environment or work culture
- seek opportunities to learn about different cultures and customs
- withhold judgment until sufficient information has been obtained
- understand and manage differences among people with varied backgrounds

What's in Your Way?

If you can't fully utilize the talent and creativity of your team members because they are different from one another, they might feel less like part of the team. Without camaraderie, team members can lose their motivation and disengage from their work. Results that might arise from those circumstances include missed opportunities for innovation, potentially making your organization less relevant and competitive. Review the following list and note the items that you believe might be getting in the way of your leveraging differences.

- ❑ You've had limited exposure to different cultures.
- ❑ You haven't had diverse experiences.
- ❑ You surround yourself with people who are like you.
- ❑ You tend to rely almost exclusively on tried-and-true methods that you trust.
- ❑ You're rigid, set in your ways.
- ❑ You prefer to talk rather than listen.
- ❑ You tend to see problems or issues from a narrow perspective.
- ❑ You make incorrect assumptions about what people need.
- ❑ You unintentionally play favorites.
- ❑ You've received feedback that you're inconsistent or unfair in your treatment of people.
- ❑ You don't take the time to understand others different from you.
- ❑ You've been told that you come off as inauthentic—people don't trust your intention to make the most of the different perspectives they bring to work.
- ❑ You expect instant results, not recognizing that tapping the power of difference is a process that requires time for building relationships.

Coach Yourself

To develop your ability to leverage differences, create goals that place you in unfamiliar circumstances, require that you work with people who are different from you, put you in a position of managing a multiregion project, and other situations that put you into contact with people different from yourself or who are geographically dispersed. These questions can help you focus on such areas:

- When has a leader made you feel valued and appreciated for who you are? What did they do to make you feel that way?

- Whose perspective or background is the most different from yours? How can you leverage that difference?

- What types of diversity do you value? How can diversity help you or the team be more effective?

- How might friction with certain individuals suggest hidden potential and highlight the value of learning more about their perspective?

- Are there any stereotypes that you're trying to overcome? How do you react when someone makes assumptions based on how you look or where you're from?

Improve Now

Practice people watching. Watching others is a good way to learn more about how people behave, and those observations can give you a chance to think about how you respond to behavior tied to difference. You can learn about such things as how different cultures view personal space, how different people use public space, whether people linger over food, and what behaviors make you uncomfortable and might cause you to react negatively toward someone else.

Experience different cultures where you are. You don't have to travel the world to experience culture firsthand—odds are that you can experience new things and unique people in your immediate surroundings.

Simple activities like trying ethnic restaurants, attending arts events, and visiting cultural enclaves can improve your appreciation of differences.

Read about other cultures. Cultural competence is quickly becoming one of the distinguishing factors between successful and unsuccessful leaders. Seek out information that will help you develop skill in this crucial domain.

Challenge yourself culturally. Are you particularly inexperienced with a particular group of people? Make a point to pay special attention to your interactions with that group. Firsthand experience is a great teacher.

Learn cultural competence from others. Seek out people in your organization who demonstrate a high level of cultural awareness and experience and solicit their services as coaches or role models.

Examine your cultural foundations. Study and reflect on your own cultural background. Consider how your cultural identity influences your perspective and behaviors.

Foster inclusion from the start. Ask your team to brainstorm ways to help new team members feel included as soon as they join the team. Some ideas to get you started:

- Look for something that new team members have in common with current team members, such as friends or attending the same school.

- Use those connections to quickly bring new team members into the team's discussions and work.

- Ask new team members to talk about their experiences at the last place they worked.

- Based on the hiring information you've received from HR, use their strengths early.

Seek professional development abroad. Attend a leadership training event or executive education course in another country. This will help you understand the business priorities and strategies used outside your home country.

Learn another language. It's natural to rely on your native language for most communication. But if you can add another language to your skill set, you create an opportunity to make a personal connection or demonstrate commitment to customers and partners from other cultures. Even a basic understanding of another language can provide a competitive advantage in your business interactions—not to mention a deeper appreciation for the beliefs of other cultures, which are often tied to language.

Hire people different from you. Recruit people whose skill set or perspective complements your own. Focus on appreciating and leveraging these differences.

Anticipate cultural differences. Be alert to the role of cultural background in your workplace and in your interactions with clients. This will help you to perform effectively across cultural boundaries.

Developmental Opportunities

■ Lead a diverse team to create a welcoming onboarding process for new employees. Seek input from people who are relatively new to the organization so that they can share from recent memory things that would have been nice to have when they started (lists of employees, terminology used, acronyms, even pictures of specific people).

■ Take an assignment in another culture. Surround yourself with people who are unlike you (for example in age, gender, race, or culture).

■ Volunteer to house a foreign student.

■ Visit ethnic festivals in your area: sample the food, learn the history, talk to the people. Even better, vacation in a city that has large ethnic areas. If you can, travel to a foreign country where you don't speak the language.

■ If your organization is geographically dispersed, make a point of visiting or working in another location to better understand the differences among the regions.

■ Manage a major multicountry project.

■ Take on global responsibility for a product, process, or function.

■ Work on a short-term service project in a foreign country.

Activity Center

Review and download these activities you can use for your development or with your team from this book's resource page at www.ccl.org/compassbook.

Difference, Diversity, Inclusion: Biases and Prejudices

Difference, Diversity, Inclusion: Hunt for Exclusionary Practices

Difference, Diversity, Inclusion: What Comes to Mind?

Related Competencies

Communication

Engagement

Flexibility

Interpersonal Savvy

Relationship Management

Self-Awareness

Team Leadership

Resources

Deal, J. J., & Levenson, A. (2016). *What millennials want from work: How to maximize engagement in today's workforce.* New York, NY: McGraw-Hill.

Deal, J. J., & Prince, D. W. (2003). *Developing cultural adaptability: How to work across differences.* Greensboro, NC: Center for Creative Leadership.

Diversity leadership: Bernard Tyson, Kaiser Permanente (Video). (n.d.). Retrieved from http://www.diversityinc.com/bernard-tyson/

Ernst, C., & Chrobot-Mason, D. (2010). *Boundary spanning leadership: Six practices for solving problems, driving innovation, and transforming organizations.* New York, NY: McGraw-Hill.

Grant, A. M. (2016). *Originals: How non-conformists move the world.* New York, NY: Viking.

Hannum, K. M. (2007). *Social identity: Knowing yourself, leading others.* Greensboro, NC: Center for Creative Leadership.

Hannum, K. M., McFeeters, B. B., & Booysen, L. (2010). *Leading across differences: Cases and perspectives*. San Francisco, CA: Pfeiffer.

McFeeters, B. B., Hannum, K. M., & Booysen, L. (2010). *Leading across differences: Cases and perspectives. Facilitator's guide.* San Francisco, CA: Pfeiffer.

McGirt, E. (2016, Feb. 1). Leading while black. *Fortune, 173*(2), 76–84. Retrieved from http://fortune.com/black-executives-men-c-suite

No. 1: Kaiser Permanente. *DiversityInc top 50.* DiversityInc (2015). Retrieved from http://www.diversityinc.com/kaiser-permanente/

22

Engagement

Unleash the hearts, minds, and energy of employees for the benefit of all.

You can have a direct influence on the level of engagement your workforce maintains with your organization. An estimated 70 percent of employees are disengaged from their work—with obvious consequences for their performance (Gallup, 2013). Fostering employee engagement motivates an organization's members to provide the best service to customers, loyalty to the company, and in general participate in the organization's overall performance.

Accept the responsibility of getting things done with and through others. Your methods of promoting engagement might differ from those of other leaders in your organization, but engagement is the constant—the difference maker separating good from great performance. Let's visit with a leader who created engagement based on his own values, which he transferred to his workers.

Leadership in Action

Bob Moore's company is more than a company. In many ways, Bob's Red Mill, which produces 284 food products derived from natural whole grains, is an expression of its founder's personal principles. Over the course of Moore's tenure as the company's CEO, he has consistently made decisions that put his own values ahead of maximum profit.

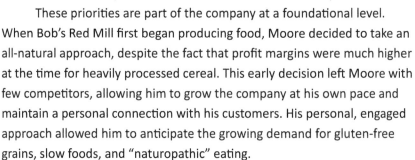

These priorities are part of the company at a foundational level. When Bob's Red Mill first began producing food, Moore decided to take an all-natural approach, despite the fact that profit margins were much higher at the time for heavily processed cereal. This early decision left Moore with few competitors, allowing him to grow the company at his own pace and maintain a personal connection with his customers. His personal, engaged approach allowed him to anticipate the growing demand for gluten-free grains, slow foods, and "naturopathic" eating.

As the company grew in size and success, Moore's company started to look more and more tempting to investors and larger competitors. As buyout offers began rolling in, Moore remained guided by his genuine connection with his employees. "In some ways I had a choice," Moore said. "But in my heart, I didn't. These people are far too good at their jobs for me to just sell it" (Snider, 2011). True to his conviction, Moore passed ownership of the company to his employees after his retirement in 2011 (Tims, 2010).

Engagement shows itself in behavior. Moore's genuine engagement in his company, not only as a business proposition but as a staging ground for his ethical principles, models that behavior for his employees, creating an environment in which people feel like part of a larger whole. This kind of common cause is what is meant by "engagement," and there is no shortcut to creating it. Engagement begins with leadership, and only when leadership models engagement can others in the organization emulate it.

What High Performance Looks Like

Leaders who create engagement

- genuinely care about the well-being of other people

- show employees that they are valued

- recognize and reward the contributions of team members and others

- treat people fairly

- understand where people fit best and how they will be most productive

- give employees opportunities to learn and grow

- provide employees with the tools and resources they need to perform well

- support employees when the work is difficult, such as during times of change, or when they take on new duties

- are generous with their time and their trust

- delegate work that provides substantial responsibility and visibility

- encourage individual initiative in determining how to achieve individual, team, and organizational goals

- involve others in making decisions

- grant people the authority to make decisions and take independent action

What's in Your Way?

If you can't create engagement, it will be difficult and perhaps impossible for you to make the most of your team's talent. Its creativity and innovation may diminish, and team members may refuse to take on responsibilities outside their normal roles. As a result, they will miss opportunities to grow and won't thrive and advance in their careers. Under these conditions, your work relationships are likely to suffer, people in and outside of your team may think you don't care, and the top levels of your organization might eventually lose faith in your ability to motivate and inspire higher levels of performance. From the list below, select those items you suspect are holding you back from developing a talent for instilling engagement in others.

- ❏ You haven't yet recognized the talent and value of your team.

- ❏ You discount your team's value to the organization.

- ❏ You neglect to invest time in the people around you.

- ❏ You have unresolved or undiscussable conflicts with coworkers.

- ❏ You don't trust the people who work for you.

- ❏ You haven't learned to delegate.

- ❏ You try to create engagement without first building alignment around the company's vision.

- ❏ People have given hints that they think you're just trying to squeeze more productivity out of them.

- ❏ Employees don't feel invested in their jobs, and you don't know how to change that.

- ❏ You rely heavily on superficial or contrived activities to motivate people—such as pizza parties or meaningless rewards—rather than basing your leadership on authentic caring and communication.

- ❏ You believe people just want to be left alone—that they want autonomy more than they want community.

Coach Yourself

To develop your ability to create engagement, create goals in areas that help you work on your motivating and coaching skills. These questions can help:

- Why are your people not engaged? Is it their jobs? Is it their attitude toward their work? Something about how you behave toward them? What can be changed and what can't?

- Who were the most motivating or engaging leaders you have worked for? What did they do that you appreciated?

- Are your colleagues truly important to you? Do you care what they think or how they feel? How might you gain a deeper appreciation?

- Do your direct reports feel empowered? Do they have enough control and personal investment in their work to stay motivated?

Improve Now

Find out why employees are disengaged. Do they dislike their jobs? Do they get along with their teammates? Do they respond to the way you manage them?

Learn about your direct reports. Take them out to lunch one at a time. Ask questions to learn more about them and their career goals.

Show that you care. Support your direct reports or help them out without taking over their work. Share your appreciation for their talent and accomplishments and their hard work and sacrifices.

Work with employees to create a development plan. Your employees want to know where they can go in the organization and what they need to do to get there.

Highlight opportunities to learn. Young workers especially appreciate the opportunities to develop new skills. Give them stretch assignments and chances to obtain other formal or informal training.

Get a coach. A professional guide can help you assess what is going wrong with your efforts to create engagement and keep you on track as you make changes to help employees feel more engaged.

Strive to give people the pay and benefits that will retain them. Even if you are a great manager or your employees love their jobs, they are still likely to go after jobs that pay better or provide better benefits.

Give your employees an opportunity to shine. Put them in visible and high-profile assignments. Acknowledge their accomplishments and the effort it took to make them happen.

Advocate for your team. Your team will work hard when they see you working hard for them. Make sure they have the time, resources, and organizational support needed to succeed.

Check the research. Organizations often regularly conduct engagement research on themselves. Check the most recent research to see what the top three items are that keep employees engaged. You might learn that the behavior of the employees' immediate supervisor is one of them.

Developmental Opportunities

- Seek experiences in which you must motivate and develop employees to be successful.

- Delegate one of your job responsibilities to a direct report. Follow up to discuss what your employee liked and disliked about the task and what the employee requires to develop further.

- Champion a change your group has been resisting by enlisting them in creating a vision for that change.

- Champion an engagement team for your department or division. Survey employees to learn what is most important to them and how they prefer to be recognized.

- Start a new group, club, or team, inside or outside your organization.

Activity Center

Review and download these activities you can use for your development or with your team from this book's resource page at www.ccl.org/compassbook.

Engagement: I Felt Valued

Engagement: Post an Idea

Related Competencies

Coach and Develop Others

Credibility and Integrity

Interpersonal Savvy

Leading with Purpose

Team Leadership

Resources

Criswell, C., & Campbell, D. (2008). *Building an authentic leadership image.* Greensboro, NC: Center for Creative Leadership.

Deal, J. J., Stawiski, S., & Gentry, W. A. (2010). *Employee engagement: Has it been a bull market?* (White paper). Center for Creative Leadership. Retrieved from https://www.ccl.org/articles/quickview -leadership-articles/employee-engagement-has-it-been-a-bull-market/

Friedman, R. (2015). *The best place to work: The art and science of creating an extraordinary workplace.* New York, NY: Penguin.

Gallup. (2013). The state of the American workplace: Employee engagement insights for U.S. business leaders. Retrieved from http://www.gallup.com/ services/178514/state-american-workplace.aspx

Gentry, W. (2016). *Be the boss everyone wants to work for: A guide for new leaders.* Oakland, CA: Berrett-Koehler.

Graves, L. M., Cullen-Lester, K. L., Ruderman, M. N., Gentry, W. A., & Lester, H. F. (2016). Motivating your managers: What's the right strategy? (White paper). Center for Creative Leadership. Retrieved from https://www.ccl.org/articles/ white-papers/motivating-your-managers-whats-the-right-strategy/

Klann, G. (2011). *Building your team's morale, pride, and spirit.* Greensboro, NC: Center for Creative Leadership.

Snider, S. (2011, April 26). Bob Moore: A man with a mill and a mission. *Washington Post*. Retrieved from https://www.washingtonpost.com/lifestyle/food/bob-moore-a-man-with-a-mill-and-a-mission/2011/04/21/AFULEerE_story.html

Tims, D. (2010, Feb. 16). Founder of Bob's Red Mill Natural Foods transfers business to employees. *The Oregonian*. Retrieved from http://www.oregonlive.com/clackamascounty/index.ssf/2010/02/bobs_red_mill_natural_foods_ro.html

23

Executive Image

Set a personal example of optimism, poise, and professionalism.

Your title and the size of your office don't make you a leader. Your role as a leader can be found in how others see you—in the way you carry yourself, the image you project, and in your daily actions. Think of these perspectives that you foster as your executive image. That image becomes incredibly valuable in challenging times, when your ability to communicate confidence and steadiness and to adapt readily to new situations dramatically affects your colleagues and your organization. Leaders projecting a strong executive image influence others more effectively and gain their respect. They also position themselves for the next promotion (Hewlett, Leader-Chivée, Sherbin, Gordon, & Dieudonné, 2012). We see in Kat Cole's story how a crafted executive image can take you from an entry-level job to a senior leadership career.

Leadership in Action

An executive image isn't about a bespoke suit, this season's fashions, or $1,000 haircuts. An executive image arises from a leader's interactions with others. What can others count on from you? What do others expect of you? How confident are people in your ability to lead people toward positive, sustainable results?

Kat Cole knows a little about executive image. Author, marketer, and speaker Kevin Daum tells of how Cole started working at 17 as a hostess at Hooters (the US casual restaurant chain famous for its beach-themed decor and its instantly recognizable "Hooters Girls"). At age 19 she was helping to establish Hooters restaurants in foreign markets. At 23 she took over global training for the organization. And at 32 she became a group president at Focus Brands, the franchiser of Cinnabon, Moe's, Carvel, and other recognizable eateries.

Cole's rise from a waitress in orange short-shorts to a brand builder stems from an executive image based on employee relationships. She is willing to go to the front lines, assumes good intentions, and, at the core, pays careful attention to trust. She goes out of her way to make sure employees feel secure to say what is on their minds, to share their ideas, and to participate in the business. The executive image she projects, as someone willing to listen, who will give honest feedback, and who genuinely cares that others succeed, creates an organization of people willing to do what it takes to achieve the results that matter most to the business.

What High Performance Looks Like

Leaders with a positive executive image

- project confidence and poise
- command attention and respect
- are optimistic and take the attitude that most problems can be solved
- set a positive personal example for the organization
- accept setbacks with grace
- tolerate stressful situations and don't overreact
- are seen as unflappable, confident, poised, charismatic, and professional
- communicate credibility
- avoid alienating people or damaging relationships
- rarely criticize other people
- are not easily rattled, distracted, or intimidated

What's in Your Way?

Leaders who don't display a positive executive image might lose the trust and respect of others. People in the organization might see them as less capable and less able to handle higher levels of responsibility. An organization might pass over such leaders when filling available executive positions. From the list below, select all the items you think stand between you and the executive image you want to project.

- ❏ You never developed healthy ways to cope with stress.
- ❏ You're overconfident.
- ❏ You lack confidence.

- [ ] You've broken down or blown up under stressful conditions.

- [ ] You don't know how others perceive you.

- [ ] You haven't learned what "good manners" are at your organization.

- [ ] You've learned that people see you as slick or manipulative.

- [ ] You've lost touch with your core values or beliefs.

- [ ] You've learned that people sense they don't know you—they can't see how you feel or what drives you.

- [ ] You're stressed by trying to be someone that you're not.

- [ ] You've received feedback that you come off as arrogant and unapproachable.

- [ ] You worry too much about how you look or what people think about you.

Coach Yourself

To develop your executive image, create goals that require you to work with others, to communicate the work ahead, to take on projects with high visibility, and that otherwise put you in a position of displaying your leadership skills. These questions can help you focus on such areas:

- Can you put yourself in the shoes of your direct reports and customers? Do you understand what they need or want? How can you show them you understand?

- When you leave the organization, how do you want others to remember you? What legacy do you want to leave behind?

- What are the three most visible actions you have taken in the last month? What might people conclude about you, based on their observations of those actions?

- Think of someone who you believe displays an ideal executive image. What does that person do to stand apart from other executives? How might you emulate his or her behavior in an authentic way?

- How did you handle the last stressful situation you found yourself in? How would you like to cope with stress? What could you do differently?

Improve Now

Be clear. Vague, contradictory, or disjointed messages harm your image and will likely leave your audience bored, confused, and feeling negative about your leadership. Conversely, a clear message can enhance your professionalism and your ability to inspire others.

Monitor your voice. If what you're saying is valuable, how you say it is just as important. A leader with a flat or monotone vocal style, inappropriate volume, or poor diction won't convey a strong executive image and will fail to inspire others.

Think "we." Simply by exchanging the words "I," "me," and "my" with more inclusive terms, you can foster a sense of community and gain trust. This will also help others recognize your collaborative spirit.

Lighten up. Leaders don't need to be overly serious for others to take them seriously. An upbeat attitude and a kind word, especially in challenging times, can lift the mood of those around you and improve your executive image.

Exude energy. Revive your love of your job, your people, and your organization, and make a point to let others know it. Passion is contagious, and an energetic leader can motivate others to be their best. Sit down and make a list of every element of your job that makes you get up in the morning and come to work and then seek to channel that commitment and enthusiasm throughout the day.

Hire an executive image coach. A professional can often give you the feedback and guidance you need to project an image that is right for you and your career path. If your intonation or vocal style isn't creating a compelling image, you may also consider getting a voice or speech coach who will help you develop your speaking skills.

Focus on managing stressful situations. Responding poorly in times of stress or conflict can tarnish your image. Find better ways to cope with adversity without losing your dignity.

Look in the mirror. Although executive image isn't altogether dependent on style, people will make judgments about your leadership capability based on how you dress, whether you take care of yourself, and how you carry yourself. Making small changes in how you look or dress, paying attention to your physical fitness, and even improving your posture support the image you create among others.

Seek a mentor. Look for someone in your organization who can give you feedback and ideas about how you can improve your leadership image. Build a partnership with this person—what can you teach him or her in exchange?

Say "Yes, and . . ." Take an improv (improvisation) class to gain practice thinking "and" rather than "but."

Show humility. There is strength in vulnerability. Accepting that you make mistakes and taking accountability for them in a genuine way, with grace and a sincere commitment to improve, can boost others' perceptions of your leadership.

Be the best. Three small but extremely powerful words. Meet with your coach, mentor, or manager and talk about how you want to improve in every way and to strive to be the best. Ask for ideas that showcase how you can be the best at all you can do.

Developmental Opportunities

- Manage a highly visible annual organizational event.
- Volunteer in a loaned-executive role for a nonprofit organization.
- Take on a responsibility previously handled by your boss, such as leading a cross-functional team.
- Work with the manager of a unit your group often has conflict with to create a better working partnership.
- Host visitors from another country.

- Manage a new customer with high potential payoff for the business.
- Represent your organization to the media.

Activity Center

Review and download these activities you can use for your development or with your team from this book's resource page at www.ccl.org/compassbook.

Executive Image: Boiling Hot Idea!

Executive Image: Build an Image

Executive Image: Your Personal Values

Related Competencies

Communication

Credibility and Integrity

Interpersonal Savvy

Leading with Purpose

Self-Awareness

Tolerating Ambiguity

Urgency

Resources

Booher, D. D. (1994). *Communicate with confidence! How to say it right the first time and every time.* New York, NY: McGraw-Hill.

Booher, D. D. (2011). *Creating personal presence: Look, talk, think, and act like a leader.* San Francisco, CA: Berrett-Koehler.

Criswell, C., & Campbell, D. (2008). *Building an authentic leadership image.* Greensboro, NC: Center for Creative Leadership.

Cuddy, A. J. C. (2015). *Presence: Bringing your boldest self to your biggest challenges.* New York, NY: Little, Brown and Company.

Daum, K. (2015, Sept. 25). 12 communication habits made this former Hooters hostess a billion-dollar-brand president at 32. *Inc*. Retrieved from http://www.inc.com/kevin-daum/these-12-communication-habits-made-this-former-hooters-girl-a-billion-dollar-bra.html

Hewlett, S. A., Leader-Chivée, L., Sherbin, L., Gordon, J., & Dieudonné, F. (2012). *Executive presence*. New York, NY: Center for Talent Innovation.

Horth, D. M., Miller, L., & Mount, P. (2016). *Leadership brand: Deliver on your promise*. Greensboro, NC: Center for Creative Leadership.

McGonigal, K. (2012). *The willpower instinct: How self-control works, why it matters, and what you can do to get more of it*. New York, NY: Avery.

24

External Partnership Management

Connect with stakeholders, peer organizations, and strategic partners.

As the business world grows increasingly complex, organizations more and more often seek expertise and opportunities beyond their own walls. According to a 2012 IBM study, 69 percent of high-performing organizations collaborate extensively with outside partners, and this figure has been rapidly increasing over the past decade. To help your organization thrive amid such forces as globalization, disruptive innovations, and shifting economies, it's vital that you develop the skills and strategies necessary to initiate and maintain successful external partnerships. Leaders skilled at building and maintaining external partnerships acquire a deeper understanding of the environment in which their organizations operate. Armed with that knowledge, they can become better equipped to foster new alliances, enter new territories, and discover new opportunities. One of the most successful US companies in recent years, Starbucks, has adopted external partnerships as a growth strategy, as we learn from the following story.

Leadership in Action

After a rapid expansion that created 5,000 Starbucks coffeehouses in 15 years, the company faced what we might call an enviable dilemma. How would Starbucks continue to grow when its ubiquitous retail shops seemed to stand on every corner across the United States? One answer came from one of Starbucks' core values: an emphasis on relationships.

The company values long-term relationships over low-cost supplies and labor. And that was the kind of external partnership leaders at Starbucks and Barnes & Noble built to put Starbucks in the bookseller's cafes. Both companies saw themselves as community gathering places—it was a fit that makes it seem almost natural to expect coffee when relaxing with a good book or magazine in your local bookstore (Gulati, Huffman, & Neilson, 2002).

What High Performance Looks Like

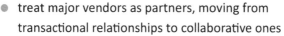

Leaders adept at building and maintaining external partnerships

- treat major vendors as partners, moving from transactional relationships to collaborative ones
- put themselves in the shoes of their audiences—customers, employees, suppliers, and vendors—and address their needs and interests
- develop strong relationships with the governing board and communities in which the organization operates
- build strong relationships with key customers
- build mutually beneficial relationships with strategic partners
- engage others with a collaborative spirit
- are self-assured and compelling partners
- are intentional and strategic about what gets communicated and to whom
- give stakeholders opportunities to provide open, honest feedback
- home in on critical issues

What's in Your Way?

Leaders unable to build or maintain external partnerships miss opportunities to collaborate and risk making their organizations less competitive. They may spread their organization's resources too thin by wanting to do everything in-house. Individuals and organizations with a reputation for being "difficult to partner with" can lose their place to more nimble collaborators. If you're having trouble developing the skills to build and maintain external partnerships, select from the list below those items that you think are holding you back.

- ❏ You don't see how partners can help you achieve your organization's vision.

- ❏ You lack empathy or appreciation for the needs of your stakeholders.

- ❏ You have a narrow definition of stakeholders that curtails your list of potential partners.

- ❏ You can't gain the trust of your stakeholders.

- ❏ You don't know how to negotiate effectively with your partners.

- ❏ You don't know how to settle conflict with stakeholders without alienating them.

- ❏ Your organization has a reputation for not delivering on its promises.

- ❏ People have unrealistic expectations of you or your organization.

- ❏ The pressures of your job prevent you from devoting time and attention to potential or current partners.

- ❏ You suspect potential partners have ulterior motives or hidden plans.

- ❏ Your potential partners are in competition or conflict with each other.

Coach Yourself

To develop competency in building and maintaining external partnerships, create goals in areas that require the participation of another organization. These questions can help you define such areas of focus:

- ● Who are your organization's most important partners? How can you help them? How can they help you?

- ● What are some of the keys to your organization's past successful partnerships? How can you replicate those success factors? What in your organization's current approach to partnerships needs augmenting or updating?

- Do you have any lingering conflicts with external stakeholders, such as key customers, vendors, or stockholders? How can you address those conflicts directly and constructively in shareholder meetings and in other venues?

- What is it about a potential partner that you believe in and for which you have passion? How can you translate your belief and passion into confidence and energy as you represent that partner to your own organization and its stakeholders?

Improve Now

Know what your organization values and stands for. Be clear about what your organization delivers to its customers and the difference it makes in their lives. What value does it provide to its customers? What value will it provide next year? In five years?

Know what you and your organization are not (yet). Where has your organization decided not to compete, what services has it decided not to provide, or what customers has it chosen not to serve? Find out the reasons behind those decisions and think about whether it might be time to enlist a partner to help your organization compete in those areas.

Know who potential partners are. Where do they compete? Whom do they serve? What are their goals and motivations? What can your organization learn from them? Where could they help your organization? Where could your organization help them? Write out your answers and then draw the connections you see among them.

Know your customers. Why do they choose your products and services? What makes you special in their eyes? What pains do they have? What gains do they hope to make? Imagine what your customers' goals are, what is important to them, and what they value. Imagine how your organization can delight them. With whom can you work to fulfill those needs and desires?

Favorite five. List your five favorite customer-service examples that have occurred since you've been with your organization. Think about the policies, procedures, and strategies your organization's leaders have put in place to ensure positive customer experiences. Now think of ways that you can replicate those experiences for future customers. Share your thoughts with others in your organization.

Interest in customers. Create a list of six to eight important guidelines your team members follow that demonstrate personal interest in customers. Then, identify how you can use those guidelines to enhance the customers' experience even more. Be creative—in a brainstorm, money and time don't matter. Next, take the guidelines you've come up with and bring them back down to reality. Decide on a couple of things that you can do to show a personal interest in customers that exceed expectations but remain within the organization's policies.

Learn more about your field—and beyond it. Look for opportunities to learn something new about the industry in which your organization operates and for ways to connect to others within the field. Be on the lookout for what other organizations could bring yours from outside your main field of interest.

Make it noteworthy. Send a handwritten thank-you note when your partner goes out of its way or does something unexpected to support the partnership.

Approach potential partners. Decide how you want to connect with partners. Think of your needs as well as theirs. What value would you bring them? How would you help them solve problems? Look for common ground that promises positive results.

Work on a common project with a potential partner. Identify an area where both organizations can collaborate easily. What people, teams, functions, and divisions can you involve? How open are they to collaborating with external partners? How will your two organizational cultures mesh? How can a blend of your two cultures form the foundation for a continuing partnership?

Set up a joint venture. Go to the next level. Identify a common project that results in a partnership. Decide how your organizations will work together (responsibilities, staffing, and communication) to complete the project.

Define and measure. Establish shared values, objectives, and metrics for success, and decide how both partners will evaluate them as your work progresses.

Developmental Opportunities

- Take a temporary assignment in the department that oversees your organization's strategic partnerships.

- Investigate outsourcing opportunities for your organization.

- Represent your group on a task force or committee searching for a partner engaged in work that your organization has designated as strategic to its aims (for example, opening a branch in an emerging market).

- Meet with your key suppliers to learn more about the key drivers in their organizations and what changes or demands they foresee in the future.

- Serve as a loaned executive to a nonprofit organization.

- Attend a conference or trade show in your organization's industry and take stock of potential partners.

- Improve a vendor relationship.

- Create a new partnership with an external organization.

Activity Center

Review and download these activities you can use for your development or with your team from this book's resource page at www.ccl.org/compassbook.

External Partnership Management: Customer Loyalty
External Partnership Management: Customer Service 101
External Partnership Management: History's Successes and Failures

Related Competencies

Boundary Spanning

Communication

Credibility and Integrity

Negotiating

Problem Solving

Relationship Management

Strategic Planning and Implementation

Resources

Bardin, L., Bardin, R., & Bardin, G. (2013). *Strategic partnering: Remove chance and deliver consistent success.* London, UK: Kogan Page.

Eisner, M. D., & Cohen, A. R. (2012). *Working together: Why great partnerships succeed.* New York, NY: HarperCollins.

Ernst, C., & Chrobot-Mason, D. (2010). *Boundary spanning leadership: Six practices for solving problems, driving innovation, and transforming organizations.* New York, NY: McGraw-Hill Education.

Gulati, R., Huffman, S., & Neilson, G. L. (2002). The barista principle—Starbucks and the rise of relational capital. *strategy+business.* Retrieved from http://www.strategy-business.com/article/20534?gko=582b3

IBM. (2012). *Leading through connections: Insights from the Global Chief Executive Officer Study.* Retrieved from http://www-935.ibm.com/services/multimedia/anz_ceo_study_2012.pdf

Johansen, B. (2012). *Leaders make the future: Ten new leadership skills for an uncertain world* (2nd ed.). San Francisco, CA: Berrett-Koehler.

Johansen, R., & Ronn, K. (2014). *The reciprocity advantage: A new way to partner for innovation and growth.* San Francisco, CA: Berrett-Koehler.

Lines, H., & Scholes-Rhodes, J. (2013). *Touchpoint leadership: Creating collaborative energy across teams and organizations.* London, UK: Kogan Page.

Nevin, M. (2014). *The strategic alliance handbook: A practitioner's guide to business-to-business collaborations.* Burlington, VT: Gower.

Osterwalder, A., & Pigneur, Y. (2014). *Business model generation: A handbook for visionaries, game changers, and challengers.* San Francisco, CA: John Wiley & Sons.

Sobel, A., & Panas, J. (2012). *Power questions: Build relationships, win new business, and influence others.* Hoboken, NJ: Wiley.

25
Feedback

Provide individuals with objective information they can use for maintaining or improving their behavior.

The Center for Creative Leadership (CCL) has a multirater assessment tool, *Benchmarks by Design*, which evaluates leaders on 91 different competencies. One of those skills is "Gives Feedback." CCL continually gathers data that calculates the average rating for each skill across all individuals who have taken the assessment and rank orders them. Out of the many skills that leaders can be evaluated on, the ability to give feedback ranks last.

The consequences associated with this low ranking affect you and everyone else in an organization where people struggle to deliver feedback effectively. Feedback lets you know what it is that you need to improve. It also lets you know if you are making progress toward your development goals. It enhances the self-awareness that is critical to helping you evaluate your strengths and weaknesses.

Just because ineffective feedback is the norm in most organizations doesn't mean it has to be that way. The following story tells how one of the world's most successful companies retooled its feedback methods to broaden its impact and link it to productivity.

Leadership in Action

In the past at GE feedback policies focused on annual employee reviews and conferences. As the nature of GE's business changed to keep up with a globalizing economy, the company also had to adjust that feedback strategy. These days, GE's operations are shorter, more agile, modular blocks in a larger whole rather than single monolithic initiatives. The company had to engineer a way to track individual contributions in a way that reflected that increased agility.

In response, GE operations executives collaborated with the HR and IT departments to create a mobile app, which managers and subordinates could use to engage in daily feedback conversations. Instead of concentrating the majority of feedback and reviews in annual conferences, the app allows for a more diffused approach (Cappelli & Tavis, 2016). The benefits are many: managers can be more precise and less confrontational, while subordinates can track their own performance and worry less about pivotal review meetings (Baldassarre & Finken, 2015). The app's language stresses forward-thinking, replacing traditional pass/fail analysis with "continue" and "consider." That shift in language creates an invitation to change, making employees into collaborators on their own development.

The results have been promising. Within a year of the premier of the new system, executives reported a "fivefold productivity increase." By transforming the nature of feedback within the organization, the team was able to create an ongoing dialogue where there had previously been only the boss's orders.

What High Performance Looks Like

Leaders skilled at feedback

- recognize the importance of giving feedback to others
- give feedback to others at the appropriate moment and in the appropriate manner
- give feedback related to specific situations and behaviors
- give feedback that describes the impact of the behavior
- deliver only firsthand feedback
- verify that feedback is clearly received
- follow up with additional feedback as needed
- demonstrate willingness to give feedback to direct reports, colleagues, and bosses
- deliver both positive and negative feedback

What's in Your Way?

Almost anyone can give effective feedback. So why is it ranked last in CCL's research in terms of effective leadership skills? The answer is twofold. One, while there is a best-practice set of "Do" behaviors related to Situation-Behavior-Impact (CCL's proven method of giving feedback), there is an even longer list of "Don't" behaviors that render feedback ineffective. Secondly, giving feedback, positive or negative, is something many leaders are apprehensive about doing. That apprehension affects their ability to deliver feedback as effectively as they would like. More often, it prevents them from delivering it at all. If you are motivated to improve your feedback-giving abilities, consider which of the following might be interfering with your developmental progress:

❏ You have few or no role models for delivering effective feedback.

❏ You don't receive enough feedback from others.

❏ You have been given ineffective feedback by others.

❏ You lack the courage to share feedback with others.

❏ You are concerned how giving feedback to others might affect your relationships with them.

❏ You are afraid that giving negative feedback to others will be reciprocated.

❏ You are concerned that giving positive feedback will be viewed as ingratiating.

❏ You assume that people are getting the feedback they need from others and don't need to be hearing it from you.

❏ You don't feel that it is your "place" in the organization to give feedback to certain individuals.

❏ You feel rushed for time to give others the feedback they need.

❏ You feel that feedback should be reserved for formal settings like performance reviews.

❏ You are not confident in your ability to express your feedback clearly and accurately.

Coach Yourself

To develop your ability to deliver feedback, create goals in areas that prompt you to deliver feedback in a timely manner that follows the principles of SBI (see page 215). These questions can help you define areas to focus your development:

● Think back to the most recent piece of feedback you delivered to someone and the resulting outcomes. How might the feedback and the results have been different had you deliberately followed the SBI process?

- Who is a role model for delivering effective feedback in your organization? What about their approach makes them effective? How might you incorporate their behaviors into your efforts to give others effective feedback?

- Reflect on feedback that was given to you ineffectively. What was the message that was intended? How might it have come out differently had they practiced SBI?

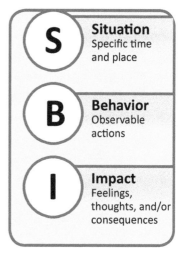

S — **Situation** Specific time and place

B — **Behavior** Observable actions

I — **Impact** Feelings, thoughts, and/or consequences

- Consider one of the most effective pieces of feedback you've received. What was it and how did it impact you? What elements of SBI were present in that feedback?

- What situational and/or emotional triggers inhibit your ability to deliver effective feedback? How can you anticipate them? What strategies might help you to eliminate or lessen their impact?

Improve Now

Commit to giving feedback. Provide feedback, both positive and developmental, to employees. Be specific. Clarify the situation, the behaviors you observed, and their impact. Give feedback often—use it  as an opportunity for development or to solve a performance problem.

Watch your language. Avoid phrases like "always" or "never" in your feedback. That puts your people on the defensive and distracts from your message, as they start to think about exceptions and extenuating circumstances rather than listening to what you have to say.

Focus on behavior. Probably the most common mistake made when giving feedback is putting it in judgmental terms. This puts others on the defensive and lessens the chance your feedback will be heard and acted on. Instead, focus your attention on people's behavior and its impact on you, not what their behavior may or may not indicate about them as a person.

Deliver your feedback. Not someone else's. Feedback needs to be authentic and accurate to have impact, so it needs to come directly from you. When others approach you with feedback about someone else, first ask them if they've shared that feedback with the other person. If not, encourage them to do so.

Describe "what" someone did. Leave motive out of the equation. Only the individual you are giving the feedback to can truly understand why he or she did something, and if this is a behavior that is a blind spot, the person might not even be aware of his or her motives. Don't get caught up in the "Why?" of someone's behavior. Instead, focus on what the specific behavior was and the impact it had on you.

Capture the setting where the behavior occurred. Highlight the specific situation in which the behavior occurred. Describing the location and time of a behavior creates context for your feedback recipients, helping them remember clearly their thinking and behavior at the time.

Describe the specific behavior you witnessed. By focusing on the action, not the impression of why it might have taken place, you can communicate clear facts that a person can understand and act on. Think in terms of verbs, not adjectives.

Explain the impact of the behavior. Relay the impact that the other person's behavior had on you. The impact you want to communicate is your reaction to a behavior. Getting just the right word to express the impact a behavior has on you is important. The right word can help keep your feedback from being vague or misconstrued.

Seize the moment. Don't wait for the "right moment" to deliver feedback. Feedback has the most impact when it is delivered close to the time the behavior in question occurred. This allows the person to have a fresh recall of the situation and better understand the impact that their behavior had on others.

Confront lack of progress. If employees fail to make changes or progress after receiving your feedback, confront that head-on. Don't let it slide so that their actions, right now a developmental opportunity, become a performance problem.

Keep it short and simple. Less is more when delivering feedback. Stick to the key elements of SBI. Don't overexplain or feel compelled to offer suggestions on what the individual could do differently. Just ensure that the feedback is clearly understood and then let feedback recipients proceed with the conversation as they wish.

They know where they stand. Ensure that all employees have a clear understanding about the level of satisfaction they're hitting with their work.

Make it a habit. Feedback is a process, not an event. It has the most impact when it is given in a regular and ongoing manner. This allows others to maintain an accurate self-awareness and better gauge which behaviors they should stop, start, or continue.

Developmental Opportunities

- Address an employee problem.
- Set goals to motivate underperformers to respond positively to the feedback they've received.
- Create a feedback schedule and monitoring system for your direct reports.
- Mentor the newest person in your group. Use feedback to help support what he or she is learning about what it takes to be a successful member of the team.
- Lead the start-up of a new team. Feedback is critical to helping others understand their individual roles and how to work together as a team.
- Reach out to a colleague who is struggling with a skill that you have expertise in and offer to coach them using CCL's SBI method.
- Delegate responsibilities to less experienced employees and use feedback to help them acquire new skills and gauge their progress.
- Assume responsibility for implementing a new process with your colleagues. Provide feedback to help guide their transition from the old to the new.

Activity Center

Review and download these activities you can use for your development or with your team from this book's resource page at www.ccl.org/compassbook.

Feedback: Feedback Checklist
Feedback: Recognition—Pass It On
Feedback: Try Feedforward

Related Competencies

Coach and Develop Others

Communication

Engagement

Interpersonal Savvy

Relationship Management

Talent Recruitment and Retention

Resources

Baldassarre, L., & Finken, B. (2015, Aug. 12). GE's real-time performance development. *Harvard Business Review*. Retrieved from https://hbr.org/2015/08/ges-real-time -performance-development

Blanchard, K., & Johnson, S. (2015). *The new one minute manager*. New York, NY: HarperCollins.

Buron, R., & McDonald-Mann, D. (1999). *Giving feedback to subordinates*. Greensboro, NC: Center for Creative Leadership.

Cappelli, P., & Tavis, A. (2016). The performance management revolution. *Harvard Business Review*, *94*(10), 58–67.

Center for Creative Leadership. (2015). *Benchmarks by Design technical manual*. Greensboro, NC: Author.

Center for Creative Leadership. (n.d.) *Feedback that works*. [eCourse]. Greensboro, NC: Author.

Center for Creative Leadership. (2016). *Feedback that works*. [Workshop kit]. Greensboro, NC: Author.

Clark, S. (2013). *Feedback that works for nonprofit organizations.* Greensboro, NC: Center for Creative Leadership.

Hart, E. W. (2011). *Feedback in performance reviews.* Greensboro, NC: Center for Creative Leadership.

Kirkland, K., & Manoogian, S. (1998). *Ongoing feedback: How to get it, how to use it.* Greensboro, NC: Center for Creative Leadership.

Weitzel, S. R. (2000). *Feedback that works.* Greensboro, NC: Center for Creative Leadership.

26
Flexibility

Adapt to meet the challenges of a dynamic environment.

Leading in today's volatile, dynamic business climate is a bit like playing a game in which the rules constantly change. Many current organizational challenges aren't technical but *adaptive*, in that there isn't a single, clear solution. Meeting adaptive challenges calls for creating new processes, systems, or skills, whereas a technical challenge requires a redistribution of resources and a well-defined plan of action. Sustainable success in an adaptive environment requires a willingness to let go of what has worked in the past and to embrace new ways of doing things, even if those new approaches initially feel awkward or don't yield immediate results. Inflexible leaders are left behind, and their organizations struggle to compete with companies that are more agile.

Demonstrate to your colleagues that you can handle the rigors of uncertainty and unexpected change. Develop the flexibility you need during those times to inspire confidence in your leadership. Make yourself a player in situations where new problems demand new solutions. And open yourself to thinking of and experimenting with new ideas, to collaboration, and to learning from others. In this story of the town of Riace, we see what flexibility makes possible.

Leadership in Action

By 1998, the village of Riace, in the Italian region of Calabria, had undergone decades of emigration, leaving it with a dwindling population and few prospects. The common response to this sort of problem is to plan out initiatives to entice citizens to stay, raise families, and grow the population back to a more sustainable level. But in Riace, the unpredictable happened instead: a boatload of Kurdish refugees came ashore. At that moment, Domenico Lucano saw a unique possibility. He had the vision and foresight to recognize those refugees as future citizens of Riace.

Emigration had left the town with numerous abandoned apartment complexes. Lucano was able to spearhead an initiative which placed the newly arrived refugees in the unused buildings and provided them with job training. This initiative transformed the formerly homeless refugees into citizens, bolstering Riace's population and winning Lucano the admiration of the town. He was later elected mayor. Since then, Riace has hosted over 6,000 asylum seekers.

Lucano's inspiration for the integration plan came from his personal social and political ideals, as well as a realistic apprehension of Riace's prospects in a modern consumerist economy. Instead of trying to solve new problems with old solutions, he adapted, solving not only Riace's population troubles but also helping thousands of people in need of aid and stability. These days, Riace's festivals bring together all kinds of populations, from stable locals to nomadic communities, in a diverse and peaceful integration (World's Greatest Leaders—Domenico Lucano, 2016).

What High Performance Looks Like

Leaders who display flexibility

- sense when situations change and call for new approaches
- adjust plans to meet changing circumstances
- try new approaches
- are open to exploring new models or methods
- are open to others' perspectives
- are willing to listen and to be influenced
- remain adaptable, agile, and unflappable in the face of uncertainty
- are perceptive
- are eager to learn and grow, seeking out new and diverse work experiences

What's in Your Way?

Volatility and unpredictability present challenges, but they also create opportunities. If you resist and stay inflexible during such times, you can miss the opportunities hiding amid the chaos. Flexible leaders know that their organization can't succeed over the long run by doing what it has always done. Stubbornness in the face of this reality undermines confidence in your long-term capabilities. Inflexibility also means that others will need to give extra attention to getting you to commit. That slows them and everyone else down. Look at the list below and mark the items that you believe contribute to any difficulty you have developing and maintaining flexibility.

- ❏ You value stability.
- ❏ You are rigid or set in your ways.

- ❏ You are slow to recognize that favored approaches aren't working.
- ❏ You are hesitant to experiment or take risks.
- ❏ You have difficulty grasping the changes going on in your business environment.
- ❏ You lose touch with your core values or beliefs.
- ❏ You worry that people might see you as a chameleon, changing to meet the needs of every situation.
- ❏ You have received feedback that others see you as inconsistent or unpredictable.
- ❏ You don't take the long view.
- ❏ You give up too quickly on new ideas and methods.

Coach Yourself

To develop your flexibility, create goals that you have to meet in a climate of ambiguity, where risk taking and resilience are needed to succeed. These questions can help you focus on such areas:

- What are some of the complex challenges in your company, industry, or environment that have required your organization to change recently? What is the impact of change on the organization? Is there anything about proposed changes that you find threatening? What do you fear about them?

- What changes in your organization excite you? What kind of change would encourage you to be flexible in how you lead?

- Who in your organization can give you a clearer picture of the changes coming in the future and the rationale for those changes?

- What are your personal strategies for remaining flexible in uncertain situations? Which strategies are healthy? Unhealthy?

- Do you have colleagues who seem to meet every challenge because they can adapt their perspectives and approaches to a solution? What are their strategies? How does their flexibility differ from yours?

Improve Now

Start and adapt. When you meet confusing or overwhelming situations, sometimes it helps to jump in and just start trying some things out. Try small-scale experiments that will help you to develop clarity and confidence over time.

Break up stale routines. Doing things the same way repeatedly, even if it works, is a detriment to learning and growth. Experiment with new ways of doing things. Observe what happens and monitor your results, including what doesn't work. Once new habits start to form, continue to push yourself to reinvent your habits.

Communication styles. Learn more about how different people communicate. Identify your employees' styles and determine their preferences so that you can more easily understand their perspectives, which might suggest alternative approaches to situations you encounter.

Reinvent. When applying everyday solutions to everyday problems, stop to ask yourself how your actions might be done differently, especially if you don't have the typical means available to you. The next time you face a routine problem, try an alternate approach toward a solution and note the outcome.

Be curious. Find the unusual in the normal. Ask questions, keep learning, and challenge the status quo.

Practice resourcefulness and perseverance. In unfamiliar circumstances, first solutions rarely work. Sometimes second, third, or fourth solutions don't either. Be nimble in generating alternative approaches and learn from each attempt. Focus on your learning, not your frustration.

Balance chaos with stability. When volatility and uncertainty are getting the best of you, maintaining order and calm in other areas of your work and personal life will be of utmost importance. Instilling stability and structure into different areas of your life will pay off when new challenges arise.

Become a continuous learner. Learn new skills, develop new understanding, and apply them during times of change. Many leaders resist learning new approaches and hold onto old behaviors and skills even when it's obvious that they don't work anymore.

Developmental Opportunities

- Take on tasks that force you out of your routine or force you to work with perspectives different from your own.

- Identify someone with whom you've had a strained relationship and identify how you can be flexible toward the difference in your styles.

- Take on part of a colleague's job while he or she is on temporary leave.

- Focus more attention on a part of your job you've been avoiding.

- Co-manage a project with someone with a different perspective from yours.

- Serve on a cross-functional task force or project.

Activity Center

Review and download these activities you can use for your development or with your team from this book's resource page at www.ccl.org/compassbook.

Flexibility: Exploring Flexibility
Flexibility: How Flexible Are You?
Flexibility: Practice Curiosity

Related Competencies

Change Acceptance
Learning Agility
Resilience
Self-Awareness
Risk Taking
Tolerating Ambiguity

Resources

Calarco, A., & Gurvis, J. (2006). *Adaptability: Responding effectively to change.* Greensboro, NC: Center for Creative Leadership.

Dalton, M. (1998). *Becoming a more versatile learner.* Greensboro, NC: Center for Creative Leadership.

Johnson, S., & Blanchard, K. (1998). *Who moved my cheese? An amazing way to deal with change in your work and in your life.* New York, NY: G. P. Putnam's Sons.

World's greatest leaders—Domenico Lucano. (2016, March 24). *Fortune.* Retrieved from http://fortune.com/worlds-greatest-leaders/domenico -lucano-40/

27

Global Perspective

Reach across international borders to leverage resources and opportunities.

Globalization requires a different kind of leadership than the kind that was practiced during times of independent economies and internationalism. Yet 30 percent of US companies fail at executing global initiatives because their leaders lack the capacity for managing global business (Ghemawat, 2012). Because the demand for a global skill set will only increase, if you can master this competency you will be recognized among your peers as a leader with the insight to lead your organization into the future. People will appreciate your understanding of how to work across cultures and geographies to convert opportunities into accomplishments. Much of what makes up the cross-cultural competence required to lead globally can also be used to lead culturally diverse groups. Let's visit with a leader whose global perspective truly operates on the world stage.

Leadership in Action

When Federica Mogherini goes to work, she represents over 500 million people on an international negotiating stage. As the High Representative of the EU for Foreign Affairs and Security Policy, she works on behalf of dozens of different nations as they work with one another and outside powers to navigate the life-or-death challenges that face the EU. Because of the European Union's limited military power, she has to leverage diplomatic and economic knowledge to benefit and protect the multicultural union she represents.

In 2015, she was instrumental in brokering a historic military missile agreement with Iran. Six world superpowers contributed to the negotiations (McNamara & Howard, 2016). Only a broad and profound global understanding made Mogherini's negotiations possible. Steven Blockmans, a research fellow at the Centre for European Policy Studies, says of Mogherini, "She's not the quiet diplomat. She's outgoing; she's using all her natural charm in a diplomatic sense to her advantage . . . in creating a more effective and visible foreign policy at a time when foreign policy is under serious stress tests" (Hansen, 2016).

With growing turmoil threatening the political stability of the nations she represents, Mogherini has a tough road ahead. Massive population shifts made up of war refugees demand a sophisticated response, even as deadly terrorist attacks against civilians make the politics of negotiation more difficult. Further, the UK's 2016 vote to leave the EU has complicated the scene at an entirely different level. Her thoughts in the face of these challenges are straightforward: "It's not just that Europe can manage, it's that Europe *has* to manage" (Hansen, 2016).

What High Performance Looks Like

Leaders who have developed a global perspective

- think beyond national and cultural boundaries
- show an interest in other cultures by asking questions and doing background research
- change approaches to meet the unique needs of other regions or markets
- monitor global trends that may affect the organization
- adapt behavior to fit different cultural norms
- integrate local and global information for multisite decision making
- discern and manage cultural influences on business practices and marketing
- display a cosmopolitan attitude
- are willing to explore
- are seen as curious, adaptable, respectful, and genuine
- can negotiate effectively in different business environments, despite a grueling travel schedule and through translation
- display a professional, credible global image
- speak more than one language
- make effective use of technologies to communicate with team members in distant locations
- are sensitive to time differences when scheduling meetings
- collaborate to create realistic growth projections for other regions or markets
- understand other currencies and financial systems

What's in Your Way?

Without the ability to lead globally, you might make uninformed business bets that don't work out. You may miss business opportunities as your organization struggles to gain a foothold in international markets. You may miss chances for your organization to reduce costs that may affect its profitability—and ultimately its competitiveness. You might not tap the unique skills and insights of the organization's most skilled people if you fail to leverage globally diverse talent. Others in the organization may regard you as narrow-minded, and you risk insulting people from other cultures, damaging your credibility. From the list below, mark any items you think are holding you back from developing a global perspective.

❏ You unknowingly break cultural norms when working with your colleagues from other regions.

❏ You need to learn more about the cultures of your coworkers.

❏ You have had limited exposure to people of other cultures.

❏ You have limited experience working or living in other cultures.

❏ You're afraid you will appear ignorant by asking questions.

❏ You're afraid of offending people.

❏ You avoid traveling to other countries.

❏ You overestimate your understanding of other cultures.

❏ You underestimate how hard it is to gain an adequate understanding of other cultures.

❏ You struggle to deal with unexpected differences between work cultures or processes.

❏ You misunderstand how business is conducted in other countries.

❏ You unintentionally violate rules or laws in other countries.

❏ You exhaust yourself with travel.

Coach Yourself

To develop your global leadership ability, create goals in areas that immerse you in different environments, require you to lead a geographically dispersed team, craft cooperative agreements that feature the work of people who don't share your national or cultural background, or simply visit museums showcasing different cultures and their histories. These questions can help you focus on such areas:

- Think of a time when you were flexible or adapted to a different way of doing business. What did you do? What were the results?

- What do you worry about the most in interacting with people from other cultures? What are your fears? How might you address them?

- Whom can you rely on to support you as an ally, role model, or mentor as you learn about doing business in other parts of the world?

- When was the last time you saw someone make a mistake while he or she was trying to work in another region or culture? What did the person do and what was the result?

- Would you ever consider living and working abroad? If not, what are your reasons for avoiding foreign assignments and opportunities?

Improve Now

Talk to global masters. Find people who have traveled and worked extensively in other parts of the world. Meet with them to learn more about experiences and knowledge. You can also talk to your friends about their world travel experiences.

Give yourself a little something. How will you reward yourself once you have mastered new culturally aware knowledge and skills? You could, for example, treat yourself to a meal at an ethnic restaurant or vacation in a new place.

Admit your ignorance. People in other cultures often appreciate your curiosity and honesty if you ask questions, even if such questions reveal how little you know.

Identify specific cultures that you want to learn more about. In what markets or cultures does your organization operate? Where are you likely to devote your time in the future? Focus your learning on where the lessons can have an immediate effect. See if there's a local university class you can attend to jumpstart your learning.

Visit a museum or art gallery to explore other cultures. Archival materials can boost your appreciation for the history and attitudes of other cultures.

Learn about a foreign sport or art form. Most cultures express themselves through games and artistic achievements. Today's sports channels on TV carry many international sports. Your local library, bookstore, or music store are sources for exploring another culture's art forms.

Conduct demographic research. Go online to explore other countries and get answers to basic questions about their culture, economy, and ways of doing business. Get smart before you get there.

Plan travel. Where will you go, and what will you do when you get there? Who will be your guide? Put your knowledge to the test. Allow yourself to make mistakes, but try to keep them small.

Enlist the help of a travel guide. You will learn much faster and avoid some mistakes if you can connect with experts and follow their lead.

Examine your cultural foundations. Study and reflect on your own cultural background. This will help you to be cognizant of how this identity influences your perspective and behaviors.

Challenge yourself culturally. Are you particularly inexperienced with a certain group of people? Make a point to pay special attention to your interactions with them. Firsthand experience is the greatest teacher.

Developmental Opportunities

- Seek an international assignment to embed yourself in another culture.

- Surround yourself with people who are unlike you (for example in age, gender, ethnicity, or culture).

- Manage a multinational project.

- Take on responsibility for a global product release, process introduction, or organizational function.

- Hire staff with international experience.

- Partner with peers in other countries to solve a shared problem.

- Take a short-term assignment in another country.

Activity Center

Review and download these activities you can use for your development or with your team from this book's resource page at www.ccl.org/compassbook.

Global Perspective: Be a Global Learner
Global Perspective: Capture, Clarify, Confirm
Global Perspective: Map Your Social Identity

Related Competencies

Boundary Spanning
Difference, Diversity, Inclusion
Global Team Management
Relationship Management
Risk Taking

Resources

Dalton, M. A., Ernst, C. T., Deal, J. J., & Leslie, J. B. (2002). *Success for the new global manager: What you need to know to work across distances, countries, and cultures.* San Francisco, CA: Jossey-Bass.

Deal, J. J., & Prince, D. W. (2003). *Developing cultural adaptability: How to work across differences.* Greensboro, NC: Center for Creative Leadership.

Denison, D. R., Hooijberg, R., Lane, N., & Lief, C. (2012). *Leading culture change in global organizations: Aligning culture and strategy.* San Francisco, CA: Jossey-Bass.

Ghemawat, P. (2012). Developing global leaders. *McKinsey Quarterly*, (3), 100–109.

Hannum, K. (2007). *Social identity: Knowing yourself, leading others.* Greensboro, N.C: Center for Creative Leadership.

Hannum, K., McFeeters, B. B., & Booysen, L. (Eds.). (2010). *Leading across difference: Cases and perspectives.* San Francisco, CA: Pfeiffer.

Hansen, S. (2016, Feb. 29). E.U. foreign-policy and security chief Federica Mogherini is often the only woman in the room. *Vogue.* Retrieved from http://www.vogue.com/13405891/federica-mogherini-european-union -foreign-policy-security-chief/

Leslie, J. B., Dalton, M. A., Ernst, C. T., & Deal, J. J. (2002). *Managerial effectiveness in a global context.* Greensboro, NC: Center for Creative Leadership.

McNamara, A., & Howard, C. (Eds.). (2016, June 6). The world's 100 most powerful women - #19 Federica Mogherini. *Forbes.* Retrieved from http://www.forbes.com/profile/federica-mogherini/?list=power-women

Prince, D. W., & Hoppe, M. H. (2000). *Communicating across cultures.* Greensboro, NC: Center for Creative Leadership.

Rush, S. (Ed.) (2013). *On leading the global organization.* Greensboro, NC: Center for Creative Leadership.

28

Global Team Management

Build effective teams by leveraging energy from widely dispersed individuals and locations.

Globalization forces organizations to operate across multiple boundaries. Teams, work groups, divisions, and other organizational functions become more culturally diverse, geographically dispersed, and temporally detached. And while this arrangement presents daunting leadership challenges, it also spawns valuable opportunities. Whether you see globalization of work as an obstacle or an asset in your organization depends on your ability to master global team management.

Leaders who can manage globally dispersed teams position themselves for the highest positions in organizations. To excel, leaders need to expand their understanding of the global market and its demands. They need to develop comfort with working across boundaries to leverage the connections of a highly diverse, mobile workforce. Such leaders develop a perspective that alerts them to business opportunities that others do not see. And opportunities can go much further than that—as we see when we look in on Michael Suffredini's job.

Leadership in Action

Look to the sky on the right night and you might see a quick, unblinking light move across the dark. That light, as bright as the moon, is the International Space Station, reflecting the light of the sun. Many of us are familiar with the ISS and its scientific missions: testing the effects of outer space on plants and animals (including humans) and paving the way for all future space stations. But the station also serves a profound political purpose: symbolizing a unity of scientific purpose shared by the participants, especially the United States, Russia, The European Space Agency, Japan, and Canada. According to NASA's website, "The ISS has been the most politically complex space exploration program ever undertaken." All of which made Michael Suffredini's job one of the most complex feats of management ever undertaken.

As program manager for the ISS, it fell to Suffredini to oversee the global effort to build, launch, and sustain the ISS. Much of the station itself was constructed in space, midflight—a job akin to building a ship on the open ocean. Participating nations build, launch, and manage their own modules. Prior to his retirement from NASA in 2015, it was Suffredini's responsibility to ensure compatibility with different equipment. Talking about the ISS in 2006, Suffredini said, "The station literally becomes a new spacecraft with each assembly mission" (Bloomberg, n.d.).

What High Performance Looks Like

Leaders adept at managing global teams

- focus others' energies on common goals, priorities, and problems

- have a track record of successful team building

- ask questions and seek guidance about other cultures and their norms

- adapt their management style to meet cultural expectations

- leverage individual differences for the good of the organization

- make effective use of technologies to communicate with team members in distant locations

- are seen as globally minded, culturally sensitive, multicultural, nimble, accepting, culturally intelligent, and empathetic

- select and develop people in many cultural settings

- evaluate the work of others while avoiding cultural bias

- encourage sharing among people who may be from different cultures, don't know each other, and seldom if ever see each other face-to-face

What's in Your Way?

If you have difficulty managing globally dispersed teams, you might fall behind in your knowledge of worldwide markets and business opportunities. Others inside and outside of your organization may see you as unsophisticated or narrow in your thinking and worldview. When others see you struggling to work across cultural differences, they can lose morale and confidence. For example, if you don't know how to leverage different time zones, your lack of skill may lead to a loss of productivity or overworked employees. Or, you might choose modes of communication (phone, email, chat), that don't fit the situation, possibly creating misunderstandings and distrust.

Leaders who struggle with this skill might be unaware of expectations or norms that differ from their own. For example, they may not know how nonverbal communications differ across cultures. As a result, those leaders may not know to adjust their personal style when necessary to meet the needs of others. They might constrain themselves with stereotypes that get in the way of their working with distant colleagues. You might have trouble developing your ability to manage a global team if you mark any of the items in the following list:

- ❏ You neglect to invest time in getting to know the people around you.
- ❏ You have limited experience working or living in other cultures.
- ❏ You unknowingly break cultural norms when working with your colleagues from other regions.
- ❏ Team members hesitate to say or do anything that might be seen in their culture as disrespectful.
- ❏ Team members don't understand the cultures of other team members.
- ❏ People hesitate to give you open feedback about your behavior in multicultural situations.
- ❏ You don't know what people from other cultures expect of you.
- ❏ You hold too many meetings.
- ❏ You make incorrect assumptions about what people need.
- ❏ You struggle to define a common set of values.
- ❏ You struggle to create collaboration among dispersed team members.
- ❏ You accidentally offend people of different cultures.
- ❏ You struggle to resolve conflicts caused by cultural differences.
- ❏ You struggle to manage time zone differences.

Coach Yourself

To develop your competence for managing global teams, create goals in areas such as distance communication, cultural immersion, and unfamiliar work. These questions can help:

- How can you build stronger relationships with team members in distant locations? Do you need to spend more time with them?
- What are your cultural blind spots? Who can help you fill in those blind spots by telling you what you need to know about working in one particular culture or another?
- Do you need to become more technologically savvy to effectively use devices and applications that connect team members across geographic distances?
- Do you fully understand the cultural differences at play in your team?
- What holds you back from expanding your cultural awareness or boundaries?

Improve Now

Watch for discomfort. It might signal cultural differences. You can use the discomfort you feel when cultural boundaries collide as an alert to be culturally sensitive and aware.

Look for nonverbal communication. Whether you're talking to someone from your own culture or to someone with a different cultural perspective, much of the conversation plays out in nonverbal cues. If you conduct all your meetings by phone or email (avoiding videoconferencing or face-to-face interactions, no matter how rare), you can't pay attention to nonverbal communications.

Use stories and analogies that can cross borders. Anecdotes and comparisons are great aids to understanding in any language and in every culture. Avoid sports and military references, stories about holidays, and other cultural touch points that may be unfamiliar or controversial to people outside of your cultural perspective.

Modify your communication style. When you work with people of other cultures, expect that differences will surface. Anticipate that differences will create a need for more thoughtful and deliberate communication choices, such as avoiding colloquialisms and slang in your native language that may not translate to a foreign language.

Welcome. Host an employee from another country or region.

Join the foreign service. Work on a short-term service project in another country.

Stay on top of team trust and relationship issues. Problems that you can easily spot in a colocated team may not be as evident when your team members are scattered around the globe.

Clearly define roles and responsibilities for team members at the start. Team leaders should do this with any team, but it's dramatically more important if your team is globally dispersed. Take the time to validate roles and responsibilities with each team member—individually and collectively—to ensure that everyone knows what he or she is accountable for and what is expected.

Set clear meeting agendas. Review the value and purpose of each meeting and consider whether all team members need to be present or if you can send meeting notes and summarize discussions with some team members later. Discuss this approach with the team before implementing it, because you don't want any team members to feel devalued if they are not part of the meeting.

Create shared goals and implement shared work. Leaders in global organizations need to create common ground while honoring differences. A key element of this task is to create alignment around the work and the mission while maintaining an appreciation for other cultural perspectives.

Address culture conflicts. Global leaders work across multiple cultural groups simultaneously. They face situations or incidents in which priorities or values embedded in those cultures may conflict. Sometimes the cultural conflict is glaring; other times the differences are subtle and easy to miss until they boil over.

Be aware of language use in other cultures. In some Asian cultures, for example, the word "no" is considered impolite. These cultures use body language to communicate indirectly a negative response. As another example, asking whether someone wants to take on an assignment might be perceived as a polite command in some cultures and a legitimate inquiry in others.

Developmental Opportunities

- Work on a multicultural team project.
- Manage a function that is globally dispersed.
- Manage a major multicountry project.
- Work on a short-term service project in a foreign country.
- Host a virtual team-building event if you have members of your team who are located at other sites.

Activity Center

Review and download these activities you can use for your development or with your team from this book's resource page at www.ccl.org/compassbook.

Global Team Management: Blending Teams
Global Team Management: Plan Your Trip

Related Competencies

Communication
Difference, Diversity, Inclusion
Flexibility
Global Perspective
Interpersonal Savvy
Relationship Management

Resources

Bloomberg. (n.d.). *Executive profile: Michael T. Suffredini.* Author. Retrieved from http://www.bloomberg.com/research/stocks/private/person.asp?personId=23614555&privcapId=13394361&previousCapId=13394361&previousTitle=Stinger%20Ghaffarian%20Technologies,%20Inc

Deal, J. J., & Prince, D. W. (2003). *Developing cultural adaptability: How to work across differences.* Greensboro, NC: Center for Creative Leadership.

Ernst, C., & Chrobot-Mason, D. (2010). *Boundary spanning leadership: Six practices for solving problems, driving innovation, and transforming organizations.* New York, NY: McGraw-Hill.

Hannum, K. M. (2007). *Social identity: Knowing yourself, leading others.* Greensboro, NC: Center for Creative Leadership.

Hannum, K. M., McFeeters, B. B., & Booysen, L. (2010). *Leading across differences: Cases and perspectives: Frequently asked questions.* San Francisco, CA: Pfeiffer.

McFeeters, B. B., Hannum, K. M., & Booysen, L. (2010). *Leading across differences: Cases and perspectives: Facilitator's guide.* San Francisco, CA: Pfeiffer.

29
Initiative

Independently assess situations, address conflicts, and lead action without hesitation.

You want to be right, achieve great things, and be rewarded and recognized for what you've done. That's good. Without ambition, it's unlikely that you will embrace challenges. Furthermore, ambition can drive success—for you and for your organization. Managing your career isn't your boss's job, and it isn't the job of your company's HR department. Gone are the days when an employee could put in the time and wait for a promotion or more responsibility. And frankly, to be a leader implies initiative. Visit the stories of two social movements, one of which lost its initiative because of a lack of leadership, and another that continues to make its voice heard because the movement's founders took initiative to see that it had a clear agenda and purpose.

Leadership in Action

Grassroots activism relies on collective will, and collective will can be fickle. In 2011, the Occupy movement appeared to manifest a huge collective dissatisfaction into a political force in the United States, but by deliberately eschewing leadership and a codified agenda, the movement surrendered its initiative and eventually fell apart. Although it could be argued that the Occupy movement changed the national conversation about income inequality, it might have influenced policy more directly with a clear list of demands. A few years later, the Black Lives Matter movement and its collection of leaders faced a similar problem: with its agenda unclear, it risked losing initiative and dissipating.

Although Black Lives Matter has no official hierarchy, it isn't deliberately leaderless in the way Occupy attempted to be. Grassroots founders steer the action and policy of the movement. Figures such as DeRay Mckesson, Brittany Packnett, and Johnetta Elzie serve as a kind of public face for a movement diffused across the entire country. It's impossible to coordinate such a group, but it is possible to rally them. For that kind of leadership, a clear statement of purpose was required.

That's why Mckesson and Packnett drafted Campaign Zero, a series of specific policy proposals. The campaign is ambitious but specific, exactly the kind of agenda their movement needs in order to rally. Had they acted with too much caution, they would have risked allowing the movement itself to diffuse. But with a set of achievable, specific goals, the organization has a real chance to create tangible, lasting reform (Baker, n.d.; Cobb, 2016; Cornish, 2015).

What High Performance Looks Like

Leaders skilled at initiative

- trust their instincts

- seize opportunities

- act when others hesitate

- take charge in the face of trouble

- follow their efforts through to completion

- are comfortable promoting their accomplishments

- have confidence in their abilities

- are driven to succeed

- seek greater challenge and responsibility

- know what they want to achieve

- understand what motivates and drives them

- take ownership of their career and long-term success

- see more than one way to reach their goals

What's in Your Way?

It's common sense—or should be—that your career won't go far if you lack initiative. You already know you need some level of initiative to achieve success. But the dark side of initiative, blind ambition, can knock your career off track. To take on a task and to talk about how you completed it is one thing, and it's something else to gloat over your achievements. The first can help people learn as they hear about the approach you chose, decisions you made, and actions you took. But their appreciation can quickly sour if you're arrogant about your successes. Maybe your challenge isn't arrogance at all but a general lack of interest in or connectedness to organizational goals—a general aimlessness in your work habits. The fact that you are using this book indicates that you have initiative. But in case you lack a reason to come into the office every day, look at the items on the following list and note those that you suspect are sabotaging your drive to succeed:

- ❏ You aren't involved with or connected to your organization's decision makers.
- ❏ Your manager oversees your work to the point of micromanaging.
- ❏ The organization you work for doesn't have an environment that accepts and encourages initiative—it's seen as ambition and politically motivated.
- ❏ You don't have or make time for creative activities.
- ❏ You don't feel responsible or accountable for team goals.
- ❏ You don't know whether others see you as competent because you haven't received feedback about your performance.
- ❏ You aren't driven by achievement, and you don't know how to channel what really drives you.
- ❏ You are risk averse.
- ❏ You want to keep a low profile.
- ❏ You are slow to recognize opportunities.
- ❏ You are content to let others take initiative.
- ❏ You look to others for direction and encouragement.

Coach Yourself

Initiative shouldn't be a problem for any potential leader, but if you need to tune yours up, create goals that bring attention to the projects you complete and that force you to seek out work and assignments on your own.
These questions can help you define areas to focus your development:

- ● Are you familiar with the team's strategy and its current state in terms of achieving its goals? What can you contribute?

- Do you have slack periods in the day when you could fit in work other than what your manager has already assigned you?

- Are you uncomfortable with showing ambition? Why?

- What's on your "someday I'm gonna" list? What's putting the "someday" into your thoughts? What's holding you back? Try making "someday I'm gonna" into "today I'm going to start" and see what happens.

- Think about situations where you have seized initiative (or at least felt tempted to). Were there any common elements to those situations? How might you shape your environment so it better motivates you to take initiative?

Improve Now

Ask for more. Finished with your tasks for the day? Ask your boss for other things you can do that would be helpful.

Aim higher. Don't automatically confine yourself to the expectations that have been set for you. If there is something further you can do that adds value and won't necessitate significantly more time or expense, give it a try.

Check it out. You may see something that should be done. If there is even a hint of a question or concern about you doing it, ask your manager and get permission to move forward on it. Someone else may have already started, or one of your colleagues may have been slated for the task. When in doubt—check it out.

Take care of your people. Sometimes those who take initiative or are practicing to take more initiative tend to look forward more often than back to ensure that everyone is with them.

Promote your employees. Initiators are often tagged for promotions early. If that is in your future, be sure you have promoted your employees verbally to everyone who needs to know.

Lead but look around. Taking initiative is admirable, bold, and an essential leadership skill, but don't lose sight of what is happening around you too.

Seek feedback. Sometimes colleagues are reluctant to provide feedback to someone who seems to be a successful leader. Ask for feedback often.

Look up. Design and deliver a class for the department or others who are interested about the skills of managing up and positive self-promotion.

Developmental Opportunities

- Facilitate a group of senior leaders to resolve a key issue—not as a participant, but in the role of facilitator. Observe how everyone in the group interacts at this level.

- Schedule a meeting with each of your mentors, coaches, and managers to discuss the advantages and disadvantages of your social style and career focus.

- Explore all nonheadquarters sites to determine their ability to maintain alignment with headquarters and make recommendations if there is misalignment.

- Supervise a product recall.

- Regain a lost customer.

- Work with others to solve a pressing business issue.

Activity Center

Review and download these activities you can use for your development or with your team from this book's resource page at www.ccl.org/compassbook.

Initiative: Leaders Go First
Initiative: No Excuses

Related Competencies

Credibility and Integrity

Executive Image

Leading with Purpose

Resourcefulness

Risk Taking

Self-Development

Urgency

Resources

Baker, B. (n.d.). Politico 50: DeRay Mckesson, Brittany Pack-nett: Co-founders, campaign zero. *Politico*.

Cartwright, T. (2007). *Setting priorities: Personal values, organizational results*. Greensboro, NC: Center for Creative Leadership.

Cobb, J. (2016, March 14). The matter of black lives: A new kind of movement found its moment. What will its future be? *The New Yorker*.

Cornish, A. (2015, Aug. 26). *All things considered: Black lives matter publishes "campaign zero'" plan to reduce police violence*. NPR.

Dweck, C. S. (2006). *Mindset: The new psychology of success*. New York, NY: Random House.

Kostanyan, A. (2014, Oct. 15). 9 ways to take more initiative at work. *Fast Company*. Retrieved from https://www.fastcompany.com/3037092/how-to-be-a-success-at-everything/9-ways-to-take-more-initiative-at-work

Lee, R. J., & King, S. N. (2001). *Discovering the leader in you: A guide to realizing your personal leadership potential*. San Francisco, CA: Jossey-Bass.

Pink, D. H. (2011). *Drive: The surprising truth about what motivates us*. New York, NY: Riverhead Books.

Scisco, P., McCauley, C. D., Leslie, J. B., & Elsey, R. (2014). *Change now! Five steps to better leadership*. Greensboro, NC: Center for Creative Leadership.

Zenger, J., Folkman, J., & Sherwin, R. H. (2012). *How to be exceptional: Drive leadership success by magnifying your strengths*. New York, NY: McGraw-Hill.

30
Innovation

Create an environment for breakthrough thinking and disruption.

Companies innovate to keep their competitive advantage and survive financially, but innovating is easier said than done. Even large companies with significant budgets struggle to create new products or services that give them an edge over their competitors or create new markets. What are they missing? They don't have leaders able to create an environment that supports innovation.

Foster a culture of innovation by developing your ability to operate in challenging, unpredictable circumstances. Set out the essential systems, tools, and thinking for organizational health and future viability. Consider the story of Alan Mulally, who took the helm of Ford Motor Company during a period of decline and just before economic disruption wreaked havoc on the automobile manufacturing industry in the United States.

Leadership in Action

Alan Mulally took over as CEO of Ford in the years just before the Great Recession. Over a decade of market share losses preceded his takeover, and he found himself in charge of a company in decline. Among the many factors contributing to Ford's struggles was the pervasive cutthroat culture within the company leadership, which strangled new ideas in favor of conservative self-preservation.

Innovation is predicated upon risk and imagination. In the fretful, fear-infused leadership culture of mid-2000s Ford, risk wasn't just impossible, it was unimaginable. Everyone knew the company was in trouble, and everyone was afraid to take the blame. In early meetings after he took on the role of CEO, his direct reports indicated that all was well within their respective departments, despite the indisputable numbers indicating otherwise. Mulally recognized these reports for what they were, but rather than take his team to task for misrepresenting their needs, he encouraged them to look closer at their departments, never mind the discomfort. It was his candor about the dire state of the company that allowed his team to take the first steps toward a cultural shift.

After loosening the stranglehold of fear that had kept his leadership team paralyzed, Mulally introduced new ideas of his own: modeling the company after consumer electronics industries that had achieved great success in the same period during which Ford floundered. The idea of reshaping public perception of what a truck could represent could never have taken root in the landscape Mulally found on his first day on the job (Caldicott, 2014).

What High Performance Looks Like

Innovative leaders

- show courage to take risks and encourage others to do so
- foster a climate of experimentation
- reward innovators
- adjust structures and strategies to accommodate new ideas
- support activities that position the business for the future
- are seen as courageous
- are inventive
- have an entrepreneurial mindset
- are receptive to new ideas, approaches, and methods
- can be demanding
- offer novel ideas and perspectives
- create dialogue about new ideas
- will represent ideas, act as an idea champion, and sell ideas to the organization
- treat failure as a learning opportunity

What's in Your Way?

Leaders unable to foster a culture of innovation miss opportunities to tap into the skills and insights of their most talented people. And they risk losing them altogether. They also see their organization become less and less competitive. Review the following list for any descriptions that apply to you and might be blocking your path to becoming a leader of innovation.

- ❑ You're afraid to fail.

- ❑ You have a conservative nature.

- ❑ You tend to rely on tried-and-true methods that you trust.

- ❑ You're too stressed from meeting your objectives to think about new ways of doing things.

- ❑ You lack resources: funding, people, or time.

- ❑ You define your job narrowly, and you don't see innovation as your responsibility.

- ❑ You struggle to view things from a different perspective.

- ❑ New initiatives are started that cannot be supported by the organization.

- ❑ Your customers are confused by a proliferation of innovation.

- ❑ You fail to criticize your ideas or solutions, being too enamored with their creativity or uniqueness.

- ❑ You lose the talent or other resources that your group needs to innovate.

- ❑ You struggle to sell your group's ideas to the organization.

- ❑ Your group gravitates toward the fun and interesting rather than focusing on what's needed for the organization or customer.

- ❑ You get a new boss who has less patience for or interest in innovation.

Coach Yourself

To develop your ability to create a culture of innovation, create goals in such areas as invention, risk, problem solving, and strategic planning and thinking. These questions can help:

- ● What are the barriers to innovation in my organization?

- ● What am I doing to develop creativity and innovation in my current employees?

- If I were to build a cross-functional team for developing breakthrough innovations, who would be on the team and why?

- What practices from the past compromise my ability to meet customer needs in the future?

- How acute is my vision for the future? Am I able to see a different world and unique new possibilities?

- Are there systems, processes, or people that I need to remove because they hold the organization back from innovating?

- How do people in the organization deal with its inherent tensions; for example, between change and stability; between innovation and the core business; between risk and safety; and between the known and the unknown?

Improve Now

Use imagery. Pictures, stories, impressions, and metaphors are powerful tools for describing situations, constructing ideas, and communicating effectively.

Explore your customers' hopes and pains. Help employees to see the world from the customer's perspective and discover what new ideas for innovation emerge. Lead employees to maintain that perspective as your organization works to implement innovative ideas.

Change it up. Take your group out of its usual environment, whether it be a literal change of scenery or a simple change of pace. Have a conversation with a group member while taking a walk, or hold a meeting over lunch. Have your team read a new book, or discuss a relevant film or news piece together. This will inspire new thinking and improve team engagement.

Delay evaluation. Ideas are most fragile when they are fresh off the ground. Hold off and explore ideas—give them some time to grow before evaluating them.

Rethink your problems. Slow down, temporarily, in order to be more deliberate in grasping the situation. Do the issues identified get at the root of the problem? Delve into the innovation obstacles faced by your organization and see if they might be a symptom of a deeper problem.

Leverage differences. Diversity in background and experience can be a boon to innovation. Make an effort to channel diverse viewpoints into positive outcomes rather than allowing them to divide your workplace.

Judge ideas fairly and constructively. Be respectful of people's ideas but open about ways to improve them.

Embrace paradox and contradiction. American novelist F. Scott Fitzgerald once said, "The test of a first-rate intelligence is the ability to hold two opposing ideas in the mind at the same time and still retain the ability to function." Innovation requires us to shed either-or thinking and see the whole as inclusive of opposition and open to a third (or fourth, or fifth) solution.

Share innovation tools. Identify innovation tools and techniques and champion them throughout the organization. Teach others how to use them.

Design an innovation system. Be as systematic with innovation as you are in other areas of management. Whether formally or informally, create a process designed to inspire new thinking, encourage the sharing of ideas, and facilitate collaboration.

Address organizational impediments. Ask your people to describe the obstacles to innovation—the current culture, leadership, resources, processes, or systems that get in the way. Tackle these challenges.

Go on a walkabout. Walk around a store or other organization that you consider innovative. What do you notice? How do people treat each other? How do you feel as the customer?

Developmental Opportunities

- Serve on a cross-functional task force or project.

- Join a team in an area unfamiliar to you in order to bring fresh perspective to the team's situation.

- Work on a new product development team.

- Spend time with internal and external customers to find out what they think their needs will be in the future.

- Work on a problem by doing quick experiments and trials.

- Visit a toy store and use the power of combination. How could this toy solve X problem at work?

Activity Center

Review and download these activities you can use for your development or with your team from this book's resource page at www.ccl.org/compassbook.

Innovation: Is It Important to Your Company?
Innovation: Championing Innovation

Related Competencies

Creativity
Organizational Savvy
Problem Solving
Resourcefulness
Strategic Planning and Implementation

Resources

Caldicott, S. M. (2014, June 25). Why Ford's Alan Mulally is an innovation CEO for the record books. *Forbes*. Retrieved from http://www.forbes.com/sites/sarahcaldicott/2014/06/25/why-fords-alan-mulally-is-an-innovation-ceo-for-the-record-books/#14e7b126779b

Clark, D. (2015). *Stand out: how to find your breakthrough idea and build a following around it*. New York, NY: Penguin.

Gryskiewicz, S. S., & Taylor, S. (2003). *Making creativity practical: Innovation that gets results*. Center for Creative Leadership.

Harvard Business Review Press. (2013). *HBR's 10 must reads on innovation*. Boston, MA: Author.

Horth, D., & Buchner, D. (2009). *Innovation leadership: How to use innovation to lead effectively, work collaboratively, and drive results*. (White paper). Center for Creative Leadership.

Horth, D., & Vehar, J. (2012). *Becoming a leader who fosters innovation*. (White paper). Center for Creative Leadership.

Horth, D. M., & Vehar, J. R. (2016). From innovation graveyard to innovation hotbed. *Developing Leaders Quarterly*, p. 23.

Sweeney, J., & Imaretska, E. (2016). *The innovative mindset: 5 behaviors for accelerating breakthroughs*. Hoboken, NJ: Wiley.

31

Interpersonal Savvy

Understand what others need and respond appropriately.

You might have great ideas and be highly accomplished, but if you struggle to connect with other people you won't be successful leading them. You need interpersonal skills to recognize and assess what others need. These skills involve not only listening to others, but also include noticing social cues that communicate how others are thinking and feeling, even if they don't say so outright.

      Interpersonal savvy helps you read and address relationships appropriately and at the right time. As business becomes more complex and as your career evolves, it's likely you will encounter an increasingly diverse set of people with whom you'll need to work. You will be able to rely on a developed interpersonal savvy to more quickly make the connection to different types of people, thereby making it easier to bring people together for a common cause. Let's visit the top government official of Canada to see what keen interpersonal savvy can accomplish.

Leadership in Action

Nowhere are the stakes for interpersonal savvy higher than in the arena of international politics. The challenges facing modern nations are daunting in their economic and ethical ramifications, and a breakdown in relations can spell disaster for thousands of people. It was into this environment that Justin Trudeau was elected prime minister of Canada in 2015.

Over the course of his election campaign and his tenure as PM, Trudeau has demonstrated an optimistic, welcoming style of leadership. People see it in his transparency and collaborative spirit. This style has made him popular among constituents and opened opportunities for dialogue with supporters and opponents alike.

Trudeau has deliberately appointed a diverse, gender-balanced Cabinet, and he has spoken candidly about his reasons for those appointments. His selections and his transparency have allowed him to redefine expectations of the PM office, which gives him more freedom when facing challenges, such as the ongoing Syrian refugee surge. It seems that his goal is to prove that more diversity, more honesty, and more dialogue lead to greater security and cohesion, not disorder.

Trudeau's interpersonal skills might be attributed to his unique job experience before his political career. Over the years, he's worked as a snowboard instructor, a nightclub bouncer, and (perhaps most importantly) a schoolteacher. All these jobs have something in common: the critical skills of communication, negotiation, and convincing others to act in accordance with the greater good. Now, Trudeau is working in a different role, one in which he must command authority while inviting productive dissent. It's a fine line to walk, but he seems to be managing it (McKernan, n.d.; Seth, 2016).

What High Performance Looks Like

Leaders with interpersonal savvy

- listen well
- learn what interests and excites other people
- tailor their communication based on others' needs and motivations
- understand their impact on situations and people
- make the first move to engage with other people
- make people feel at ease in tense situations
- build rapport with others
- practice emotional intelligence
- are seen as perceptive, adaptive, patient, responsive, and sociable
- try to understand another person's experiences before making judgments about that person
- can connect with diverse audiences
- can relate to people one-on-one
- ask questions to learn about and understand others
- build confidence in others

What's in Your Way?

If you struggle to develop interpersonal savvy, you might not pick up on cues to how others are thinking and feeling until small misunderstandings grow into problems and conflicts. Others may not feel personally connected to you and may avoid coming to you with issues or may hesitate to give you helpful feedback. In the short term, lack of interpersonal savvy can lead to an absence of trust on your team and loss of confidence in your leadership. In the long term, it may be difficult for you to advance if you can't rely on personal connections for a network of support or make important political contacts. Take a look at the descriptions below and mark any that you believe are getting in the way of your developing interpersonal savvy.

- ❏ Your social skills are underdeveloped.
- ❏ You are impatient with people.
- ❏ Your role models lack interpersonal sensitivity.
- ❏ You prefer to talk rather than listen.
- ❏ You've received feedback that you're self-centered and insensitive to others' needs.
- ❏ You are quick to judge other people.
- ❏ You tend to focus on the business more than on people.
- ❏ You lack diplomacy or tact.
- ❏ You've learned that others see you as slick or manipulative.
- ❏ You lose touch with your core values or beliefs.
- ❏ People see you as a chameleon, changing to meet the needs of every situation.
- ❏ Upper management sees you as too soft on people and not willing to demand excellence.
- ❏ You come off as inauthentic—people don't trust their interactions with you.

Coach Yourself

To develop interpersonal savvy, create goals in areas that have you working with different groups, that push you to build a leadership network, and that otherwise contain situations in which you must get along with others and understand them to produce positive results. These questions can help you focus on such areas:

- How well do you really know the people around you?

- Do you focus on work tasks at the expense of learning about the people you work with? What distracts you from focusing on the people around you?

- Do you spend enough time networking or building new relationships?

- How would stronger rapport with others help you be more effective or get more done?

- How do you think other people perceive you? What feedback have you received about your interpersonal skills?

- How much are you focused on understanding and meeting the needs of others rather than only on your own interests?

Improve Now

Think before you speak. Managers with interpersonal savvy exercise impulse control. They choose their battles wisely and size up situations before deciding how to present ideas to others.

Clarify. Ask follow-up questions, especially open-ended ones, and probe for more information. This serves to improve your own understanding and to help others develop their thoughts and ideas.

Summarize. Restating key themes as your conversation progresses helps to prevent misunderstanding and to ensure that everyone involved is on common ground.

Meet others where they are. First, understand others' interests, needs, and motivations. Demonstrate that you understand by responding to them in ways that highlight areas where your interests align. Then, depending on your assessment of any gaps between or among you, offer and listen to alternate perspectives.

Read and adjust. Social interactions are a back-and-forth affair, not a one-way street. Instead of just working your agenda or waiting to make your point, pay close attention to how others react to you and form your response accordingly.

Lay the groundwork. Approach interactions with a sense of purpose and be transparent about what you hope to accomplish. That doesn't mean you can't engage in some small talk to ease into things, but don't engage in small talk at the expense of the important issues.

Hone your powers of perception. Socially astute managers tend to be observers of others and of social situations. They can comprehend social interaction, and in social settings they accurately interpret their own behavior as well as that of others. They have strong powers of discernment and high self-awareness.

Learn to network. Leaders who possess a strong networking ability build friendships and beneficial working relationships by garnering support, negotiating, and managing conflict. Skilled networkers know when to call on others and have a reputation for reciprocating.

Practice influence. Interpersonal-savvy leaders make effective influencers because they have built strong interpersonal relationships and have good rapport with others. This aspect of emotional intelligence isn't necessarily or overtly political, but it operates within the borders of the organization's political landscape.

Become a people reader. Learn to read body language and to respond appropriately. Practice all the time: at work, during social events, with your neighbors, and at home with your family.

Learn your environment. Organizations are complex. Knowing how to navigate your organization's formal and informal systems and cultures will improve your interpersonal savvy by making your responses fit the time and situation.

Developmental Opportunities

- Serve on multiple project teams simultaneously.

- Ask your group to generate a new idea to implement. Work to move that idea through the organization and get the necessary support from others.

- Head a new initiative for a community or professional organization.

- Create a networking group in your organization.

- Serve as a campus recruiter for your organization.

- Volunteer with an organization that works with underserved populations in your community.

Activity Center

Review and download these activities you can use for your development or with your team from this book's resource page at www.ccl.org/compassbook.

Interpersonal Savvy: Choose to Be Interpersonally Savvy

Interpersonal Savvy: How They Perceive You

Related Competencies

Communication

Credibility and Integrity

Influence

Organizational Savvy

Relationship Management

Self-Awareness

Resources

Booher, D. (2015). *What more can I say? Why communication fails and what to do about it*. New York, NY: Prentice Hall.

Cain, S. (2013). *Quiet: The power of introverts in a world that can't stop talking*. New York, NY: Broadway Books.

Cartwright, T. (2003). *Managing conflict with peers*. Greensboro, NC: Center for Creative Leadership.

Cartwright, T. (2009). *Changing yourself and your reputation*. Greensboro, NC: Center for Creative Leadership.

Center for Creative Leadership. (2013). *Interpersonal savvy: Building and maintaining solid working relationships*. Greensboro, NC: Author.

Center for Creative Leadership. (n.d.). *Be grateful to lead*. (Video). Author. Retrieved from https://vimeo.com/160131385.

Gentry, W. A. (2016). *Be the boss everyone wants to work for: A guide for new leaders*. Oakland, CA: Berrett-Koehler.

Gentry, W. A., & Leslie, J. B. (2013). *Developing political savvy*. Greensboro, NC: Center for Creative Leadership.

McCauley, C. D. (2012). Reflection and integration: Supervisor-employee relationships. In L. T. de Tormes Eby & T. D. Allen (Eds.), *Personal relationships: The effect on employee attitudes, behavior, and well-being* (pp. 95–105). New York, NY: Taylor & Francis.

McKernan, B. (n.d.). 19 reasons why the world has fallen in love with Canada's prime minister Justin Trudeau. *Indy100*. Retrieved from http://indy100 .independent.co.uk/article/19-reasons-why-the-world-has-fallen-in-love -with-canadas-prime-minister-justin-trudeau--Z1nJRgUCcx

Popejoy, B., & McManigle, B. J. (2002). *Managing conflict with direct reports*. Greensboro, NC: Center for Creative Leadership.

Scharlatt, H. (2016). *Resolving conflict: Ten steps for turning negatives to positives*. Greensboro, NC: Center for Creative Leadership.

Seth, R. (2016, June 29). 5 leadership lessons from Canadian prime minister Justin Trudeau. *Fast Company*. Retrieved from http://www.fastcompany .com/3061046/lessons-learned/5-leadership-lessons-from-canadian-prime -minister-justin-trudeau

Sharpe, D., & Johnson, E. (2002). *Managing conflict with your boss*. Greensboro, NC: Center for Creative Leadership.

Zack, D. (2010). *Networking for people who hate networking: A field guide for introverts, the overwhelmed, and the underconnected*. San Francisco, CA: Berrett-Koehler.

32

Leading the Culture

Build a healthy, productive work climate while paying attention to unwritten rules and assumptions.

Your employees' norms, attitudes, beliefs, and habits constitute the culture of your organization. Leaders are an important part of that dynamic mix. Empirical evidence shows that an organization's culture is a consequence of its leadership and that a productive organizational culture results in high levels of organizational performance (Holloway, 2012; Ogbonna & Harris, 2000). You can instill a positive, performance-oriented culture within your organization by honing the crucial skills of culture-oriented leadership within yourself.

Leaders act as ambassadors within their organizations. They personify "how things are done here" and contribute to the attractiveness and efficiency of their organizations' practices and processes. Along with others, leaders instill the distinct knowledge and practices of the organization into a vibrant system and help fuel sustainable organizational success for the benefit of all.

Leadership in Action

What happens to an organization's culture when 18 percent of its employees leave? Tony Hsieh, CEO of online retailer Zappos, might say the organization gains an entrepreneurial spirit and eliminates the constraining bureaucracy that comes with growth. In 2015, Zappos began implementing author and former software company executive Brian Robertson's notion of "holacracy," a self-managed, self-directed organizational structure that eliminates much of the traditional organizational hierarchy.

Hsieh admits the change hasn't been easy for some people in the organization, but he maintains that the radical culture shift will help the company by helping each employee become more like an entrepreneur and less like someone dependent on a manager to set priorities and assign tasks. Hsieh wants the people at Zappos to adopt and share that mindset. He believes Zappos must leave behind the boss-worker paradigm and shift from principally an e-commerce site to a mobile-first retailer. He believes that the way holacracy distributes power in organizations will fuel that shift and help Zappos keep its competitive edge and sustain itself in an ultra-competitive marketplace (Feloni, 2016).

What High Performance Looks Like

Leaders capable of leading the organization's culture

- question the value of the organization's current culture and beliefs that are counterproductive or inaccurate

- establish clear organizational values

- cast a vision for how people will work together in the organization

- define culture needed to enact business strategy

- align the executive team around the organization's vision, strategy, and culture

- set a positive personal example for the organization

- ensure that executive team members model the culture in their behavior

- are seen as inspirational, motivating, exemplary, encouraging, questioning, and accountable

- reflect on the beliefs and assumptions that drive key decisions

- encourage others to question their beliefs or assumptions about the organization

- create a sense of accountability and personal ownership

- stay in touch with how people in the organization think and what they believe

What's in Your Way?

People unable to lead organizational culture can't promote the best, most efficient, and healthiest way of accomplishing the business's goals. They may fail to make the organization attractive to employees and prospective new hires. To the extent that the cultural practices they promote come across as counterproductive, their motives, loyalty, and fit with the organization may be questioned. Take a look at the following descriptions and mark any that you believe are getting in the way of your ability to lead your organization's culture.

- ❏ You have a good grasp of the desired culture but your communication style is uninspiring.

- ❏ You're not sure what you want to stand for in your organization.

- ❏ You're unwilling to engage the organization in thoughtful exploration of culture.

- ❏ You're committed to doing things the way they have always been done.

- ❏ You lack curiosity about the organization's underlying beliefs and assumptions.

- ❏ Your values are out of alignment with the majority of the organization's members.

- ❏ The culture you envision conflicts with how the work is currently organized or with the processes used to carry out the work.

- ❏ Harsh business conditions force you to make decisions that may conflict with the culture.

- ❏ Your cultural changes are seen as a fad.

- ❏ You focus just on operational systems, structure, and process at the expense of the human side of the business.

- ❏ You try to push the culture too far, too fast.

- ❏ You don't change yourself or your team first.

- ❏ You try to change aspects of the culture that are fundamental or sacred to the organization.

Coach Yourself

To develop your ability to lead the culture at your organization, create goals in areas that invite communication across the business, that make you familiar with your organization's hiring and orientation processes, and that can give you a voice in the organization's strategic planning. These questions can help you focus on such areas:

- What are the barriers to excellence in your organization? For example, are there unwritten rules about how work should be accomplished that should be questioned?

- Do you have a full understanding of your organization's current culture? How does it expect people to act? What principles does your organization stand for?

- Whom do people look to as culture-setters in your organization? Other than the top leaders, who else is most visible to and influential among employees?

- How does your organization communicate its cultural norms to new hires?

- How does your organization's culture align with the needs of your customers and other stakeholders?

Improve Now

Make your case. List the benefits of the culture you want the organization to adopt. What would it bring to your organization? Consider the role of culture in aligning business functions. The culture you envision should encourage among other things superior execution, employee motivation, and cohesion. Connect each element of the culture to your organization's business strategy.

Cut the act. Identify one behavior that is no longer welcome at your organization. Explain how this kind of behavior is counterproductive and must be abandoned. Give feedback when you see others engage in old behaviors that run counter to the culture you want to see adopted. Be open to feedback if you lapse into old behaviors too.

Status quo challenge. Ask a friend who works at a different company (any industry) and whom you trust to share how employees challenge the status quo at his or her company. Ask what is acceptable, what works, and what doesn't work. Relate this to your organization and identify how you can incorporate this information into your efforts to improve.

Be a role model. Everybody who reports to you and even people not directly under your supervision continually observe and interpret what you do (and what you don't do). Become part of a positive change by championing the culture your organization needs, influencing people toward that goal, and supporting them as they shift their beliefs and actions to create that culture.

Invest time in your people. Invite them to share what is important to them and what they need to work at their best. Compare and contrast what they say with what the organization officially sanctions.

Draw a crowd. Identify key players, communicators, stakeholders, and supporters throughout the organization who will motivate others to listen, reflect on, and engage with the culture.

Be everywhere your message can be. Visit different locations in your organization wherever they are, from the mailroom at company headquarters to the satellite division on the other side of the world. Make your presence known with constant enterprise communications and with small face-to-face gatherings.

Picture this. Send your team out to the other parts of the organization to take pictures around the company of how other departments live the culture. Bring everyone together to discuss and to share what they learned. Ask them to suggest ways that you could do a better job of leading the culture.

Celebrate culture. Seize any opportunity to display positive behaviors that reinforce the culture you are trying to create and highlight what those actions bring to the organization.

Align learning with culture. Connect with your training and development staff or your human resources department to ensure that training aligns with the culture you want to put in place.

Align culture with strategy. Culture can wreak havoc on organizational strategy. Connect your culture to your business strategy by identifying the crucial links between them. What happens to your organization's strategic plan if it doesn't stand on a supportive culture?

Connect with your human resources staff. Work with them to figure out how to explain the culture to prospective hires. Help them assess methods for determining whether a prospect is a good fit at the organization.

Rituals and symbols. Identify the rituals, symbols, ceremonies, customs, practices, and other signs that you believe represent the organization. Make a list of as many as you can think of. How do these relate to the culture? Schedule a meeting with your coach or supervisor to discuss these cultural symbols. Also ask if you could share your observations at a staff meeting or a lunch-and-learn event.

Developmental Opportunities

- Investigate the cultures of partner organizations and think about how changes to your organization's culture will affect your partners. How could you work better together if your cultures were aligned or complementary?

- Make speeches to external groups as a representative of your organization. Be an ambassador and role model for your culture. Collect stories to use to make these presentations come alive.

- Study cultures around you. Go to your favorite store and look at how people carry out their jobs. What works well? What could work better?

- Take on a boundary-spanning role for a community or professional organization. How could you help it integrate its cultures?

- Create a blog or become active on social media. Be the visible ambassador of your organization's culture, the champion of its success.

- Volunteer to write and give a presentation at the next new-employee orientation that presents the company's vision. Clear it with your supervisor.

■ Prepare a community speech you could give to the Chamber of Commerce, Civic League, or other civic organizations that explains your company's vision. Have your supervisor or coach critique it.

Activity Center

Review and download these activities you can use for your development or with your team from this book's resource page at www.ccl.org/compassbook.

Leading the Culture: Leader as Culture Ambassador
Leading the Culture: Values–Culture–Vision

Related Competencies

Communication
Credibility and Integrity
Organizational Savvy
Self-Awareness
Strategic Planning and Implementation
Vision

Resources

Axelrod, R. H. (2010). *Terms of engagement: New ways of leading and changing organizations* (2nd ed.). San Francisco, CA: Berrett-Koehler.

Ernst, C., & Chrobot-Mason, D. (2011). *Boundary spanning leadership: Six practices for solving problems, driving innovation, and transforming organizations*. New York, NY: McGraw-Hill.

Feloni, R. (2016, Jan. 28). Zappos CEO Tony Hsieh reveals what it was like losing 18% of his employees in a radical management experiment and why it was worth it. *Business Insider*. Retrieved from http://www.businessinsider.com/tony-hsieh-explains-how-zappos-rebounded-from-employee-exodus-2016-1

Gullette, E. C. D. (2015). Coaching in context: The individual relation to organizational culture. In D. D. Riddle, E. R. Hoole, & E. C. D. Gullette (Eds.), *The Center for Creative Leadership handbook of coaching in organizations* (pp. 289–309). San Francisco, CA: Jossey-Bass.

Holloway, J. B. (2012). Leadership behavior and organizational climate: An empirical study in a nonprofit organization. *Emerging Leadership Journeys, 5*(1), 9–35. Retrieved from https://www.researchgate .netpublication/305397374_leadership_behavior_and_organizational_ climate_an_empirical_study_in_a_nonprofit_organization

Hughes, R. L., Beatty, K. C., & Dinwoodie, D. L. (2014). *Becoming a strategic leader: Your role in your organization's enduring success*. San Francisco, CA: Jossey-Bass.

Laloux, F. (2014). *Reinventing organizations: A guide to creating organizations inspired by the next stage in human consciousness*. Brussels, Belgium: Nelson Parker.

Lewis, R. D. (2005). *When cultures collide: Leading across cultures.* (3rd ed.). Boston, MA: Nicholas Brealey International.

McGuire, J. B., & Rhodes, G. (2009). *Transforming your leadership culture*. San Francisco, CA: Jossey-Bass.

Ogbonna, E., & Harris, L. (2000). Leadership style, organizational culture and performance: Empirical evidence from UK companies. *International Journal of Human Resources Management, 11*(4), 766–788. Retrieved from http:// faculty.mu.edu.sa/public/uploads/1360753037.3351organizational%20 cult31.pdf

Robertson, B. J. (2015). *Holacracy: The new management system for a rapidly changing world*. New York, NY: Henry Holt and Co.

Studer, Q. (2006). *Results that last: Hardwiring behaviors that will take your company to the top*. Hoboken, NJ: Wiley.

33

Leading with Purpose

Energize others by demonstrating passion, commitment, and focus.

Are you leading work that you love in an organization you care about with people you enjoy? If so, then you have some idea of the power of purposeful leadership. Leading with purpose channels enthusiasm and zeal into an intense energy and drive. Leaders with purpose stay focused and committed—a critically important perspective in an environment filled with obstacles and distractions.

When you lead with purpose, you radiate an energy and passion for work. Your passion affects everyone around you. It inspires and motivates others. When people are searching for direction, they often turn to a leader who personifies purpose. Those leaders have a reputation in their organizations for attracting talent to their teams and inspiring achievement—sometimes beyond what is thought possible. If you need evidence of the power of purpose, consider Ray Anderson's story of organizational transformation.

Leadership in Action

Ray Anderson had a single-minded purpose: to move the textile company he founded, Interface, to a model of sustainability. Anderson wasn't looking for sustainability in terms of a long company lifespan, but in terms of the resources it used and its effect on the environment. In a manufacturing business heavily dependent on petrochemicals for production, sustainability seemed more like an impossible dream than a guiding purpose.

Nevertheless, guiding the company toward sustainability is what he did. Interface started with the easy stuff—reducing waste in its manufacturing process. Recycled textiles became backing for the carpet the company produced. Interface created a program in which its customers leased carpet and tile, which the company replaced as needed, recycling the worn and damaged pieces back into its manufacturing. Interface's approach to a closed-loop manufacturing process will make the company completely sustainable by 2020 (Todd, 2006).

Ray Anderson's purpose was simple and ambitious. Following his purpose put him at odds with competitors and others. The company's stock took a hit but has since rebounded. And most importantly, Interface is making Anderson's purpose manifest: using nothing from the Earth that isn't renewable and doing no damage to the Earth's ecosystem.

What High Performance Looks Like

Leaders with purpose

- are passionate about seeing the business succeed
- attack work with a sense of urgency
- demonstrate energy, drive, and ambition
- have a strong work ethic
- create a productive atmosphere
- have a personal direction or focus
- keep purpose front and center as they make daily decisions
- can visualize the impact they want to have on their organization or on others
- are seen as driven, determined, focused, disciplined, inspired, and passionate
- are not easily sidetracked
- see how their work ties in with the organization's vision and mission
- overcome obstacles in striving to achieve long-term, positive, sustainable results
- talk about their purpose in terms of its impact on the organization
- rise above immediate concerns to see the bigger picture

What's in Your Way?

If you lack purpose in your work, it will show up in how you lead. Others will notice your obvious lack of direction and commitment. Those absences are likely to trigger unwillingness to contribute to group efforts, and results will suffer. Others will see you as someone who manages rather than leads and inspires. Take a look at the following descriptions and mark any that you believe are getting in the way of your developing purpose to ground your leadership.

- ❑ You don't interact enough with the people you want to inspire.
- ❑ You don't reflect on what the work means and why you do it.
- ❑ Your work doesn't engage you.
- ❑ You live in the moment, without much thought about your long-term impact.
- ❑ The work and the goals that inspire you aren't supported by the organization.
- ❑ Your purpose feels like a distraction from business.
- ❑ You talk about your purpose without taking action.
- ❑ You focus on the future at the expense of the present.
- ❑ You get frustrated and give up.
- ❑ You have inadequate resources to execute your plans.

Coach Yourself

To develop leadership purpose, create goals in areas that put you in a role to provide service to others. Such roles aren't necessarily tuned to your personal benefit (even though they will benefit you). These questions can help you focus on such areas:

- ● What do you have passion for? What brings you joy? How can you use this passion or joy to lead others in the organization?
- ● What types of work give you energy, and what types drain you?

- When was the last time you encountered a setback or frustration in your organization? How did you react? How did the situation turn out?

- What epitaph would you like to see on your tombstone? What do you need to do to justify that?

- What are you looking to give to your community or society?

Improve Now

Make time. Spend a little time each day to think about your purpose. Over the next 30 days, spend some time thinking about how you define the purpose that drives you. What do you care about? How do you want to spend your time and talent?

Know why. Explore thoroughly the reason you want to be a leader. What are the advantages, disadvantages, rewards, and drawbacks? Take your thoughts to at least two people who have been in the role you are considering and ask them about those four aspects. Gather your thoughts and meet with your manager for the same discussion.

Identify your uniqueness. What can you do that no one else can do? A unique set of talents can highlight or inspire a sense of purpose.

Partner up. Look for someone who shares your sense of purpose. You're more likely to stay focused if you surround yourself with people with similar vision or values.

Track your time against your values. Look at how you invest your time and money relative to what you care about.

Explore why you do what you do. Take a personality assessment. It may help you understand how your personal preferences influence your behavior in various situations and how you can capitalize alternative skills and behaviors at work.

Reflect and pull forward. Reflect on those times in your career when your direction was clear and you were brimming with enthusiasm. What was it about both you and your work that made that possible? How might you re-create those conditions in your current circumstances?

Eliminate or minimize distractions. While still honoring your responsibilities, explore how you can declutter your current work and hone in on core responsibilities that align with your purpose. Delegate tasks to your direct reports or share responsibilities with a peer, at least temporarily, as a means of establishing focus.

Find meaning in your current work. Reflect on your last few days at work. What kind of activities were you involved in? What kind of outcomes did you produce? What impact did they have on your customers, your business, your team, and yourself? What does that impact say about what you contribute and your purpose? Keep the answers to these questions in mind during your daily activities.

Developmental Opportunities

- Participate in a volunteer initiative in your organization. Find an issue that means something to you and help to gather support for this cause.

- Take a leadership role in your company's corporate social responsibility initiatives and gain experience communicating important issues to a variety of audiences.

- If you're feeling burned out or stuck in your current position, take on a project or assignment that can rekindle what used to excite you about work. Even a short-term project can reconnect you with your purpose.

- Guide or coach a coworker or direct report toward finding his or her purpose.

Activity Center

Review and download these activities you can use for your development or with your team from this book's resource page at www.ccl.org/compassbook.

Leading with Purpose: A Job for an Authentic Leader
Leading with Purpose: Rules for Leading with Purpose

Related Competencies

Resourcefulness

Risk Taking

Team Leadership

Vision

Working through Others

Resources

Center for Creative Leadership. (n.d.). *Life entrepreneurship: Creating a life of significance and increasing your team's performance* [Webinar]. Author. Retrieved from http://insights.ccl.org/webinars/life-entrepreneurship-creating-a-life-of-significance-and-increasing-your-teams-performance/

Duckworth, A. (2016). *Grit: The power of passion and perseverance.* New York, NY: Scribner.

Dweck, C. S. (2006). *Mindset: The new psychology of success.* New York, NY: Random House.

Hams, B. (2012). *Ownership thinking: How to end entitlement and create a culture of accountability, purpose, and profit.* New York, NY: McGraw-Hill.

King, S. N., Altman, D. G., & Lee, R. J. (2011). *Discovering the leader in you* (Rev. ed.). San Francisco, CA: Jossey-Bass.

King, S. N., & Altman, D. G. (2011). *Discovering the leader in you workbook.* San Francisco, CA: Jossey-Bass.

Koehler, M., & Marquet, L. D. (2015). *Leading with purpose: How to engage, empower, and encourage your people to reach their full potential.* Los Angeles, CA: Over and Above Press.

Pink, D. H. (2009). *Drive: The surprising truth about what motivates us.* New York, NY: Riverhead Books.

Todd, R. (2006, Nov. 1). The sustainable industrialist: Ray Anderson of Interface. *Inc.* Retrieved from http://www.inc.com/magazine/20061101/green50_industrialist.html

34

Negotiating

Reach consensus while maintaining positive, sustainable relationships.

Negotiation is a collection of several skills, including influence, communication, self-awareness, and conflict resolution. Competence in all these areas and in others will help you reach consensus on a specific question, ironing out agreements, and otherwise bringing diverse interests together to support a specific goal. That's what it's all about. Negotiation isn't always about winning but about creating sustainable value for all sides.

As you move higher in an organization, your negotiations take on increasingly higher stakes. When you can get your way without deception, bullying, or manipulation—that's when you become a skilled negotiator. As a skilled negotiator, you know when to stand firm and when to compromise. In an ever-changing and even chaotic business environment, you can fashion common agreement and make the difference between a successful venture and a failed one. Few if any of us might hope to live up to his example, but Nelson Mandela's long negotiation—from inside prison—gives us more than a glimpse of the give-and-take behind negotiating for the highest stakes there are.

Leadership in Action

Nelson Mandela spent 27 years of his life in prison after being convicted of a conspiracy to overthrow the state. The state system he sought to dismantle was, of course, the South African apartheid system, which derived power from discrimination along racial lines and concentrated that power in the hands of a small elite. It deserved to end.

Despite his imprisonment, Mandela continued to negotiate, and amid rising political pressure, then-president F. W. de Klerk released Mandela from prison and instituted an integrated election, which Mandela won. As president, it was within his power to instigate retribution, but instead Mandela chose negotiation and reconciliation. He created the Truth and Reconciliation Commission with the goal of investigating, discussing, and understanding violations of human rights throughout decades of South African history. His goal: to reunite a fractured population, to dial back tension from the brink of a seemingly inevitable civil war (Abramson, 2016).

His approach earned Mandela criticism from all sides, but time has vindicated his decision. He shared the Nobel Peace Prize with de Klerk in 1993. Most importantly, he is still revered and respected by the people he led.

What High Performance Looks Like

Skilled negotiators

- know what they want from the negotiation process—their ultimate goal
- ask open-ended questions to learn what the other side wants or needs
- listen without judgment and confirm their understanding of the other side's position
- treat the other side with respect
- stay calm during the negotiation
- use good timing and common sense in negotiating
- understand what the other side might interpret as too difficult a demand
- are seen as focused, perceptive, flexible, patient, inventive, credible, realistic, and solution-oriented
- are prepared to walk away from negotiation
- pursue the highest possible rewards or outcomes in a negotiation
- ensure that the other side maintains its dignity and is not humiliated by its compromises
- create a relaxed and trusting environment for negotiation

What's in Your Way?

Leaders who struggle with negotiation may lack confidence in themselves or their organization. They may feel stress in high-pressure situations or rely extensively on a few go-to strategies because they don't have a broad range of negotiating approaches and tactics to draw from. They may underprepare and thus not understand or appreciate the goals and the constraints of the other side. They may be afraid of walking away from a bad deal or having overly optimistic expectations. They may lack the patience to work out the details or alternatively burden themselves with details and miss the real opportunity that negotiating can bring. Look at the following descriptions and mark any that you believe are getting in the way of your becoming a better negotiator.

- ❏ You're not interested in what others want but only what you want.
- ❏ You struggle to understand the perspective or intentions of others.
- ❏ You give up too soon.
- ❏ You're inflexible or dogmatic, unwilling to find a different path to your goals.
- ❏ You see too few options and can't imagine different paths toward agreement.
- ❏ You become flustered by conflict or competition.
- ❏ You bring unrealistic expectations to the negotiation.
- ❏ People respond to you as if they think you're out to win at their expense.
- ❏ You ask for too much.
- ❏ You're seen as overly aggressive during negotiations.
- ❏ You misread the needs or motivations of the other party.
- ❏ You try to close a deal too fast.
- ❏ You push a solution without fully understanding the needs of the other side.

☐ You put yourself under time pressure that can lead to the wrong decisions or approaches.

Coach Yourself

To develop your negotiating skill, create goals in the areas of influence, communication, self-awareness, and active listening. These questions can help you focus on such areas:

- Do you understand the goals or motivations of the people with whom you negotiate? What can you do to gain more insight into what's important to them?

- Are you clear about your goals or bottom-line needs when you negotiate? How and when during the negotiation process will you communicate what's important to you?

- Have you prepared to negotiate based on what you've learned about the other side's position? How can you gain more insight and shore up your approach before entering negotiations?

- Are you afraid of direct confrontation? Why? How can you change your response to become a more effective negotiator?

- What have you learned from watching skilled negotiators? What do they do that is effective? How do they manage the relationship or process? What qualities do they bring to the situation?

Improve Now

Expect conflict. Every negotiation involves some conflict. Accept it and anticipate it. Use it as an opportunity to explore the needs and potential solutions for both sides.

Avoid ultimatums. Drawing a line in the sand can cause other people to dig in their feet and halt the negotiation process. Watch out for terms such as "must" or "have to" that indicate a potentially inflexible position. This is especially important if you're working across cultures, which may house different views on how to address negotiating points.

Ask questions. Ask until you are confident you understand the needs of the other side. Don't sacrifice or shortchange what the other side needs in exchange for the specifics of what it's asking for. Needs and demands are different, which opens room for negotiation. There are many ways to meet needs, but fewer choices if you're answering to demands.

Be yourself. Genuine leadership inspires trust and goodwill among negotiating partners. It's easy to see through someone who's trying to be something they aren't, and it's easy to be found out if you are pretending to be something other than what you are. Negotiations have to allow a level of trust to develop if they are to produce benefits.

Take time. Stay committed to what you want, be patient, and allow time to work in your favor. Sometimes taking a break or stepping back from the problem allows perspectives to shift and new possibilities to emerge.

Work together to solve problems. Focus on mutual needs and goals and try to imagine different scenarios in which you and your negotiation partner can address those needs and goals. Keep the focus of the negotiations on what's already been agreed upon and use that as a foundation for addressing areas of difference.

Listen carefully. If you find yourself talking a lot, ask questions instead. Paraphrase what the other side is saying to show them you are listening and to ensure that you understand them. Ask follow-up questions. Listen with a desire to learn.

Understand what is nonnegotiable for you. What can you and should you be able to ask for? What pains are you trying to address? What new capability do you need? What results do you want from this negotiation?

Be flexible. Frame your objectives in a way that allows different paths to get to them. Be ready to solve problems creatively and make adjustments on the fly.

Have a backup plan. What will you do if the negotiations fail? A fall-back position can give you the courage to walk away from the negotiations and pursue other options.

Developmental Opportunities

■ Be a member of a team that negotiates a contract for space, supplies, raw materials, or other goods or services.

■ Represent your organization's management to the union, if it has one.

■ Put together a coalition of peers that lobbies the organization for a new process, system, or technology. Write a business case for why you believe a change is required.

■ Register for a negotiation-skills class.

■ Work on a project that requires coordination across the organization.

Activity Center

Review and download these activities you can use for your development or with your team from this book's resource page at www.ccl.org/compassbook.

Negotiating: Negotiating Tools and Tactics
Negotiating: Prepare

Related Competencies

Communication

Conflict Resolution

Influence

Interpersonal Savvy

Problem Solving

Relationship Management

Resources

Abramson, H. I. (2016). Nelson Mandela as negotiator: What can we learn from him? (2016). 31 *Ohio St. J. on Disp. Resol.* 19 (2016); Touro Law Center Legal Studies Research Paper Series No. 16-22. Retrieved from SSRN: https://ssrn .com/abstract=2808740

Cartwright, T. (2003). *Managing conflict with peers.* Greensboro, NC: Center for Creative Leadership.

Fisher, R., & Ury, W. (1983). *Getting to yes: Negotiating agreement without giving in.* (B. Patton, Ed.). New York, NY: Penguin.

Gentry, W. A., & Leslie, J. B. (2013). *Developing political savvy.* Greensboro, NC: Center for Creative Leadership.

Patterson, K., Grenny, J., McMillan, R., & Switzler, A. (2012). *Crucial conversations: Tools for talking when stakes are high* (2nd ed.). New York, NY: McGraw-Hill.

Scharlatt, H. (2011). *Selling your ideas to your organization.* Greensboro, NC: Center for Creative Leadership.

Scharlatt, H. (2016). *Resolving conflict: Ten steps for turning negatives to positives.* Greensboro, NC: Center for Creative Leadership.

Scharlatt, H., & Smith, R. (2011). *Influence: Gaining commitment, getting results* (2nd ed.). Greensboro, NC: Center for Creative Leadership.

Sharpe, D., & Johnson, E. (2002). *Managing conflict with your boss.* Greensboro, NC: Center for Creative Leadership.

Voss, C., & Raz, T. (2016). *Never split the difference: Negotiating as if your life depended on it.* New York, NY: HarperBusiness.

35

Organizational Savvy

Navigate organizational ambiguity, politics, dilemmas, and trade-offs.

Leading does not follow a straight or predictable path, especially in complex organizations. Moving yourself and others toward a goal requires anticipating, understanding, and addressing a variety of obstacles and trade-offs. Recognize and accept the realities of organizations to more skillfully deal with the tensions between your interests, your team's interests, and the interests of others, over the short term and long term.

Businesses compete in an increasingly uncertain and complex global environment. Surviving, let alone thriving, as a leader in this environment requires you to clearly understand and quickly adapt to the many dilemmas you face. Step into the executive suite at General Motors to get a close-up view of a savvy organizational leader.

Leadership in Action

Before she was named CEO of General Motors in 2013, Mary Barra worked as an engineer, a plant manager, the head of corporate human resources, and, since 2011, the senior executive overseeing GM's global product development. With over 33 years of experience at a variety of levels within the company, she brought an incredible level of organizational awareness and knowledge to her new position.

Her experience and comprehensive understanding of the business machinery within GM allowed her to make fundamental, efficiency-minded changes to leadership. She was able to rearrange management to eliminate redundant layers and smooth the communication between design, engineering, marketing, and production. According to a *New York Times* report regarding her appointment as CEO, "She is known inside GM as a consensus builder who calls her staff together on a moment's notice to brainstorm on pressing issues" (Vlasic, 2013).

Seeking to spread her inside-out knowledge of GM's products and processes, Barra has spearheaded an initiative that assigns engineers to work directly in car dealerships. The idea: help designers of new products get a real-world idea of what car buyers want and need. The results produced by these kinds of initiatives can be subtle, but they add up to a more effective and useful product.

With her company emerging from the 2009 government bailout that saved it from bankruptcy and the last of the government shares sold, Barra has an opportunity to leverage her unique perspective and experience to bring out new ideas and initiatives.

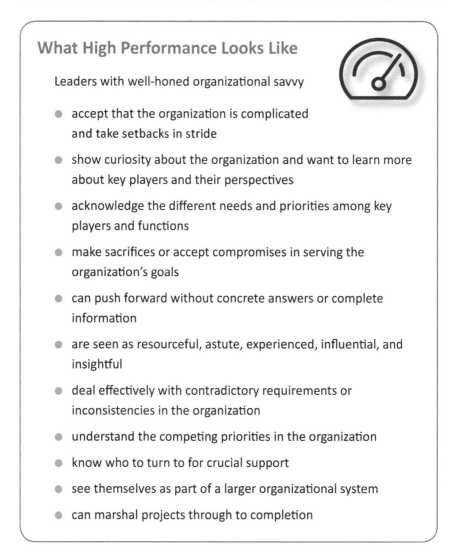

What High Performance Looks Like

Leaders with well-honed organizational savvy

- accept that the organization is complicated and take setbacks in stride
- show curiosity about the organization and want to learn more about key players and their perspectives
- acknowledge the different needs and priorities among key players and functions
- make sacrifices or accept compromises in serving the organization's goals
- can push forward without concrete answers or complete information
- are seen as resourceful, astute, experienced, influential, and insightful
- deal effectively with contradictory requirements or inconsistencies in the organization
- understand the competing priorities in the organization
- know who to turn to for crucial support
- see themselves as part of a larger organizational system
- can marshal projects through to completion

What's in Your Way?

Struggling to navigate complex organizational environments makes it very difficult to get things done, especially when competing for resources when time is of the essence. A leader more in tune to the workings and culture of the organization might well outmaneuver your play for resources. As you move higher in the organization, the ability to deal with the informal organization is as important as following the formal policies, practices, and rules. Take a look at the following descriptions and mark any that you believe are hindering your development of organizational savvy.

- ❏ You're new to the organization.
- ❏ You tend to focus on your own interests.
- ❏ You're impatient.
- ❏ You have yet to establish relationships with key people from other functions.
- ❏ You lack experience in complex organizations.
- ❏ You tend to oversimplify difficult circumstances.
- ❏ You've been told that you're seen as a people-pleaser.
- ❏ You've been told that you're seen as slick or manipulative.
- ❏ You don't pay close attention to the more mundane aspects of your job.

Coach Yourself

To develop your organizational savvy, create goals in areas outside your specific expertise or in areas that require you to sell new ideas to your organization. These questions can help you focus on such areas:

- Whom do you need to influence to achieve the results you need?
- Who are the key players who can help you achieve your goals in the organization?
- Whom in your organization do you respect for their ability to influence and get things done? What special skills or knowledge do they demonstrate? What are their approaches?
- When was the last time you encountered a setback or frustration in your organization? How did you react? How did the situation turn out?
- Who in this organization frustrates you the most and why? What are their goals? How can you get to know these people better?

Improve Now

Ask questions and listen. Don't make assumptions about others' ideas, opinions, or concerns. Allow them to reveal themselves to you before making judgments.

Lend a hand. Go beyond your job description to help others excel and grow. As the mantra goes, you reap what you sow, and leaders who others see as caring and responsive will enjoy closer work relationships and improved performance.

Study success. Look at a major organizational initiative that appears to have been successful. Who were the champions? What obstacles did they address? What was the secret to their success?

Spend time observing. Take a day to just ask questions and to listen to stakeholders and leaders throughout the organization. Note their positions on strategic issues, resource alignment, and other organizational aspects.

Plan ahead. Think about and plan how you can make a positive impression on others but still remain genuine. Tailor your interactions with others based on your analysis of their motives. Adapt your style to meet others' needs.

Political savvy. How do you approach people who are obviously "political"? What behaviors annoy you? What's missing in their behaviors? How can you ensure you do not come across the same way?

Know the key players. Get to know them. Find out what they care about and who they trust.

Plan your message. Design your communication to be simple and compelling to different stakeholders. The key to effective messages is for you to know what you want to say before you say it and make changes and practice it over time. Request feedback on your message.

Work on your timing. Not everything needs to happen all at once, and demanding action from others or rushing headlong into a new initiative might be detrimental over the long run. Think carefully about when to take action, what goals are the priority, what else is happening in the organization, how priorities may have changed, and how you can best schedule your progress toward goals.

Be flexible. In organizations that operate in volatile environments, your plans might have to change at a moment's notice. Expect the unexpected and be ready to pivot toward a different approach.

Do your research. Study one of your organization's successful initiatives. What hurdles did people encounter, and how did they get past them?

Walk in bigger shoes. Interview people above your level and ask them about their pressures and challenges. What's most important to them, and what's keeping them up at night?

Keep a journal. Collect your thoughts about how you are attempting to influence the organization and what appears to be working or not working. Take notes about key stakeholders and what they appear to want.

Developmental Opportunities

- Take a temporary assignment in another part of the business to understand how it sets its priorities and how it operates.

- Attend an executive-level meeting and observe the interactions. Discuss anything that confuses you with a trusted senior manager.

- Select five or six key people in your area and determine what motivates them. Identify the organizational incentives and agendas that drive their behavior.

- Meet regularly with your mentor or coach for advice on solving complex problems.

- Serve on the board of a community nonprofit organization.

- Take a temporary assignment in your organization's strategy group.

Activity Center

Review and download these activities you can use for your development or with your team from this book's resource page at www.ccl.org/compassbook.

Organizational Savvy: How Savvy Are You?

Organizational Savvy: Map Your Network

Organizational Savvy: Mastering Politics

Related Competencies

Boundary Spanning

Influence

Interpersonal Savvy

Relationship Management

Resourcefulness

Systems Thinking

Vision

Resources

Brandon, R., & Seldman, M. (2004). *Survival of the savvy: High-integrity political tactics for career and company success.* New York, NY: Free Press.

Cartwright, T., & Baldwin, D. (2011). *Communicating your vision.* Greensboro, NC: Center for Creative Leadership.

Center for Creative Leadership. (2013). *Interpersonal savvy: Building and maintaining solid working relationships.* Greensboro, NC: Center for Creative Leadership.

Criswell, C., & Cartwright, T. (2011). *Creating a vision.* Greensboro, NC: Center for Creative Leadership.

Gentry, W. A., & Leslie, J. B. (2013). *Developing political savvy.* Greensboro, NC: Center for Creative Leadership.

Scharlatt, H. (2008). *Selling your ideas to your organization.* Greensboro, NC: Center for Creative Leadership.

Van Velsor, E. (2013). *Broadening your organizational perspective.* Greensboro, NC: Center for Creative Leadership.

Vlasic, B. (2013, Dec. 10). New G.M. chief is company woman, born to it. *The New York Times.*

Zack, D. (2010). *Networking for people who hate networking: A field guide for introverts, the overwhelmed, and the underconnected.* San Francisco, CA: Berrett-Koehler.

36
Problem Solving

Bring fresh solutions to difficult problems.

Leaders, their teams, and even their organizations all too often hit a roadblock when their usual problem-solving methods fail. These situations call for leaders to offer creative solutions that get the wheels turning again.

Organizations see innovative problem solving as essential to continued growth and to maintaining a competitive edge. When you demonstrate a knack for innovating solutions when all else fails, you will find yourself called on to play a role in solving some of the organization's most important and perplexing problems. Your ability to generate and apply novel solutions inspires others and can move organizations in new directions. See how far it moved our perceptions of education by looking in on the Khan Academy.

Leadership in Action

Millions of people around the world know the Khan Academy through direct experience or through stories about it and its creator, Salman Khan. Khan Academy originated as a solution to a problem—Khan was tutoring his cousins remotely, and he needed a way to give lessons that weren't dependent on everyone being in the same place at the same time. So he made videos of his lessons.

When his cousins told him they preferred his videos to seeing him in person, Khan realized the power of his solution. He decided to make his videos public on YouTube, and he soon received comments from people who stumbled across them and learned from them (Temple, 2009). Now, millions of people use the site every month to learn about math, science, history, and other school subjects. Teachers are using the videos to move lectures from class to home. Homework becomes classwork, classwork becomes homework, and teachers guide and coach their students as they practice the lessons learned from the videos. Khan's innovative solution to his tutoring dilemma was simple and immediately intuitive—and it has flipped the idea of how to use a classroom.

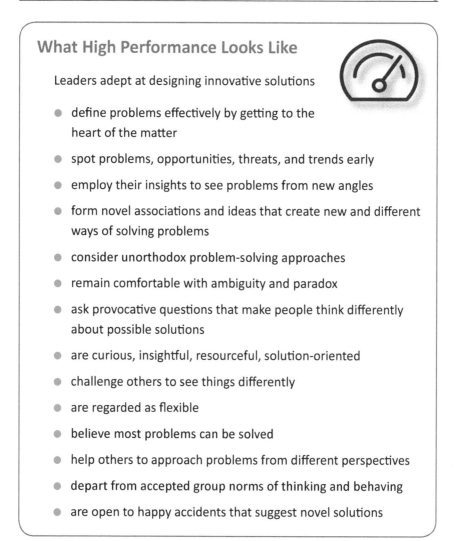

What High Performance Looks Like

Leaders adept at designing innovative solutions

- define problems effectively by getting to the heart of the matter

- spot problems, opportunities, threats, and trends early

- employ their insights to see problems from new angles

- form novel associations and ideas that create new and different ways of solving problems

- consider unorthodox problem-solving approaches

- remain comfortable with ambiguity and paradox

- ask provocative questions that make people think differently about possible solutions

- are curious, insightful, resourceful, solution-oriented

- challenge others to see things differently

- are regarded as flexible

- believe most problems can be solved

- help others to approach problems from different perspectives

- depart from accepted group norms of thinking and behaving

- are open to happy accidents that suggest novel solutions

What's in Your Way?

When you fail to develop innovative problem-solving skills, you waste the time, money, and talent of your team or organization because critical challenges go unresolved. Your inaction or unskilled approach can make problems worse, damaging your career as a leader. When the same problems arise repeatedly, other people may see you as weak or ineffective, your boss can lose faith in you, and you risk losing the respect

305

of your coworkers. As the problem defies solution, your organization becomes less competitive. Review the following list and note the items that you believe interfere with developing your problem-solving skills.

- ❏ You tend to see problems or issues from a narrow perspective, making them difficult to define.
- ❏ You see yourself as the expert.
- ❏ You are too quick to judge ideas.
- ❏ You don't think beyond your function or role.
- ❏ You are removed from the people affected by problems.
- ❏ You give up too easily.
- ❏ You focus on creativity at the expense of practicality.
- ❏ You fail to critique your ideas or solutions, becoming too enamored with their creativity or uniqueness.
- ❏ Your potential solutions are mostly unrealistic or impractical.
- ❏ You break existing processes that work just fine.
- ❏ You lose touch with the traditions of your organization, always looking for a better way to do things.

Coach Yourself

To develop your problem-solving skills, create goals in areas that bring unexpected challenges, in new product development, and in other unfamiliar terrain. These questions can help you focus on such areas:

- What are the most challenging business problems for you? How can you attack these problems with a fresh perspective or new approach?
- To what extent do you focus on problems as opposed to solutions? Are you a solutions-oriented person?
- Are there unspoken organizational rules that get in your way when trying to address problems? If so, what are they?

- What are your strategies for inventing solutions radically different from those tried before?

- How can you take your mind off the pressing problem before you so that you can come back to it with a fresh perspective?

- What function in your organization has the deepest knowledge of what your customers want or need in the future?

- Who on your team is often the best at solving problems? How can you tap the ideas and talent of this person and share them more broadly?

Improve Now

See your actions from the other side of things. Take a moment to consider how others might perceive your actions and decisions. That knowledge will help you make choices that draw from common sense rather than from isolated sparks of inspiration that may not solve the problem in a way that others can accept and build from.

Adopt new lenses. Training and experience often teach us to analyze problems in a prescribed manner, sometimes to our detriment. Look at each issue from multiple perspectives to gain a more complete insight into all of its elements and possible solutions.

Ask provocative questions. Predictable questions result in predictable solutions. Ask something unexpected. This may be as simple as What's missing? or What are the patterns? Try odd what-if scenarios, or challenge long-held beliefs. Innovation often emerges from questions that no one has previously asked.

Apply S-C-A-M-P-E-R to the problem, challenge, or opportunity. In the next meeting devoted to solving the problem, try using these prompts to stretch your and your team's thinking (Mindwerx, 2017).

- *Substitute.* Are there any components of our current solution that can be substituted or replaced with something else?
- *Combine.* Can we combine our current solution with other ideas to create a new solution?

- *Adapt.* Are there ideas from other industries that we can borrow and apply to our current solution?
- *Maximize or minimize.* What components of our current solution can we enlarge or reduce? Can we enlarge or reduce the scope of the problem?
- *Put to other uses.* Are there problems different from the current one to which we can put our current solution?
- *Eliminate.* Are there components or features of the current solution that we can eliminate?
- *Rearrange or reverse.* What happens when we rearrange the process associated with the current solution?

View obstacles as opportunities. Under the right leadership, difficult times can inspire innovative ideas and organizational growth. When confronted with a problem, approach it as a chance to improve how your team or your organization solves similar challenges. Convey this sense of opportunity to others in your organization.

Find passion for change. Energy and optimism fuel innovation, and that passion can transform new ideas into positive results. Energize your employees to develop new ways of getting things done and to demonstrate the courage to defy the status quo.

Leverage differences. Diversity in background and experience among team members can boost innovation. Lead an effort to channel diverse viewpoints toward positive outcomes rather than allowing them to divide your team.

Bring people together. Physical proximity promotes collaboration, trust, and communication. Create opportunities for your employees to interact in order to develop bonds that improve group performance.

Design an innovation system. Be as systematic with innovation as you are in other areas of management. Whether formally or informally, create a process designed to inspire new thinking, encourage free sharing of ideas, and facilitate collaboration.

Developmental Opportunities

- Take an assignment to work on an ill-defined or recurring organizational problem that requires input from others across the organization to solve.

- Serve on a team assigned to make decisions that groups have avoided addressing.

- Go on an adventure (for example, travel somewhere you haven't been, go to events you never attend, seek out people you don't normally meet).

- Work on a new-product development team.

- Work on a task force tackling a thorny business challenge.

- Spend time with customers to find out what they think their needs will be in the future, and use those answers to pose potential problems your organization might face.

- Ask your management team to give you one new problem a year to solve.

- Ask your boss to assign a problem to you that has defied easy solutions.

Activity Center

Review and download these activities you can use for your development or with your team from this book's resource page at www.ccl.org/compassbook.

Problem Solving: 25-Minute Problem-Solving Team
Problem Solving: Become a Brainstormer
Problem Solving: Learn About Problem Solving

Related Competencies

Difference, Diversity, Inclusion

Innovation

Organizational Savvy

Resourcefulness

Risk Taking

Urgency

Vision

Resources

Cartwright, T. (2004). *Developing your intuition: A guide to reflective practice*. Greensboro, NC: Center for Creative Leadership.

Ernst, C., & Chrobot-Mason, D. (2010). *Boundary spanning leadership: Six practices for solving problems, driving innovation, and transforming organizations*. New York, NY: McGraw-Hill.

Ernst, C., & Martin, A. (2006). *Critical reflections: How groups can learn from success and failure*. Greensboro, NC: Center for Creative Leadership.

Gryskiewicz, S. S., & Taylor, S. (2003). *Making creativity practical: Innovation that gets results*. Greensboro, NC: Center for Creative Leadership.

Kallet, M. (2014). *Think smarter: Critical thinking to improve problem-solving and decision-making skills*. Hoboken, NJ: Wiley.

Mindwerx. (2017). History S.C.A.M.P.E.R. [Blog post]. Author. Retrieved from https://mindwerx.com/history-s-c-m-p-e-r/

Palus, C. J., & Horth, D. M. (2002). *The leader's edge: Six creative competencies for navigating complex challenges*. San Francisco, CA: Jossey-Bass.

Palus, C. J., & Horth, D. M. (2010). *Visual explorer facilitator's guide*. Greensboro, NC: Center for Creative Leadership.

Temple, J. (2009, Dec. 14). Salman Khan, math master of the internet. *San Francisco Chronicle*. Retrieved from http://www.sfgate.com/business/article/Salman-Khan-math-master-of-the-Internet-3278578.php

Tracy, B. (2015). *Creativity and problem solving*. New York, NY: American Management Association.

37

Relationship Management

Create and nourish healthy, strong relationships among employees, peers, and customers.

At its most fundamental level, an organization is a collection of relationships. Because of that, leaders should build close bonds with and among the people associated with their organizations. Your skill at building and maintaining relationships leads to a strong network of allies in and outside your organization. Become a strong partner who contributes to alignment and support in large-scale projects and among teams and individuals. Successful leaders make relationships a priority, because they know that building relationships is how organizations sustain themselves and achieve their goals—through influence, inspiration, and coordinated activity. Check out the story of Market Basket to see the power of relationships in action.

Leadership in Action

When in June 2014 the board of Market Basket, a budget grocery chain in New England, decided to fire the CEO, Arthur T. Demoulas, the board probably did not expect that 5,000 of the company's employees would show up at its headquarters to protest. They weren't unionized workers— but they were unified. As Simone Pathe reported for the PBS *Newshour* in 2014, employees and customers stood together against the board's actions because of one overwhelming fact: they felt a personal relationship to Demoulas. How did he create such loyalty?

For one, employees believed Demoulas cared about them. Workers tell stories of hospital visits, attendance at funerals, and other human connections. Beyond that, Demoulas gave workers a stake in Market Basket's success: profit-sharing, wages above the minimum set by the Commonwealth of Massachusetts, and even scholarship programs. A CEO of a company as large as Market Basket can't have a personal relationship with every employee, but Demoulas showed how to forge personal connections with real action.

No leader is perfect. Demoulas may not be completely innocent in his benevolence. The family-owned business included family and board members seeking better profits—which meant cutting people, raising prices, and reducing benefits. Demoulas's adversaries dismissed his employee relationships as a defensive tactic against his ouster. Every story can be told differently. Nevertheless, Demoulas built relationships with action and empathy. As a leader, he understood that without employees committed to the enterprise, no organization can long sustain itself.

What High Performance Looks Like

Leaders adept at building and maintaining relationships

- reach out to people and engage them in a common cause
- listen and are willing to be influenced
- quickly gain trust and respect from customers
- reconcile conflicts to support smooth, effective working relationships
- achieve results without creating unnecessary adversaries
- display emotional intelligence
- are good listeners
- care about people
- are seen as open and nonjudgmental
- put people at ease
- display warmth and a good sense of humor
- try to understand what other people think before judging their positions
- seek common ground in an effort to build relationships
- seek first to understand others before being understood by them
- help or advocate for other people

What's in Your Way?

Leaders who struggle to build and maintain relationships can become isolated, excluded from the most important work as colleagues and partners lose interest in working with them. They are less likely to be trusted, which prevents the honest collaboration needed to succeed in contemporary organizations. Take a look at the following descriptions and mark any that you believe are blocking you from improving how you manage your work relationships.

❏ You try interpersonal tactics that work well for other people but not for you because your social skills are underdeveloped.

❏ You are new to the organization.

❏ You're not interested in what others want—only what you are after.

❏ You focus more on tasks than people.

❏ You don't trust other people.

❏ You have been hurt or let down by people in the past.

❏ You don't balance your interest in what other people need with what the organization needs.

❏ People have told you that you have an agenda or hidden motive.

❏ People with whom you try to build connections don't reciprocate.

❏ You expect too much of other people.

❏ You try hard to relate to others, but you've received feedback that it comes off as desperate.

Coach Yourself

To develop your ability to build and maintain relationships, create goals that put you into contact with a variety of people and that depend on collaboration and support. These questions can help you define such areas of focus:

- How do other people perceive you? What feedback have others given you about your behavior and the impact it has had on them? How can you use that feedback to better your working relationships?

- Are your colleagues truly important to you? Do you care what they think or how they feel?

- Do you regard other people as instruments for pursuing your agenda? Do you care about their needs and the needs of the organization?

- Whom do you know at work who could benefit most from your support or guidance?

- How would you assess the quality of your current relationships with your coworkers? What words come to mind to describe these relationships? How do you feel about that?

Improve Now

Smile. It's a small gesture, but smiling makes you more approachable to others, makes you seem more trustworthy, and can even boost your productivity by strengthening your resolve and commitment. All of these results can be used to build strong working relationships.

Listen for ideas. You're surrounded by people with different perspectives and beliefs than your own. Listen to them. If you listen long enough, you will learn something you can use to strengthen your relationship with them.

Mind your nonverbal communication. People don't only listen to the words you say but react to your presence. They will note your posture, the way you breathe, your facial expressions, even your hand gestures. What does your nonverbal communication say about your intent?

Focus on Yes. If your default response to requests is No, see how responding Yes can improve your relationships with colleagues, direct reports, bosses, and peers. Express criticism in helpful, supportive terms. Focus on being constructive.

Enjoy work. Try to focus on what you love about what you do—that joy can affect how you treat other people and how they respond to you.

Royal matchmaker. Become the King or Queen of introductions. Introduce customers to employees, suppliers to customers. In-person introductions are best, but if the people you're introducing to one another are at different sites or in different countries, a virtual introduction by email takes very little time and gives you a chance to say something worthy about each person.

Ask others for their opinions, perspectives, and ideas. Ask questions and show that you are listening. Demonstrate that you care about what they think about the organization, projects, and teammates.

Your treat. Take your team out for lunch or for some other reason and use the time to get to know each team member a little better.

Allow others to influence you. Be open to their perspectives. Where you see potential alignment, pursue it with them, to your mutual benefit.

Help others. Remember the golden rule—people will treat you as you treat them. And you ought to keep the platinum rule in mind as well: "Treat others as they want to be treated."

Spend time with others. Build trust by letting people get to know you better. Be kind and generous. Communicate clearly and openly. Above all, be sincere in your dealings with others.

Don't burn bridges. You may know the adage, "the people you meet on the way up are the people you will meet on the way down." Remember that you are likely to run into the same people over your career. Treat them as an asset to be treasured and become an asset yourself.

Maintain your relationship network. Your relationships need regular attention. Keep your network vibrant by recognizing and acting on the challenges of staying connected. Bolster your relationships by getting below the surface. Look for someone who can teach you how to become better at what you do and find out what you can teach them.

Developmental Opportunities

- Take on your unit's most dissatisfied customer or its most difficult supplier.

- Manage by walking around. Meet, greet, and get to know your staff.

- Work to retain a valued employee who is thinking about leaving the organization.

- Guide or coach a coworker or direct report.

- Handle conflict with another person or group.

- Volunteer in a setting where you can practice giving and gratitude, such as a meals-on-wheels program, a food bank, or a refugee relocation center.

Activity Center

Review and download these activities you can use for your development or with your team from this book's resource page at www.ccl.org/compassbook.

Relationship Management: Check Yourself
Relationship Management: Partner with Me

Related Competencies

Communication
Conflict Resolution
Interpersonal Savvy
Influence
Team Leadership

Resources

Center for Creative Leadership. (2013). *Interpersonal savvy: Building and maintaining solid working relationships.* Greensboro, NC: Author.

Gentry, W. A., & Leslie, J. B. *Developing political savvy.* (2012). Greensboro, NC: Center for Creative Leadership.

Goleman, D. (1998). *Working with emotional intelligence.* New York, NY: Bantam Books.

Goleman, D. (2011). *Leadership: The power of emotional intelligence.* Northampton, MA: More Than Sound.

Grayson, C., & Baldwin, D. (2007). *Leadership networking: Connect, collaborate, create.* (Webinar). Greensboro, NC: Center for Creative Leadership.

Klann, G. (2004). *Building your team's morale, pride, and spirit.* Greensboro, NC: Center for Creative Leadership.

Kram, K. E., & Ting, S. (2006). Coaching for emotional competence. In S. Ting & P. Scisco (Eds.), *The CCL handbook of coaching: A guide for the leader coach* (pp. 179–202). San Francisco, CA: Jossey-Bass.

Maxwell, J. C. (2004). *Relationships 101: What every leader needs to know.* Nashville, TN: Thomas Nelson Publishers.

Pathe, S. (2014, Aug. 13). With jobs on the line, why are Market Basket employees so loyal to Artie T? (Television series episode.) *PBS Newshour.* Retrieved from http://www.pbs.org/newshour/making-sense/with-jobs-on -the-line-why-are-market-basket-employees-so-loyal-to-artie-t/

Sobel, A., & Panas, J. (2012). *Power questions: Build relationships, win new business, and influence others.* Hoboken, NJ: Wiley.

Zack, D. (2010). *Networking for people who hate networking: A field guide for introverts, the overwhelmed, and the underconnected.* San Francisco, CA: Berrett-Koehler.

38
Resilience

Cope positively with stress, uncertainty, and setbacks.

We often think of resilient people as unflappable, strong, or unaffected. But resilience isn't just a matter of "toughing it out." Bearing up under pressure and in stressful situations is certainly part of being resilient, but it's just one part. Marathon runners, for example, have to be tough to endure a grueling 26-mile run, and yet it's often their ability to handle the intangibles (weather, unknown competition, attitude about ability, a nagging injury at the 20-mile marker) that puts them across the finish line.

Resilience provides the ability to recover quickly from change, hardship, or misfortune. It's the product of a broad perspective. You can bolster it with a supportive network of professional and personal relationships and use it to become comfortable with change. Resilience taps into your ability to adapt even as it relies on your own knowledge about yourself—your values, confidence, and optimism. Make it a key element of your leadership success at all levels—from your pursuit of personal goals and well-being to your capability to lead others through times of transition, stress, and uncertainty.

Leadership in Action

In 2010, game developer Jane McGonigal suffered a concussion that almost completely disabled her for two years. She had to avoid all triggers that led to the intense headaches that resulted from the concussion: reading, writing, games, alcohol, and caffeine. She jokingly calls it "everything worth living for."

McGonigal isn't your run-of-the-mill video game designer. She is an industry thought leader and a fervent believer in the power of games to make lives better. And so her strategy to overcome her injury drew from her years of experience as a game designer: "I said, 'I am either going to kill myself or I'm going to turn this into a game.'" She called it "Jane the Concussion Slayer."

The game was simple. Adopt a secret identity, recruit allies, battle enemies, gain power-ups. In her case, McGonigal recruited her sister and her husband (allies), and together they battled the triggers (enemies) that slowed her recovery and sought small actions, like taking short walks, that counted as power-ups. Almost immediately, her despair and feelings of helplessness began to lift. And although her full recovery took another year, her game's challenges and rewards kept her from giving up.

In her resilience, McGonigal tapped into her passion for game design, her belief in its positive effects, and her own experience. When resilient leaders get knocked down, these are the kinds of sources they draw from to answer the question: How will you get back up?

What High Performance Looks Like

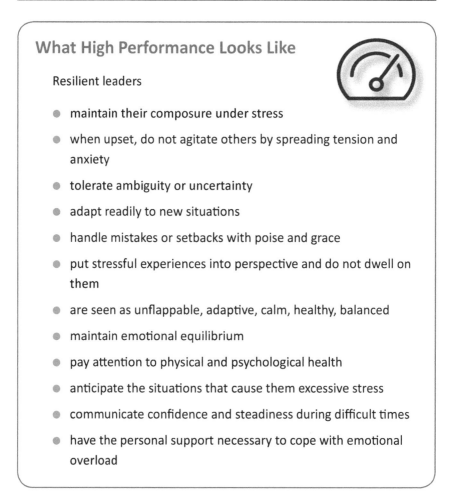

Resilient leaders

- maintain their composure under stress
- when upset, do not agitate others by spreading tension and anxiety
- tolerate ambiguity or uncertainty
- adapt readily to new situations
- handle mistakes or setbacks with poise and grace
- put stressful experiences into perspective and do not dwell on them
- are seen as unflappable, adaptive, calm, healthy, balanced
- maintain emotional equilibrium
- pay attention to physical and psychological health
- anticipate the situations that cause them excessive stress
- communicate confidence and steadiness during difficult times
- have the personal support necessary to cope with emotional overload

What's in Your Way?

Without resilience, your health, productivity, and relationships can suffer. You may also be slower to recover after a setback, which can prove especially difficult in volatile environments. Take a look at the following descriptions and mark any that you believe block you from developing resilience.

- ❏ You have a difficult time saying no to requests.
- ❏ You struggle to prioritize.

- ❏ After a difficult conversation or conflict you ruminate about it, which keeps you in a stressed state.

- ❏ You're unaware of just how overcommitted you've become.

- ❏ You work in a highly competitive culture and sacrifice periodic reflection for constant action.

- ❏ You have little control over your work or what assignments you take on.

- ❏ You sacrifice empathy for toughness.

- ❏ Your optimism is perceived as unrealistic.

- ❏ Your self-reliance keeps you from trusting others.

- ❏ In stressful situations, you rely on your strengths and don't lean on less-used skills.

Coach Yourself

To develop your resilience, create goals that challenge you and move you past your comfort zone. These questions can help you define that area of focus:

- ● What stresses you at work?

- ● What healthy strategies have you developed for coping with stress?

- ● What unhealthy strategies do you use for coping with stress?

- ● How does your stress affect other people?

- ● What programs or support does your organization provide to help people cope with stress?

- ● Think of people you know who stay calm and collected during stressful situations. What are their strategies?

- ● Did you exercise today? How much time do you spend taking care of yourself?

- ● How do you get away during the work day to gain a new perspective when you experience stress or become stuck on a problem?

Improve Now

Recognize the signals of stress. Pay attention to your body's response to stress. What triggers a feeling of stress, and what are your physiological responses? Do you feel your heart rate going up? Do you get hot? Do you clench your jaw? The sooner you recognize that your body is going into stress, the sooner you can do something to manage it.

Regroup. When a task becomes stressful, look for ways to organize and streamline your work. Effective strategies include defining roles and clarifying expectations, managing a project schedule, and completing tasks ahead of deadline. Gaining focus may reduce stress before or during a task.

Develop self-care rituals. These can be as simple as taking a walk around the office, getting some fresh air, or practicing some stretches at your desk. These short breaks won't significantly eat into your work time and in fact can boost your productivity.

Put setbacks in perspective. Don't run away from mistakes and failures, but don't dwell on them either. Strive to get beyond the pain and disappointment and refocus on what you can learn from the experience and apply to future stressful circumstances.

Take time to recover. Make your health, happiness, and well-being a priority. You are at your best when you are energized, positive, and engaged, and maintaining these attributes requires your attention.

Best-laid plans. With the help of your manager or coach, create your personal resilience development plan. With that experience under your belt, help your team develop a "team" resilience development plan.

Recharge. Build time into your schedule to recharge your energy. Let go of unimportant, nonurgent work or delegate those tasks to others. In place of that work, do something that inspires and rejuvenates you. You may believe that your stamina is boundless, but it is not.

Get away from work. As passionate as you are about your job, making time for other activities actually improves your long-term performance. Manage the boundaries between your work life and personal life to find fulfillment in both domains by separating or integrating those parts of your life, according to your preferences.

Redefine work-life balance. The balance among all the aspects of your life is complicated. Demands and interests change over time, and

323

what feels like balance at one point quickly becomes outdated. If your life revolves around who you are and what you value, you will feel balanced— even when you have to temporarily prioritize one part of your life over other parts.

Develop a support system. Seek and build a diverse group of peers, supervisors, and personal contacts on whom you can rely in difficult times. Social support is essential to avoiding the burnout associated with stress and sustaining your optimal level of performance.

Become a continuous learner. Learn new skills, gain new under-standing, and apply those lessons during times of stress and change. Many managers resist learning new approaches to their work and hold onto old behaviors and skills even when those actions don't work anymore.

Volunteer in a hospital or school. See firsthand how doctors, nurses, and teachers constantly address stressful situations and interruptions and note what they do to cope.

Developmental Opportunities

- Serve on a team dealing with a business downturn, a merger, or an environmental crisis.

- Represent your organization to the media.

- Work on a political campaign.

- Train a course on stress management.

- Manage an unexpected opportunity with high potential payoff for the business (a new customer, for example, or a new partner).

- Take on a project with a short deadline from your boss's boss.

- Serve on a high-visibility task force.

Activity Center

Review and download these activities you can use for your development or with your team from this book's resource page at www.ccl.org/compassbook.

Resilience: An Assessment
Resilience: Mistakes Are a Gift
Resilience: Three Actions to Resilience

Related Competencies

Conflict Resolution
Flexibility
Learning Agility
Self-Awareness
Tolerating Ambiguity

Resources

Clerkin, C., & Ronayne. P. (Webinar). *Resilience isn't futile: How brain-science can help us thrive in increasingly complex work environments*. Center for Creative Leadership. Retrieved from http://insights.ccl.org/webinars/resilience-isnt-futile-how-brain-science-can-help-us-thrive-in-increasingly-complex-work-environments

Greitens, E. (2016). *Resilience: Hard-won wisdom for living a better life.* Boston, MA: Houghton Mifflin Harcourt.

Kossek, E. E., Ruderman, M. N., Braddy, P. W., & Hannum, K. M. (2011). *WorkLife indicator: Increasing your effectiveness on and off the job.* (Feedback report and development planning guide). Greensboro, NC: Center for Creative Leadership.

McGonigal, J. (2012). *The game that can give you 10 extra years of life.* (Video). Retrieved from http://www.ted.com/talks/jane_mcgonigal_the_game_that_can_give_you_10_extra_years_of_life

Pulley, M. L., & Wakefield, M. (2001). *Building resiliency: How to thrive in times of change.* Greensboro, NC: Center for Creative Leadership.

Roger, D., & Petrie, N. (2016). *Work without stress: Building a resilient mindset for lasting success.* New York, NY: McGraw-Hill.

Ruderman, M. N., Braddy, P. W., Hannum, K. M., & Kossek, E. E. (2013). *Managing your whole life*. Greensboro, NC: Center for Creative Leadership.

Zolli, A., & Healy, A. M. (2012). *Resilience: Why things bounce back*. New York, NY: Free Press.

39
Resourcefulness

Accomplish what you can, when you can, with what you have—no matter what.

You know the type. The "get it done" leader. You can develop the same dexterity and intent to complete tasks and projects when resources are few and obstacles are many. Resourceful leaders aren't discouraged in these circumstances. They don't give up when they are frustrated that their first few attempts didn't pan out. Every unsuccessful approach they take becomes an opportunity for resilience and an invitation to try different approaches until one works. Develop a reputation as someone who knows how to get results, even on challenging projects—someone willing to do whatever it takes. Be one of those leaders. For inspiration, take a look into a devastating natural event and the resourcefulness that rose in response.

Leadership in Action

The famine that struck Malawi in 2001 was devastating. By early 2002, the BBC reported that nearly 70 percent of the population was on the verge of starvation. During that calamity, William Kamkwamba had his idea.

Kamkwamba's family lived among many families who tended fields of maize for food and profit. At the height of the famine, his family had only a single meal a day: a few mouthfuls of meal paste. It became impossible for his family to continue his education. But Kamkwamba had already had a taste of learning and was determined to keep at it. He visited a small local library and brought back science books, focusing on physics. Despite his lack of facility with the English language, he was able to decipher the diagrams in these books to learn about the machine he decided to build: a windmill.

In the story he tells, Kamkwamba had no money and no hardware store. But there was a local scrapyard. Picking through the junk, he found a fan, PVC pipes, and bicycle parts (including a frame and an old headlight generator). With these, he constructed a windmill that provided electricity to his home and allowed neighbors to charge batteries for mobile phones and other devices. The second windmill, with a larger fan, pumped water. Bit by bit, his inventions improved, eventually saving his family from the famine (2009).

Though he had nearly nothing at his disposal, Kamkwamba was able to put together enough information and knowledge to change his family's fate. Instead of wishing for material, money, or information he couldn't access, he used everything available to him, along with his own ingenuity, to build something great.

What High Performance Looks Like

Resourceful leaders

- attack goals or problems with vigor and zeal
- act with a sense of urgency
- know the organizational system
- find the resources needed to get the job done
- cultivate access to key organizational resources
- are seen as savvy, inventive, pragmatic, adaptive, persistent, and determined
- thrive in the absence of rules or established methods
- relish the challenge obstacles pose
- anticipate problems or challenges and respond proactively
- learn in real time about what works and what does not
- make practical sacrifices to overcome hurdles

What's in Your Way?

Leaders without a proven resourcefulness may not be promoted to projects or job roles that carry greater complexity or ambiguity than their current roles. Senior leaders in the organization may see them as less creative or innovative than their peers. Take a look at the following descriptions and mark any that you believe give you trouble as you develop a resourceful attitude.

- ❑ You haven't cultivated resources or relationships at work.
- ❑ You don't fully understand what resources are available.
- ❑ You often see a limited number of ways to deal with obstacles.
- ❑ You tend to rely on rules or tradition when tackling a problem.

- ❑ You lean on tried and true methods that you trust when facing an obstacle.

- ❑ Challenges quickly frustrate you.

- ❑ You attack problems by yourself, without seeking support.

- ❑ You set goals that are too big—you overreach.

- ❑ You take foolish risks.

- ❑ Other people tell you that you're a rule breaker.

- ❑ You create confusion in your team and among other people by frequently shifting your approach to tasks.

Coach Yourself

To develop your resourcefulness, create goals in areas that are unfamiliar to you or that are underdeveloped. These questions can help you focus on such areas:

- Think about people who you think were particularly resourceful and productive. What did they do? What resources did they rely upon? How were they regarded in the organization?

- How has lack of resourcefulness made things difficult for you in the past? What has it kept you from doing or achieving?

- Can you anticipate situations or challenges that will call for your resourcefulness? How might you approach these challenges?

- How would increasing your resourcefulness affect your ability to respond to challenges?

- When was the last time you passed over a well-accepted approach for the chance to try something different?

Improve Now

Reinvent. When applying everyday solutions to everyday problems, stop to ask yourself how things might be done differently. What if you didn't have access to the typical means you use? Try an alternate approach and see what the outcome is.

Reach out to experts. Next time you find yourself struggling with a challenge, ask yourself if you know people who can do it better. Reach out to them, enlist their help, and see what you can learn.

Apply analogous solutions. Resourceful problem solvers often recognize solutions to similar problems that they can apply to their current situation. When you encounter a problem with no apparent solution, consider how it is like another situation you have encountered. Think about how you might apply the successful solution to that past situation to your current problem.

Study role models. Watch people whom you consider resourceful. How do they approach problems? To whom do they turn for help? How would you describe the spirit with which they approach obstacles?

Cultivate resources. Refresh your network of contacts. Think about the people you know or want to know and seek more information about the skills, connections, or other resources that they can access. Seek opportunities to bring them into problem-solving situations where their capabilities can make a difference.

Build your own brand of resourcefulness. Everyone is different. Look at what's unique about you and how you approach hurdles. Do you go over? Under? Around? Through? Ask for feedback about how you deal with adversity.

Turn obstacles into challenges. The next time you encounter a problem or obstacle, look at it as a small test. Focus attention on the obstacle and keep attacking it until you find your way past it. Apply the lessons you learned to future challenges.

Look at people in a different light. One of the keys to resourcefulness is knowing how to leverage others' skills. Get beyond their reputations. Resourceful people observe others closely and can detect their often subtle, hidden strengths that often prove useful for solving problems.

Exploit ambiguity. Ambiguity can be daunting, even paralyzing, for many people. Highly resourceful people often engage in a clever reframing of ambiguous circumstances. Instead of allowing the lack of a clear problem or solution to inhibit them, resourceful people find freedom in defining the problem and the solution in a way that suits their needs. No rules, no problem!

Question tradition. Inefficient methods often persist for a long time because they are accepted as "the way things are done around here." A better solution may be well within reach, but it takes someone willing to question the status quo and invite new ideas to put it into action.

Developmental Opportunities

- Agree to lead a complex task with multiple stakeholders.

- Take on an assignment in uncharted territory, something that has never been done before and that comes with no set approaches.

- Learn more about an impossible customer expectation and meet it—or better, exceed it.

- Lead a start-up of a unit department or branch in a new region.

- Become active in a nonprofit organization.

- Take on a problem where previous solutions no longer seem to work sufficiently.

Activity Center

Review and download these activities you can use for your development or with your team from this book's resource page at www.ccl.org/compassbook.

Resourcefulness: The Many Faces of Resourcefulness
Resourcefulness: Looking for the Value

Related Competencies

Boundary Spanning

Flexibility

Learning Agility

Negotiating

Organizational Savvy

Problem Solving

Risk Taking

Resources

Baldoni, J. (2010, Jan. 13). The importance of resourcefulness. *Harvard Business Review*. Retrieved from https://hbr .org/2010/01/leaders-can-learn-to-make-do-a

Gryskiewicz, S. S., & Taylor, S. (2003). *Making creativity practical: Innovation that gets results*. Greensboro, NC: Center for Creative Leadership.

Kamkwamba, W. (2009). *How I harnessed the wind*. (Video). Ted.com. Retrieved from https://www.ted.com/talks/william_kamkwamba_how_i_harnessed_ the_wind?language=en

Morgan, A., & Barden, M. (2015). *A beautiful constraint: How to transform your limitations into advantages, and why it's everyone's business*. Hoboken, NJ: Wiley.

Paulson, T. L. (2010). *The optimism advantage: 50 simple truths to transform your attitudes and actions into results*. Hoboken, NJ: Wiley.

40

Risk Taking

Take calculated risks to create and seize opportunities for making your organization better.

With great opportunities come great risks. Don't become paralyzed by uncertainty. Take necessary, considered risks and you will advance further in your career and outperform your more cautious peers, according to a 2005 survey by auditing firm Grant Thornton. But, as the survey report indicates, too many leaders don't have the will to persevere in the face of risk. You can challenge others and push for change and growth—for yourself, your team, and your organization. Increase your comfort with and skill at taking risks and position yourself to take advantage of opportunities as they arise. Don't wait for your competitors to try new things and fail. Because if they learn and succeed, it will be too late for you to respond. Consider how Amazon's Jeff Bezos refuses to wait for all the answers before moving into new ventures.

Leadership in Action

Amazon is the fastest company ever to reach $100 billion in sales, according to a shareholder letter published by CEO Jeff Bezos in 2016. In that same letter, Bezos referred to his company as "the best place in the world to fail." That sounds counterintuitive, but as Ryan Mac explains in his *Forbes* article, a closer inspection reveals that Amazon's enormous success is proportional to the risks its founder seems willing to take (2016).

For example, consider the Amazon Fire Phone. Despite an enthusiastic launch, despite the Amazon pedigree and the incredible brand recognition it provides, the device frustrated consumers and never caught on. Before long it was a clearance item, and the investment Amazon poured into the venture never paid dividends.

However, a similar risk (perhaps a greater risk) in the form of Amazon Web Services (AWS) has grown massively since its debut in 2006. While a smartphone was already a recognizable product when the Fire Phone launched, at the inception of Amazon Web Services the idea of cloud computing was just beginning to take root in the public consciousness. The product met a growing demand, and today AWS is at $10 billion in annual sales.

The thing to remember is that Bezos' willingness to take risks is what allowed for the success of AWS. Without the will to risk a failure like the Fire Phone, there might not have been AWS at all.

What High Performance Looks Like

Leaders who take risks

- acknowledge the risk and move ahead, aware of potential failure

- are entrepreneurial and eager to seize opportunities

- will experiment and try things before they are completely vetted

- don't give up when the going gets tough

- absorb the repercussions and responsibility of failure

- enjoy not knowing exactly how things will turn out and are comfortable in that situation

- are seen as innovative, persistent, adventurous, courageous, future-oriented, confident, flexible

- analyze risks and provide data on various scenarios and the potential costs and benefits to the organization

- strive toward the extraordinary and against all odds

- deviate from the norm when necessary

- learn and adjust approach through trial and error

- prove ideas with successful small-scale demonstrations

What's in Your Way?

If you are unable or unwilling to take risks, you might miss opportunities to contribute significantly to the growth of your organization. Courage is necessary to take part in bold ventures. You might also limit your opportunities for personal growth and development, because taking risks, including those that don't work out, and being accountable for the results, form powerful on-the-job learning experiences. Look at the following descriptions and mark any that you believe are getting in your way to becoming comfortable with risk.

- ❏ You're afraid to fail.
- ❏ You're not comfortable changing your work situation or work processes.
- ❏ You've been burned in the past by risky ventures.
- ❏ You're a cautious person.
- ❏ You lack confidence.
- ❏ Your organization rewards avoiding risky decisions.
- ❏ You feel responsible for protecting the well-being of your organization and colleagues.
- ❏ You pursue exciting ideas without fully understanding the risks and drawbacks.
- ❏ You've received feedback that others see you as a maverick and not a team member.
- ❏ You're impatient and push people and processes too fast.
- ❏ You don't make adjustments along the way.
- ❏ You pursue a new area in which you don't have the knowledge or connections you need to be successful.
- ❏ You can't sell the organization on the benefits of investing in an unproven area.
- ❏ People are unwilling to provide the honest guidance or feedback that you need to mitigate risk.

Coach Yourself

To develop your tolerance for risk taking, create goals that put you in the role of arguing for an unpopular position, that let you work on new ideas, and that expose you to the possibility of failure. These questions can help you find such a focus area:

- ● What unsuccessful risks have you taken in the past and what, based on what you learned, would you do differently to decrease that risk?

- ● How can you create an environment that encourages experimentation and learning from failure?

- How can your organization fail fast, improve, and move on, minimizing the cost and maximizing the value of trial and error?

- What is your strategy and process for testing new ideas?

- What are the potential costs of avoiding risk in a particular area (for example, product development, entering new markets, expanding into new locations)? What opportunity will you lose by pursuing the risky path?

Improve Now

Just start. Step into unproven areas to collect feedback and learn from your experience. Try small experiments to explore, prove, and refine ideas.

Learn to manage risk. You can't expect to take risks without knowing something about risk management. Learn more about the process of risk management.

Define the benefits of taking risks. What specifically can the organization gain if you succeed? What can the organization gain if you fail? What comes from doing nothing?

Define the cost of missed opportunities. Avoiding risk usually means you have to make a trade-off. That means you will miss opportunities. What do missed opportunities cost the organization?

Look into your heart. What do you care about enough that you're willing to put yourself on the line to make it happen? Is the cause important enough to you that you're willing to make sacrifices or flirt with failure? Can your passion for the idea balance or overcome your anxiety of risk?

Define areas for experimentation. Certain organizational areas may be sacrosanct and off limits for experimentation, such as financial systems or complicated manufacturing processes. But other areas may be ripe for innovation and risk taking. Understand the difference.

Stretch yourself. Sign up for a course in an area you're unfamiliar with but have always wanted to try (scuba diving, for example). Note your responses to the stress of learning in an unfamiliar environment.

Set aside a budget for risky activity. Taking risks includes tolerating waste as you try new approaches and abandon what doesn't work. Decide how many resources you are willing to risk and protect those resources from other organizational needs.

Move quickly with low-cost, low-risk prototypes and trials. Moving too slowly and not getting the feedback you need from clients, customers, and staff until it's too late to change direction pose the greatest risks to any project. Create the means for your team to try different approaches, gather responses, and figure out what works.

Fail fast. The most entrepreneurial organizations accept failure as inevitable. From that perspective, it's best to fail as quickly and cheaply as possible, learn from the experience, and move on smarter and more capable of succeeding.

Gather collective wisdom. Bring colleagues together to share their wisdom, experience, and opinions. Exploit and distill the wisdom of the crowd to inform your decisions and decrease risk.

Build a team of advisers. Surround yourself with people who have more experience than you do and are willing to guide you through a high-risk situation. Don't put together a group that is like you. Seek differences in cultures, ethnicities, demographics, geography, and roles. The English poet John Donne once wrote that no one is an island. If you take risks only on your own island, it may soon be a deserted one.

Go on an adventure. Travel somewhere you haven't been, go to events you never attend, seek out people you don't normally meet. Getting used to discomfort will increase your tolerance for risk.

Developmental Opportunities

- Work on a new-product development team.

- Join a task force tackling an emerging business issue.

- Work on a problem by doing quick experiments and trials.

- Advocate for an idea that you feel strongly about but that is unpopular with some of your peers.

- Run for office in a professional or community organization.

- Volunteer to develop a risk mitigation plan for a project in your organization.

- Take on a problem that others in your organization have failed to solve.

Activity Center

Review and download these activities you can use for your development or with your team from this book's resource page at www.ccl.org/compassbook.

Risk Taking: Manage Risk
Risk Taking: Take a Risk to Lunch

Related Competencies

Creativity
Problem Solving
Resourcefulness
Vision

Resources

Ernst, C., & Chrobot-Mason, D. (2010). *Boundary spanning leadership: Six practices for solving problems, driving innovation, and transforming organizations.* New York, NY: McGraw-Hill.

Horth, D. M., & Vehar, J. R. (2016). From innovation graveyard to innovation hotbed. *Developing Leaders Quarterly*, p. 23.

Johansen, B. (2012). *Leaders make the future: Ten new leadership skills for an uncertain world* (2nd ed.). San Francisco, CA: Berrett-Koehler.

Mac, R. (2016, April 5). Jeff Bezos calls Amazon 'best place in the world to fail' in shareholder letter. *Forbes*. Retrieved from http://www.forbes.com/sites/ryanmac/2016/04/05/jeff-bezos-calls-amazon-best-place-in-the-world-to-fail-in-shareholder-letter/#4bd7a50e62f4

Riddle, D. (2009). *Tense. Worry. Choke.* (Blog post). Center for Creative Leadership. Retrieved from https://www.ccl.org/blog/tense-worry-choke/

Thornton, G. (2005). *What makes a good leader? Grant Thornton's leadership survey suggests that today's leaders may have lost their risk taking bottle.* Author. Retrieved from http://docplayer.net/8690591-What-makes-a-good-leader-grant-thornton-s-leadership-survey-suggests-that-today-s-leaders-may-have-lost-their-risk-taking-bottle.html

41

Self-Development

Take charge of your future—set and achieve leadership improvement goals and revise as necessary.

Learning beyond the classroom. Commit to that, and you'll grow as a leader. However, if you let your self-development fall behind your other responsibilities, you may find yourself using the same tools for every problem—even when it's obvious they don't work. Let your profile as a continually self-developing leader inspire others in your organization to follow suit. Watch how all that learning raises your organization's performance. What does continual development look like? Let's visit with an unconventional, unlikely example.

Leadership in Action

When the rock band Queen was on the cusp of fame, guitarist Brian May was in the midst of earning his PhD and teaching. Painful though it was for him to set aside his academic pursuits, he eventually faced the music and threw himself full force into the band, with results that are now immortalized in pop culture history. Years later, when the band's life cycle had entered a quieter stage, he returned to the science that had inspired him as a child: stereoscopy.

May completed his doctorate 30 years after beginning the process, and since then he has been busy in his personal workshop. Among his inventions are the Red Special guitar and his latest creation: the Owl VR Smartphone Kit. Based on Victorian methods of stereoscopy, the Owl allows viewers to see 360-degree videos and pictures in stereoscopic 3D. For May, these innovations are an attempt to recapture the magical experience in his childhood when he first used a toy stereoscope to see a picture of a hippopotamus. Furthermore, he believes the Owl can affect animal rights activism as well. As he told the *Guardian*'s Nicola Davis in 2016, "If you could put virtual reality in an abattoir and if people could see what happens to those animals that they were eating, I think we'd see a lot of people turning vegan overnight."

All of May's activity comes after what many would consider the achievements of a lifetime, playing for one of the most widely recognized and beloved musical acts of the past century. Instead of contenting himself with what he has already done, May pushes forward, layering new skills over old to create something entirely new.

What High Performance Looks Like

Leaders who pay attention to and work on their self-development

- seek opportunities to learn from their experiences by taking on challenging assignments

- stay curious because they know they don't know everything

- integrate feedback with self-reflection for a balanced view of themselves

- accept responsibility for their development

- identify where to focus their development attention and energy

- set clear and achievable leadership goals that energize them

- identify and overcome obstacles to development

- stay on course by reviewing progress and anticipating roadblocks

- celebrate successes

- revise goals over time, as necessary

- seek candid feedback on their performance

- question their assumptions

- engage colleagues in their development to learn from others

- anticipate how their personal changes affect others

- manage time well

- incorporate development into their daily routines

- align their goals with their values

- are often seen as adaptive, open to change, self-aware, humble, curious, interpersonally savvy, courageous, purposeful, learning agile, reflective, and persistent

What's in Your Way?

Leaders unwilling to continuously develop tend to repeat their mistakes. Their careers can stall. Other people in the organization may question their ability to grow, adapt, and adjust as circumstances demand. They may level off in a role that maximizes their current abilities but doesn't offer a career path to rise in the organization. Take a look at the following descriptions and mark any that you believe are blocking you from taking on the commitment to and the work of self-development.

- ❏ You don't take time to reflect on what you're learning.
- ❏ You're overwhelmed by how much you have to learn.
- ❏ You lack curiosity.
- ❏ You have been successful in the past and don't see a need to change.
- ❏ You're afraid of what people will say if you seek their feedback.
- ❏ You believe self-development calls attention to your weaknesses.
- ❏ You believe training time takes you away from your work.
- ❏ You don't want to involve others in your development, and you fail to pursue a developmental relationship with them.
- ❏ No one notices that you've improved, and you infer that other people prefer you remain the same.
- ❏ You worry that you will come off as self-obsessed.
- ❏ You're satisfied in your current role and don't want to take on another.
- ❏ You're unable to fit your developmental commitments into your life.
- ❏ You fear that other people will react negatively to the changes you make.
- ❏ You're unable to connect your progress to positive impact on others.

- You cannot clearly communicate your changes so that others notice.

- Your work priorities crowd out your attempts to develop new leadership skills.

- You worry that the changes you make may evoke conflicts.

- You don't feel safe and supported in your organization while you pursue your leadership goals.

- You're stuck because you believe there's a downside to achieving your goals that you can't anticipate.

Coach Yourself

To work on your self-development, create goals in areas that call on you to take on new skills or refine old ones. These questions can help you focus on such areas:

- When you finish projects, do you review your performance and look for ways to improve?

- Is there anything that your friends or your spouse have been telling you that could help you improve personally and professionally?

- What are you trying to achieve—where do you want to be in 12 months?

- What are some of the most important developmental experiences you've had? What lessons did you learn?

- What kind of leader do you want to be?

- What do you want to do more of, do differently, or stop doing?

- What resources are available to you in terms of money, time, and people?

Improve Now

Challenge yourself. Identify areas in which you want to develop, and then immerse yourself in situations that will push you to your limits in these areas. It will be uncomfortable at first, but learning from experience is the surest way to real and lasting self-improvement.

Create a plan and focus. Write an action plan that defines how you want to change, what you will do, and how you will assess your progress. Narrow your focus to one or two areas for improvement. Which areas might have the greatest impact on your overall effectiveness as a leader?

Follow up. Check with your colleagues to see if they have perceived a change in your leadership abilities and to solicit additional feedback and guidance.

Seek challenges outside work. Other areas of your life often provide challenges equal to those found on the job. You'll find plenty of leadership responsibilities in nonprofit, religious, social, and professional organizations, as well as schools, sports teams, and family life. There are many opportunities to learn lessons of leadership through personal experiences.

Seek training. Find development programs and classes designed to give you feedback so you can direct your experiences to your benefit.

Create developmental relationships. Search for members of your organization who exemplify expertise in the areas where you wish to develop. Such people don't need to be, and often aren't, found in your immediate work group. You can use their guidance to hone your skills and to convey your commitment to development.

Pursue lifelong development. Identify your long-term growth goals, and regularly assess whether you are making progress towards achieving these goals. Stagnation can block even the most promising leaders from achieving their full potential.

Think about the alternative. Create alternative scenarios of different strategies your organization could pursue. Consider what's common among those alternatives. Think about what kinds of leadership and which competencies your organization will need to be successful in those scenarios.

The job after next. Identify the job you would like to have after your next job. What skills and knowledge will you need to be successful?

Similarly, you can think one level up. Whatever your role or position in your organization, consider what your boss needs to handle his or her responsibilities. Think about what is keeping you from performing at that level. Ask yourself what is getting in your way of working at that level. Design an action plan that identifies the skills and knowledge you will need and how you intend to acquire them.

Identify an area of change. You can't set goals for every leadership competency you want to develop. Narrow your goals to those that you feel passionate about, those that benefit you or can reduce mistakes, and those that are not too difficult to achieve but still stretch your abilities.

Learn about the different kinds of goals. Not all goals are the same. There are goals that change how you act (behavioral), goals that improve a skill (competency), and goals that meet a target (outcome). Set the kind of leadership goals that promise the results you want.

Get tactical. Break your goals down. List the smaller steps you need to take to achieve the outcome. Figure out what you are going to do and when you are going to do it. And put it in writing.

Enlist an accountability partner. During the time you are setting leadership goals and working toward them, ask a trusted colleague to hold you accountable and provide feedback.

Stay the course. Regularly revisit your goals, track your progress, and adapt as needed. Keep your momentum in the face of obstacles and your eyes on the finish line.

Celebrate your progress. Each step you take in setting leadership goals and every step you take toward achieving those goals is worth special mention. Be good to yourself.

Start a leadership reading club. Choose several top business or professional development books from this year (or classics from the past). Invite a group of people to read the books and to get together to discuss them and how their ideas could be integrated into your organization.

Developmental Opportunities

- Reshape your current job by adding new responsibilities, trading tasks with a colleague, or otherwise restructuring it.

- Take on part of a colleague's job while he or she is on leave.

- Focus more attention on a part of your job you've been avoiding.

- Ask your boss to delegate to you one of his or her responsibilities that incorporates one of the skills you want to develop. Ask for specific feedback on your performance.

- Locate someone whom you admire because of his or her skill in the area you want to develop. Ask that person if he or she will provide expertise and support to your development.

- If your goal is in a specific technical area, such as information technology or financial management, for example, sign up for formal classes. If your area of development lies in "soft skills," consider training for that, too. Classes can provide safe spaces in which you can try, fail, learn, and practice.

- Put yourself in front of customers and clients. Focusing on what other people need can help you reach goals in such areas as interpersonal savvy, negotiating, and active listening.

- Shadow someone for a day or a week. Choose someone in another capacity than yours, someone in another location but in a similar job, or someone in a leadership or management role a level or two higher than yours. Note questions that come up for you and follow up with a meeting where you can get your questions answered.

- Lead a group of community volunteers. Volunteers often work with few resources, and they are not as accountable as people on the job. Taking on an opportunity like this can help you set and achieve practice goals in such areas as resourcefulness, leveraging differences, and problem solving.

Activity Center

Review and download these activities you can use for your development or with your team from this book's resource page at www.ccl.org/compassbook.

Self-Development: Brand You

Self-Development: Learn to Learn

Related Competencies

Flexibility

Learning Agility

Resourcefulness

Self-Awareness

Resources

Bradt, G. B., Check, J. A., & Lawler, J. A. (2016). *The new leader's 100-day action plan: How to take charge, build or merge your team, and get immediate results* (4th ed.). Hoboken, NJ: Wiley.

Chappelow, C., & Leslie, J. B. (2004). *Keeping your career on track: Twenty success strategies.* Greensboro, NC: Center for Creative Leadership.

Davis, N. (2016, May 29). Brian May: 'All sorts of stuff happens in my workshop.' *The Guardian.* Retrieved from https://www.theguardian.com/technology/2016/may/29/brian-may-owl-stereoscope-interview

George, B. (2015). *Discover your true north* (expanded and updated ed.). Hoboken, NJ: Wiley.

Goldsmith, M., & Reiter, M. (2015). *Triggers: Creating behavior that lasts— becoming the person you want to be.* New York, NY: Crown Business.

Hallenbeck, G. (2016). *Learning agility: Unlock the lessons of experience.* Greensboro, NC: Center for Creative Leadership.

Hallenbeck, G. (2017). *Lead 4 success: Learn the essentials of true leadership.* Greensboro, NC: Center for Creative Leadership.

Klann, G. (n.d.) *Building character: Strengthening the heart of good leadership.* [Podcast]. Greensboro, NC: Center for Creative Leadership. Retrieved from http://insights.ccl.org/multimedia/podcast/building-character-strengthening-the-heart-of-good-leadership/

McCauley, C. D. (2006). *Developmental assignments: Creating learning experiences without changing jobs.* Greensboro, NC: Center for Creative Leadership.

McCauley, C. D., DeRue, D. S., Yost, P. R., & Taylor, S. (Eds.). (2014). *Experience-driven leader development: Models, tools, best practices, and advice for on-the-job-development.* San Francisco, CA: Wiley.

Rath, T. (2007). *Strengths finder 2.0.* New York, NY: Gallup Press.

Ruderman, M. N., & Ohlott, P. J. (2000). *Learning from life: Turning life's lessons into leadership experience.* Greensboro, NC: Center for Creative Leadership.

Ruderman, M. N., & Ohlott, P. J. (2014). Learning from personal life experiences. In C. D. McCauley, D. S. DeRue, P. R. Yost, & S. Taylor (Eds.), *Experience-driven leader development: Models, tools, best practices, and advice for on-the-job-development* (pp. 77–80). San Francisco, CA: Wiley.

Scisco, P., McCauley, C. D., Leslie, J. B., & Elsey, R. (2013). *Change now!: Five steps to better leadership.* Greensboro, NC: Center for Creative Leadership.

Stanier, M. B. (2016). *The coaching habit: Say less, ask more, and change the way you lead forever.* Toronto, Canada: Box of Crayons Press.

Johansen, B. (2012). *Leaders make the future: Ten new leadership skills for an uncertain world* (2nd ed.). San Francisco, CA: Berrett-Koehler.

Wilson, M. S., & Chandrasekar, N. A. (2014). *Experience explorer facilitator's set.* Greensboro, NC: Center for Creative Leadership.

42

Strategic Alignment

Rally the organization around a common strategy.

Even the most brilliant strategies won't produce expected outcomes if they conflict with one another or contain mixed messages. And a leader can't go it alone when developing a strategy. Research suggests that individual strategies have negligible effects on organizational performance; coordinated, aligned strategies are what is needed for growth (O'Reilly, Caldwell, Chatman, Lapiz, & Self, 2010). Play an instrumental role in ensuring that senior leaders, culture, message, and all elements of strategy are unified and cohesive.

When you create strategic alignment between systems and people, you set up everyone to more easily achieve individual, group, and organizational objectives. You contribute to the organization's shared efforts. You save it from wasting energy and resources. And you can be counted among the leaders whose actions enable the direction, alignment, and commitment that sustain the organization and propel it into the future. Consider the challenge Airbnb faced in focusing its strategy during its explosive growth.

Leadership in Action

Airbnb (originally Air Bed & Breakfast) launched in 2008 and started small. Its goal: operate as a facilitation marketplace connecting people with spare bedrooms to people who needed a place to stay on short notice. At first the company's focus was narrow, targeting areas in which large business conventions had sold out available hotel space. Slowly at first, their targeted approach began to take off. Somewhere around 2011, as the company expanded into tourist and vacation rentals, came the tipping point. The company started to grow faster than its leadership could keep up.

This sounds like a good problem to have. But for Brian Chesky, the cofounder and CEO, the overgrowth demanded a solution. The rapid expansion of the company's market came with concurrent strategic bloat, rendering Airbnb's goals too scattershot to set reasonable goals. In order to focus the strategy, Austin Carr writes in *Fast Company*, Chesky assigned his leadership team the goal of shrinking the company's entire corporate strategy down to a single page. This challenge forced the issue of the company's future identity, eschewing the old "chase every possibility" approach for a more linear concentration on hospitality. To complement the one-page strategy, Chesky commissioned a Pixar animator to create an outline of the conceptual goal. The result was a series of 30 images called "Snow White," which brings to life the emotional impact of travel.

By tailoring leadership decisions to conform to the one-sheet strategy or resonate with the vision of "Snow White," Chesky's team assures Airbnb's strategic alignment. These tools allow his team to maintain clarity and working harmony, leaving opportunities for growth while maintaining a strategic anchor.

What High Performance Looks Like

Leaders who create strategic alignment

- involve other people in the organization in strategic planning

- recognize and understand the different strategies at play in the organization

- deal quickly with lack of alignment in the executive team to ensure that it integrates the agreed-upon strategy into its planning processes

- ensure that people have clear, shared priorities

- hold people responsible for focusing on and implementing the strategy

- collaborate with others, listening and learning to gain a broader view

- measure progress toward strategic goals

- communicate with managers at all levels to ensure that they understand the organization's overall strategy

- build talent or operational capacity to meet strategic needs

- invest in capabilities needed to support anticipated market demands

- create a compelling message about long-range strategy

- make appropriate course corrections when executing the strategic plan

What's in Your Way?

Without a doubt, you don't want teams working at cross-purposes or making your organization less nimble and competitive. Time spent dealing with the noise of misaligned strategies subverts group effort. Build your reputation as a leader who can get people to work together toward a common goal. Mark any of the items in the following list that might give you trouble developing your ability to create strategic alignment.

- ❏ You focus on the present more than the future.
- ❏ You are overly confident or complacent about your organization.
- ❏ You avoid conflict.
- ❏ You don't look beyond the needs of your immediate work group or function.
- ❏ You don't have relationships with key people from other functions.
- ❏ You haven't invested in building a long-term strategy.
- ❏ Your organization's culture is diverse or fragmented.
- ❏ Your organization places a high value on independence.
- ❏ You try to make everyone happy.
- ❏ You overlook people who are pivotal for creating alignment.
- ❏ Your industry or competition changes, rendering strategies obsolete.
- ❏ You push your group, function, division, or organization too hard and too fast.
- ❏ You underestimate how long it takes to reach alignment.
- ❏ You can't communicate a compelling message for the strategy.
- ❏ People resist aligning strategies.
- ❏ You haven't given consideration to aligning leadership and talent to the strategy.
- ❏ The company's business strategy has suddenly shifted, rendering the current talent strategy obsolete.

Coach Yourself

To develop your ability to create strategic alignment, look to gain broad knowledge about the organization. Create goals in the areas of collaboration, communication, and conflict resolution, goals that demand you think systemically about organizational alignment. Use the following questions to define an area of focus:

- Do you fully understand your organization's business model? For example, do you know what your organization's various functions do and the full range of products or services that your organization provides?

- What challenges or changes could damage your organization in the future? How can your organization better align its strategy to prepare for that?

- Who on the organization's senior team can you work with to build a compelling, shared strategy?

- How aligned is the talent in your group to the business strategy? What are the most critical talent gaps your organization needs to close?

- Do senior leaders believe in your vision and strategy? Do they recognize the kind of talent required to execute it?

- What is your personal or team's intent, and are you willing to put that aside to pursue a shared strategy?

Improve Now

Get connected. Link your responsibilities to your organization's mission and strategy. Establish how your own personal duties contribute to the strategy of your organization. Look to what you can do in your own area to better align with the organization.

Reframe conflict. While it's easy to see conflict as an obstacle to progress, conflict can also point to areas where greater collaboration would push the organization forward.

Explore possibilities. If envisioning long-term possibilities proves difficult, consider what-if scenarios. What if a new competitor challenges your organization's position? What if your organization joined with another company from another industry or field? What could you create together? What would be the impact on your organization? On your division?

Monthly alignment. Add the topic of strategic alignment to your regular staff meetings. Ask your team members to bring in examples of decisions they made during the week. Ask how their decisions align with the organization's strategic plan. Sharing information and ideas ensures that everyone is in the loop regarding the strategy and that you are monitoring results to make certain that the best decisions have been made.

Build alliances with your peers. Leaders who can create strategic alignment do not only have a good understanding of where they want their team to go—they also understand the different strategies at play in the organization. Learn who is dependent or otherwise has a stake in your strategy's success. Listen and learn from them to broaden your views. Look for synergy among strategic plans. What can your team bring to making another team's strategy successful? What can other teams bring to yours?

Create interdependencies. If you see a lack of collaboration among teams, consider approaches to help them span organizational boundaries. Ask the teams involved to define and manage their boundaries. Help them look for common ground. Then invite them to define what they can do together.

Translate strategic plans into tactics. What will an aligned strategy mean for you? For your teams? What will be the benefits? What changes will it induce on your own responsibilities? What are the implications of continual misalignment? How can you start planning for possible contingencies?

Zero in on misalignments. Consider not what, but why. This will reveal the core issues to address to create alignment. To create momentum, build on shared objectives and aspects of the strategy that do align.

Use the "5 Whys" technique. Originally conceived and used at Toyota Motor Corp., probing a problem by asking Why five times (observations revealed that five was the usual number of questions needed to get to a result) has been adopted and modified in many organizations. In terms of strategic alignment, the technique can uncover deeply rooted assumptions and reveal similarities among different teams.

Developmental Opportunities

- Serve on a team responsible for setting the organization's strategic vision.

- Work on a strategic plan for your unit.

- Present a workshop to help colleagues better understand common concerns across functions and groups.

- Help a community or professional organization create a strategic plan.

- Develop five-year business scenarios for your unit.

- Develop processes for tracking progress toward long-term goals.

- Take a temporary assignment in the strategic planning group.

Activity Center

Review and download these activities you can use for your development or with your team from this book's resource page at www.ccl.org/compassbook.

Strategic Alignment: Evaluate Your Strategic-Thinking Skills
Strategic Alignment: Interview an Executive
Strategic Alignment: Strategic Decision Review

Related Competencies

Boundary Spanning
Conflict Resolution
Organizational Savvy
Relationship Management
Strategic Planning and Implementation
Systems Thinking

Resources

Carr, A. (2014, March 17). Inside Airbnb's grand hotel plans. *Fast Company*. Retrieved from http://www.fastcompany. com/3027107/punk-meet-rock-airbnb-brian-chesky-chip-conley

Ernst, C., & Chrobot-Mason, D. (2010). *Boundary spanning leadership: Six practices for solving problems, driving innovation, and transforming organizations.* New York, NY: McGraw-Hill.

Hughes, R. L., Beatty, K. C., & Dinwoodie, D. L. (2014). *Becoming a strategic leader: Your role in your organization's enduring success* (2nd ed.). San Francisco, CA: Jossey-Bass.

McCauley C. D., & Fick-Cooper, L. (2015). *Direction, alignment, commitment: Achieving better results through leadership.* Greensboro, NC: Center for Creative Leadership.

O'Reilly, C. A., Caldwell, D. F., Chatman, J. A., Lapiz, M., & Self, W. (2010). How leadership matters: The effects of leaders' alignment on strategy implementation. *Leadership Quarterly, 21*(1), 104–113.

Van Velsor, E. (2013). *Broadening your organizational perspective.* Greensboro, NC: Center for Creative Leadership.

43

Strategic Planning and Implementation

Develop and execute data-driven long-range plans.

Leaders who make a difference develop the ability to see beyond the day-to-day tasks of organizational life. CCL research reports that 86 percent of managers believe strategic planning will be a critical skill in the future, and yet 59 percent of those managers say their organizations are deficient in strategic leadership capacity (Leslie, 2009).

Avoid being part of that number and foster a broad view of how your organization works and how its parts operate together. Connect this perspective with a solid strategic plan, and you have a blueprint for implementing that strategy. A big job, sure. But pull it off and make it stick, and you will cement your place among the top leaders in your company. Angela Merkel's story illustrates the kind of planning and implementation that moves beyond borders—even if it's a story that hasn't yet ended.

Leadership in Action

Before she became chancellor of Germany and the de facto leader of the European Union, Angela Merkel earned a PhD in quantum chemistry. Such an undertaking requires a great ability for analysis, as well as great patience. These are the capacities she draws on when the EU is in crisis, whether from a gradual economic unspooling or a shockingly quick population shift.

When the Greek financial collapse faced the EU with the possibility of dissolution (or at the very least, prolonged discord) Merkel encouraged the associated parties to take the long view. A simple fire-and-forget bailout would create only a temporary distraction from the real problem of sustainability. "I come from a country in which I experienced economic collapse," Merkel reminded reporters in 2012. If Greece's debt was not reduced "sustainably and with a view to the long term, Europe simply will no longer be the prosperous continent that the world listens to and that gets people's attention" (Vick, 2015).

Now her country and her continent face a different problem. Thousands of refugees flee the wars in Syria and other parts of the Middle East and northern Africa. Can space be made for them in Europe? Can they be expected to return to countries in which stability and safety are no longer likely? Merkel will need to draw on all her powers of analysis and patience to navigate the solution.

What High Performance Looks Like

Leaders with expertise in strategic planning and implementation

- balance the present with the future
- stay current on trends in the market, including global, political, and economic trends
- anticipate what their competitors will do next and what direction the industry will take
- anticipate what customers will need in the future
- understand how the organization produces revenue and which of its products and services produce the greatest margins
- know what trade-offs to make in the short term to achieve long-term goals
- invest time early to involve the organization in strategic planning
- see beyond quarterly commitments to a long-term competitive position and vision
- keep watch on customers and what drives their purchases
- spend time with employees throughout the organization to gather input and to see the business through their eyes
- understand the needs of various business units
- make investments in potential high-growth areas
- understand operational processes
- see opportunities for increasing efficiencies and cutting costs
- modify the corporate structure to address strategic leadership and talent needs
- are seen as astute, discerning, excellent planners, connected, future-oriented, and results-driven

What's in Your Way?

A deficiency in strategic planning and implementation might lead to lost business opportunities. Without competence in this area, you might take your group or organization down the wrong path and squander time and money. Such shortsightedness will make it difficult for you to gain support and commitment for your projects and to influence other people. Review the following list and note the items that you believe block you from developing skill in strategic planning and implementation.

- ❏ You don't fully understand the business or marketplace your organization is in.

- ❏ You won't admit what you don't know about the business.

- ❏ Your experience is too narrow—it's hard for you to imagine bigger possibilities.

- ❏ You focus more on the present than on the future.

- ❏ You focus on the future at the expense of the present.

- ❏ You rely too much on your own knowledge and experience.

- ❏ You plan too far into the future.

- ❏ You are told your dreams or plans are too ambitious.

- ❏ You struggle to communicate your strategic ideas.

- ❏ You struggle to develop a practical plan for implementing your ideas.

- ❏ You think too much about your competition and too little about the unique value of your organization's products and services.

- ❏ You have unrealistic expectations and push the organization too hard and too fast.

- ❏ Employees feel threatened by the changes that you promote.

- ❏ You don't see the link between business strategy and talent planning.

- ❏ Few people in the organization are concerned with aligning leadership and talent with the business strategy.

❑ Your organization lacks proven systems and processes to address critical talent needs.

❑ You underestimate the time required to align talent strategy with business strategy.

❑ The business strategy suddenly shifts, rendering the current talent strategy obsolete.

Coach Yourself

To develop skill in strategic planning and implementation, create goals in areas that require you to plan for the future, give you a role in developing organizational strategy, place you in a team outside of your  usual responsibilities, require you to develop broad knowledge about the organization, or otherwise encourage you to trade short-term planning for long-term planning. These questions can help you define that area of focus:

● How can you develop deep knowledge of your organization's competitive challenges and opportunities?

● Do you fully understand your company's business strategy? Who can give you deeper insight into the strategy?

● What dramatic challenges or changes might negatively affect your organization in the future?

● What are the technological, demographic, and political trends that will affect your organization in the next five years? The next ten years?

● What challenges or changes could threaten the sustainability of your organization in the future? Do you have a sense for the moves planned by your competitors and how your organization will counter them?

● How willing are you to listen to other opinions about the potential direction of the organization? Are you willing to engage in a process that might produce opinions with which you disagree? Do you trust people around you to help build a leadership and talent strategy?

- How aligned is the talent in your group to the business strategy? What are the most critical gaps you need to close?

- What challenges or changes could threaten the sustainability of your organization in the future? How can talented people buffer or exploit the impact of those changes?

Improve Now

Think systemically. A strategic leader sees the organization as interdependent and interconnected parts and is mindful that actions and decisions made in one part of the organization affect other parts of the organization.

Focus on the future. Operate with a far-reaching timetable, integrating short-term results and a long-term focus.

Keep a firm grasp on what's happening in the company. Know the systems as well as the details. Circulate through the company so you can see it through the perspective of employees.

Stay attuned to your organization's external environment. Always scan the external climate for patterns and trends that may affect your organization. Stay informed about your customers' needs and your competitors' updates.

Consider the customers' perspectives. Pay attention to the choices they make and their response to your organization's services. Feedback from your customers is as valuable as feedback from people in your organization.

Check your course. Systematically gather feedback information from your team and direct reports to ensure the organization is headed in the desired direction.

Use information wisely. Develop systems and filters to distill information down to what is essential for setting the organization's strategic direction.

Seek alignment. Consider how systems, culture, and organizational structure match up with your strategic planning.

Involve others. If you engage others in imagining your organization's future, they are more likely to own and follow the resulting strategy. Listen and learn from others to broaden your view and deepen your understanding of possible future circumstances. What do they anticipate as being their biggest leadership and talent needs? How might those needs be addressed?

Developmental Opportunities

- Craft alternative scenarios for strategic business moves your organization could make in the near future.
- Work on a strategic plan for a community or professional organization.
- Work on a strategic plan for your unit.
- Develop a five-year business scenario for your unit.
- Study and report on the impact of emerging technologies on your work.
- Take a temporary assignment in new product development.

Activity Center

Review and download these activities you can use for your development or with your team from this book's resource page at www.ccl.org/compassbook.

> Strategic Planning and Implementation: Develop Strategic-Plan Awareness
> Strategic Planning and Implementation: Dust Off Your Strategy
> Strategic Planning and Implementation: How's Your Execution?

Related Competencies

Boundary Spanning
Business Development
Strategic Alignment
Systems Thinking
Vision

Resources

Adair, J. E. (2010). *Strategic leadership: How to think and plan strategically and provide direction.* Philadelphia, PA: Kogan Page.

Ernst, C., & Chrobot-Mason, D. (2010). *Boundary spanning leadership: Six practices for solving problems, driving innovation, and transforming organizations.* New York, NY: McGraw-Hill.

Hughes, R. L., Beatty, K. C., & Dinwoodie, D. (2014). *Becoming a strategic leader: Your role in your organization's enduring success* (2nd ed.). San Francisco, CA: Jossey-Bass.

Krogerus, M., & Tschäppeler, R. (2012). *The decision book: Fifty models for strategic thinking.* (J. Piening, Trans.). New York, NY: W.W. Norton.

Leslie, J. (2009). *The leadership gap.* (White paper). Center for Creative Leadership. Retrieved from https://www.ccl.org/articles/white-papers/the -leadership-gap/

Levinson, J. C., & Khan, S. (2014). *Guerrilla marketing and joint ventures: Million dollar partnering strategies for growing any business in any economy.* New York, NY: Morgan James Publishing.

Nevin, M. (2016). *The strategic alliance handbook: A practitioner's guide to business-to-business collaborations.* New York, NY: Routledge.

Pasmore, B. (2015). *Leading continuous change: Navigating churn in the real world.* Oakland, CA: Berrett-Koehler.

Steinhilber, S. (2008). *Strategic alliances: Three ways to make them work.* Boston, MA: Harvard Business Press.

Vick, K. (2015). Angela Merkel: Person of the year. *Time Magazine.* Retrieved from http://time.com/time-person-of-the-year-2015-angela-merkel/

44

Systems Thinking

Focus on the needs of the entire organization or division.

The proverb "You can't see the forest for the trees" captures the difficulty of systems thinking. Organizations are complex, and many leaders fall into the trap of becoming absorbed in the minutia of day-to-day to the exclusion of the bigger picture. Systems thinking—or lack of it—will profoundly affect your career. In moving from individual contributor to first-time manager, and from there higher in the organization, you come to understand and to act on behalf of an increasingly larger number of organizational functions. As the complexity of organizational challenges increases, the responsibility for solving the problems they pose spreads from the top of the organization to different levels. Even if you are early in your management career, you will call upon systems thinking to make decisions and to move projects forward. Take a look inside Netflix to see systems thinking at work.

Leadership in Action

Netflix is a household name now, a company redefining television for an entire generation. But it started out with a pretty simple idea: DVDs are thin and weigh next to nothing, so they are cheap to send through the mail. It turns out people love getting movies in the mail, and the idea was so popular that CEO Reed Hastings now finds himself in charge of a company worth $23 billion.

Obviously, Netflix does a lot more than mail out discs these days. Its streaming service is synonymous with the very idea of TV on the Internet, and its original studio programs are among the most popular, award-winning shows of recent years. How does Hastings stay on top of such a complicated operation? "You're much stronger being a distributed set of great thinkers," he says.

Instead of focusing his attention on individual initiatives or products offered by Netflix, Hastings pulls back and runs the company with a big-picture scope. For example, he delegates innovation and product development, traditionally ascribed to the CEO, to his fellow leaders and direct reports. Instead of creating rigid, all-encompassing processes to direct every move made within the company, Hastings relies on the good judgment of his employees, and gives himself the final word (Satell, 2014).

Much of what Hastings has created is cultural, built into the operating philosophy of the company. But his decision to keep a bit of distance from individual operations gives him a view of the entire enterprise.

What High Performance Looks Like

Leaders with systems thinking skills

- understand entire situations and the details within them

- take a broad organizational perspective on new ideas or initiatives

- think about what's best for the organization

- consider the impact of their actions, and the actions of their team, on the organization

- establish collaborative relationships and alliances throughout the organization

- understand the political nature of the organization and work appropriately within it

- guide and shape new ideas so they are more likely to succeed in the organization

- know whose support is needed for new initiatives to take hold— who needs to be involved early and who will be affected later

- listen and ask questions with the needs of the organization in mind

- quickly spot organizational opportunities and ramifications when presented with new ideas

- are seen as systematic, pragmatic, collaborative, reflective, broad-minded, critical thinkers, and integrative

What's in Your Way?

If you struggle with thinking and acting from a systems perspective, you can become isolated from other parts of your organization. Working from the outside can negatively affect your peer relationships, and your efforts are weakened by organizational boundaries. You might be communicating a narrow view of the organization and its needs to your direct reports. Review the following list and note the items that you believe block you from developing your capacity for systems thinking:

- ❏ You feel too stressed in meeting your objectives to think about the broader needs of the organization.

- ❏ You don't feel a responsibility to address broader organizational needs.

- ❏ You prefer to play your own role and let more senior leaders make systemic decisions.

- ❏ You have had limited opportunities to move around and gain experience in other areas of the organization.

- ❏ You have narrow functional expertise.

- ❏ You neglect your individual responsibilities and focus too much on the work of other managers and their units.

- ❏ You don't fight for what your team needs.

- ❏ You focus on consensus at the risk of reducing quality outcomes or excellent performance.

- ❏ You overlook important details.

- ❏ You focus on your organization at the expense of your customer.

- ❏ You underestimate or misunderstand the politics of a given situation.

Coach Yourself

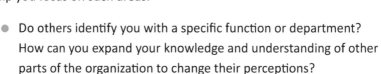

To develop your ability to think and act systemically, create goals in areas that require you to look and work beyond your own team, unit, or function. These questions can help you focus on such areas:

- Do others identify you with a specific function or department? How can you expand your knowledge and understanding of other parts of the organization to change their perceptions?

- If you have worked with someone who was not a systemic thinker, who focused mainly on his or her role or function, consider how that person's actions affected other people and groups.

- How does your work affect other people in your organization? Who are your internal clients—those people and groups who depend on your work?

- Do you understand your business's operational model? Do you know what its various functions contribute to your organization's range of products or services?

- What work experiences, career path, or on-the-job assignments would help you better understand the organization as a whole?

Improve Now

Consider the long term. Think about the future consequences of your decisions on all levels of your organization.

Map your organization. Don't just rely on an organizational chart. Create your own map of the organization's various groups, stakeholders, and their relationships.

Invent a mechanical metaphor. If your organization were a finely tuned machine, what would its parts be and how would they interact? Test this metaphor out on others and see how it aligns with their understanding of the organization.

Create reminders about the overall needs of the organization to keep them fresh in your mind. For example, place a note on your phone or create a screen saver stating your organization's or your group's mission. Relate your current work and role to the mission.

Team learning. Conduct sessions with your team in which you discuss how changes in one part of the organization affect its other parts. How would a flexible system deal with those interdependencies?

Get to know other managers of different functions. Reach out to others to build collaborative relationships. Ask people from other parts of the business to lunch or spend time with them on the job.

Build a network of collaborators. Look for common interests and work with others to achieve them. Allow for give-and-take when collaborating.

Customer first. You know your company's customers. But who are your internal customers? Where would they say you need to improve your processes? Customers judge your work on its results, and your processes are your path to results. Start with the right stuff, end with the right stuff.

Ask experts for their insights. Sometimes the best way to expand your knowledge about an organization is to see it through the eyes of more experienced people. Consider how you might access and use their wisdom to improve your contributions to the organization's mission and goals.

Ask the newbie. Ask the newest person on your team for his or her insights. No one likes to hear "the way we did it on my last job" stories, but often there is a nugget of wisdom that you and your organization can tap into—perhaps not exactly as described, but a version that makes sense in your situation.

Focus on your organization's ultimate vision. Talk to others about the vision and about how you can work together to achieve it.

Focus on the whole organization. If you are not the president or CEO, imagine that you are and you're trying to do what's best for the organization. How does this reinforce or change your view of what you are doing?

Developmental Opportunities

■ Take on a cross-functional assignment, such as setting up different reporting structures.

■ Take a temporary assignment in another part of the business to better understand its priorities and how it fits into the entire system.

■ Work on a process change or strategic plan that crosses functional or unit boundaries.

■ Work with a colleague in another function on a project proposal.

■ Facilitate a quarterly review of your group's actions and assess alignment with strategic goals. Invite your boss to observe.

■ Serve on the board of a nonprofit or community organization.

■ Take a temporary assignment in your organization's human resources office.

Activity Center

Review and download these activities you can use for your development or with your team from this book's resource page at www.ccl.org/compassbook.

Systems Thinking: Input/Output
Systems Thinking: Thinking About Systems

Related Competencies

Boundary Spanning
Differences, Diversity, Inclusion
Organizational Savvy
Relationship Management
Resourcefulness
Strategic Planning and Implementation
Vision

Resources

Adams, B. (2010, Feb. 18). Cross-silo communication: All talk and no action? (Blog). *The Washington Post*. Retrieved from http://views.washingtonpost.com/leadership/guestinsights/2010/02/interagency-communication.html

Beatty, K., & Byington, B. (2010). Developing strategic leadership. In C. D. McCauley, E. Van Velsor, & M. N. Ruderman (Eds.), *The Center for Creative Leadership handbook of leader development* (3rd ed., pp. 313–344). San Francisco, CA: Jossey-Bass.

Ernst, C., & Chrobot-Mason, D. (2010). *Boundary spanning leadership: Six practices for solving problems, driving innovation, and transforming organizations.* New York, NY: McGraw-Hill.

Hughes, R. L., Beatty, K. C., & Dinwoodie, D. (2014). *Becoming a strategic leader: Your role in your organization's enduring success* (2nd ed.). San Francisco, CA: Jossey-Bass.

Kahneman, D. (2013). *Thinking, fast and slow*. New York, NY: Farrar, Straus and Giroux.

Kallet, M. (2014). *Think smarter: Critical thinking to improve problem-solving and decision-making skills.* Hoboken, NJ: Wiley.

Satell, G. (2014, Sept. 5). A look back at why Blockbuster really failed and why it didn't have to. *Forbes*.

Senge, P. (2006). *The fifth discipline: The art and practice of the learning organization.* New York, NY: Doubleday.

Van Velsor, E. (2013). *Broadening your organizational perspective.* Greensboro, NC: Center for Creative Leadership.

45

Talent Recruitment and Retention

Find, recruit, and retain talented people for the organization.

Much of your organization's competitive advantage depends on its teams of talented people. To make sure that's the case, you use a systematic and focused resolve to identify the best candidates, recruit them to the organization, develop them into high performers, and retain them over time. It's an ongoing, dynamic effort. As the competitive landscape shifts and your organization's strategy evolves, so too will your definition of the talent your organization needs. Leaders who excel at acquiring and retaining talent often develop reputations that make their organizations more attractive to talented people. Doris Kearns Goodwin's political history of US president Abraham Lincoln gives us a look at a leader absolutely set on recruiting and building talent to meet the drastic challenges to the United States at the outset of its Civil War.

Leadership in Action

The 1860 US presidential nominating process was tempestuous, to put it mildly. But at the end, Abraham Lincoln emerged the winner. Lincoln was intent on surrounding himself with talented people who made up for his own shortcomings. And so he appointed to his Cabinet his three political opponents from the 1860 Republican contest for the presidential nomination.

No doubt Lincoln expected some rough terrain given the ambitions of these three men and their disdain for his winning the presidency. Goodwin attributes Lincoln's success in managing their talents to his ability to listen to each of them and to consider what each contributed, without falling prey to the political and personal bickering that defined their connections to one another. Each brought a different perspective and different purposes to the work of Lincoln's wartime Cabinet (Goodwin, 2005). Lincoln's story reminds us that building talent isn't just finding the right, supremely skilled people and "getting them on the bus," but getting them to ride together toward a common destination. No matter your own capabilities, your organization can't sustain itself without a community of highly capable, engaged people.

What High Performance Looks Like

Leaders who can recruit and retain the talented workers their organizations need

- recognize raw talent and potential in others
- identify the right development needs to focus others' improvement
- show a genuine interest in the career goals and development of direct reports
- talk with employees about what they value and what motivates them
- are good judges of people
- are attentive
- encourage others
- are interested in other people
- are accessible
- work with direct reports to create development plans
- believe that developing people is important to the performance of the organization or team
- know the special skills or qualities the team or organization needs
- talk with employees with high potential about what the organization can do to help them get better or advance

What's in Your Way?

Difficulties with attracting, developing, and keeping top talent can make achieving your day-to-day and long-term goals difficult. Review the following list and note the items that you believe block you from developing skill in recruiting and retaining talented people for your team or organization.

- ❏ You focus on your own interests.

- ❏ You succeed by competing with people rather than helping them.

- ❏ You feel threatened by talented people.

- ❏ You have a reputation for being difficult to work with.

- ❏ You focus on immediate objectives rather than long-term results.

- ❏ You focus on talented people to the detriment of people with untapped potential in need of development.

- ❏ You hire for talent that is needed now rather than what is needed for the future.

- ❏ You lose patience with the process of developing others.

- ❏ You treat everyone the same rather than tailoring your approach to each person's unique development needs.

Coach Yourself

To develop your ability to acquire and retain talented people, create goals in areas that put you into contact with your organization's human resources function to understand current processes, require you to work across boundaries to give you a broader perspective on the talent currently in the organization, and put you into contact with organizational strategy makers. These questions can help define such areas of focus:

- ● What specific strategic issues could your organization address with new talent?

- As you look into the future, what new skills will your team need to meet its goals?

- Who was the last person you identified as talented and a good fit for your team or organization? What was your process and were you successful in bringing that person in? Why or why not?

- What are the career aspirations of your direct reports? What are their development needs? Their unique skills or knowledge?

- What activities promote the kind of development you're looking for?

- How do you think other people learn best?

Improve Now

Find your way. Think about what energizes you in terms of developing others. Play on that energy to increase the scope of your acquiring talented people.

Share yourself. Decide on the special talent you possess that you can impart to up-and-coming employees for the benefit of the organization.

Talk to people considered to be good developers of people. You have preferred ways for developing others. So do your colleagues. Talk to them about their process, what they do to help their people develop, and what benefit it has been for them and their employees. Take what makes sense to use in your situation and merge it with your own approach.

Selection role play. Role play with your manager or coach an interview for a key position that you have open. Ask for feedback and identify how you can build these skills to be a better interviewer.

Set the stage. Tell prospective employees about other people who have come into the organization and successfully advanced in their career. Help the people you're recruiting to imagine themselves as characters in a similar success story.

Explore and listen. Ask employees about their ambitions and perceptions of their development needs. Solicit their ideas about the best ways for them to learn and grow. Talk less and listen more.

Involve others in finding and keeping talent. Talk with your peers and boss about their perception of the talent the organization needs. Find out who they identify as high potential. Use that information to inform how you develop the talent your organization needs for the future.

Hold people accountable for development. You can bring in fresh talent, and you can work to retain talented employees. You can even work with them to further develop their talents. But make sure they understand that developing new capabilities is their responsibility and a requirement for promotion.

Explore organizational resources for seeking and developing talented employees. Make yourself familiar with the recruitment and development programs that your organization uses to keep its talent pipeline flowing. Consider how your people can benefit from these resources.

Develop people with carefully selected assignments. When you assign work to your direct reports, make each assignment somewhat more challenging or somehow different from the other work they do so that they stretch their abilities. What they do, how they do it, and what they learn from the experience is more important and more effective than whatever wisdom you can pass on to them.

Developmental Opportunities

- Serve on a hiring committee.
- Hire and develop an employee who shows promise but doesn't have the needed experience for the job.
- Work to retain a valued employee who is thinking about leaving the organization.
- Take a temporary assignment with your organization's human resources office.
- Take on the job of recruiting for a position and track how the hiring process plays out. Discuss what you're learning with your manager.
- Volunteer as a Big Brother or Big Sister to learn how to measure people's potential but yet unrealized talents.

Activity Center

Review and download these activities you can use for your development or with your team from this book's resource page at www.ccl.org/compassbook.

Talent Recruitment and Retention: Inspire Commitment

Talent Recruitment and Retention: Investing in Retention

Talent Recruitment and Retention: Select for Leadership

Related Competencies

Coach and Develop Others

Engagement

Influence

Leading with Purpose

Strategic Alignment

Resources

Axelrod, W., & Coyle, J. (2011). *Make talent your business: How exceptional managers develop people while getting results.* San Francisco, CA: Berrett-Koehler.

Byham, W. C., Smith, A. B., & Paese, M. J. (2002). *Grow your own leaders: How to identify, develop, and retain leadership talent.* Upper Saddle River, NJ: Prentice Hall PTR.

Charan, R., Drotter, S. J., & Noel, J. L. (2011). *The leadership pipeline: How to build the leadership powered company* (2nd ed.). San Francisco, CA: Jossey-Bass.

Goodwin, D. K. (2005). *Team of rivals: The political genius of Abraham Lincoln.* New York, NY: Simon & Schuster.

Hampel, B., & Bruce, A. (2014). *The talent assessment and development pocket tool kit: How to get the most out of your best people.* New York, NY: McGraw-Hill Education.

Klann, G. (2011). *Building your team's morale, pride, and spirit.* Greensboro, NC: Center for Creative Leadership.

McCauley, C. D. (2006). *Developmental assignments: Creating learning experiences without changing jobs.* Greensboro, NC: Center for Creative Leadership.

McCauley, C. D., DeRue, D. S., Yost, P. R., & Taylor, S. (Eds.). (2014). *Experience-driven leader development: Models, tools, best practices, and advice for on-the-job development*. San Francisco, CA: Wiley.

McCauley, C. D., & McCall, M. W., Jr. (2014). *Using experience to develop leadership talent: How organizations leverage on-the-job development*. San Francisco, CA: Jossey-Bass.

Rush, S. (Ed.) (2012). *The leadership in action series: On selecting, developing, and managing talent*. Greensboro, NC: Center for Creative Leadership.

Smith, R., & Campbell, M. (2011). *Talent conversations: What they are, why they're crucial, and how to do them right*. Greensboro, NC: Center for Creative Leadership.

Ting, S., & Scisco, P. (Eds.). (2006). *The CCL handbook of coaching: A guide for the leader coach*. San Francisco, CA: Jossey-Bass.

46

Team Leadership

Unite and engage a group of people to pursue a common goal.

No one works alone. Not even leaders. Especially not leaders. And so leaders learn how to produce results through others. No easy task. Managing teamwork is complicated, which may explain why so few teams meet their organizations' expectations. Elevate your ability to lead teams and gain a reputation for pulling people together around a common goal. You are a consensus maker, and you get the best from the people you lead. Trace that to your developing the ability to inspire common goals and strategies, ease positive interpersonal communication, work across differences and geographical space, resolve conflicts, and ultimately transform a group of individual employees into a team committed to group and organizational goals. Simply put, assemble highly efficient teams and get more done. Watch how Christiana Figueres handles her monumental team challenge.

Leadership in Action

Maybe it's impossible to organize the efforts of 195 countries without a little bureaucracy and a few alphabet-soup style acronyms. Every country on Earth has ratified the United Nations Framework Convention on Climate Change (UNFCCC), which obligates them to send delegates  to the annual Conference of the Parties (COP), which is a meeting that contains another meeting: the Meeting of the Parties (MOP). It falls to Christiana Figueres of Costa Rica to manage these delegates and attempt the monumental task of steering global efforts through them. The goal: to prevent total ecological collapse resulting from humans' effects on the environment.

Her job "may possess the very highest ratio of responsibility (preventing global collapse) to authority (practically none)." Nonetheless, she takes a positive attitude toward her work. As an anthropologist, she has more than a few keen-eyed observations about people. "I have not met a single human being who's motivated by bad news," she says. "Not a single human being." As a result, she takes an optimistic approach, spotlighting successes while treating failures as learning opportunities (Kolbert, 2015).

What High Performance Looks Like

Leaders adept at leading teams

- promote camaraderie among team members
- work with the team to establish a clear mission and goals
- engage everyone on the team
- set the expectation that everyone will come together to tackle a challenge
- facilitate team efforts and learning
- hold team members accountable
- are good coaches
- are seen as positive, affirming, inspiring, challenging, and fair
- size up strengths of individual team members and look for ways to leverage those strengths
- give people a sense of their individual purpose
- provide and seek feedback and guidance

What's in Your Way?

Leaders who have difficulty building teams can fail to deliver the results they have promised. Their team members may feel undervalued, leading to dysfunction and ultimately departures from the team. Review the following list and note the items that you believe block you from developing the skills of a great team leader.

- ❏ You don't have a compelling vision for your team.
- ❏ You focus more on tasks than people.
- ❏ You're afraid to speak up when you disagree with the team.
- ❏ You don't trust the people who work for you.

- ❏ Your team members don't trust each other.

- ❏ Team members are separated geographically.

- ❏ Your company rewards individual achievement over team achievement.

- ❏ You neglect your individual work responsibilities, focusing too much on managing other resources.

- ❏ You spend time and resources building a team when the work could be done by just one or two talented people.

- ❏ You focus on superficial team building, neglecting the fundamental conflicts affecting the team.

- ❏ You put too much emphasis on team members getting along and not enough emphasis on meeting team objectives or providing value to the organization.

- ❏ You feel you need to take control to deliver on an aggressive schedule.

- ❏ You spend too much time getting consensus and fail to exercise strong decision-making skill when it's needed.

Coach Yourself

To develop your ability to lead a team, create goals that put you in a position to lead a work group or large project requiring teamwork. These questions can help you focus on such areas:

- ● Have you conveyed a compelling vision to your team? Do people know and believe in what you call success?

- ● Have you clarified team norms—the rules about what is acceptable or unacceptable during teamwork?

- ● Are there specific conflicts pulling your team apart? How might you address them?

- ● Do you see the business advantages of collaborating as a team?

- ● What are the barriers to teamwork in your organization?

Improve Now

Set the team's direction—together. Work with your team to develop a vision for the team's work. What is the purpose of this team? What does it stand for? Align the team's work with its vision. The work of the team should be traceable to its vision.

Check the course. Systematically gather feedback to ensure the team is on track toward meeting its goals.

Identify important stakeholders. Help your team to understand the necessity of building and maintaining solid relationships with people affected by its work, such as other groups within your organization, groups outside your organization, partners, customers, and so forth.

Draw clear lines of authority. Explain to the team how you intend to share or retain authority. Exercise the control you need while team members gravitate to work they can control.

Get to know your team members. Connect with each of them one-on-one to learn more about their special skills, connections, perspectives, and approaches to their work. Find out what they know and how you can help them have a greater impact on the team's work.

Create consensus. Early during team formation, establish a concrete goal, define member responsibilities, and decide on group norms. This will ensure consistency and prevent conflicts before they start.

Celebrate and play. Find reasons to celebrate: birthdays, awards, recognition. Make work fun and rewarding.

Create a liberating team structure. Clarify members' roles and responsibilities, but ensure that they have room to work freely within these roles. Balance between maintaining order and giving each member a sense of ownership and voice.

Secure organizational support. Make special efforts to ensure that your organization provides your team with adequate resources, organizational sponsorship, recognition of team member responsibility, team authority, feedback on team performance, and a team-oriented reward system.

Stay attuned to your environment. Your team is vulnerable to outside influences, demands, and changes. Being aware and responsive to these external forces will ensure your team's long-term performance.

Developmental Opportunities

- Lead a multinational or multicultural team.

- Lead a cross-functional team.

- Lead a virtual team.

- Lead a short-term, task-focused team.

- Lead a long-term project team.

- Lead a team of volunteers.

- Work with a professional team builder who can recommend surveys, activities, events, or processes that can build your team.

Activity Center

Review and download these activities you can use for your development or with your team from this book's resource page at www.ccl.org/compassbook.

Team Leadership: A Winning Team

Team Leadership: Rate Your Leadership

Team Leadership: Teamwork Is Fun, Too

Related Competencies

Coach and Develop Others

Credibility and Integrity

Global Team Management

Leading with Purpose

Talent Recruitment and Retention

Working through Others

Resources

Harvey, F. (2016, July 7). Christiana Figueres nominated for post of UN secretary general. *The Guardian*. Retrieved from https://www.theguardian.com/environment/2016/jul/07/christiana-figueres-nominated-for-post-of-un-secretary-general

Kanaga, K., & Browning, H. (2003). *Maintaining team performance*. Greensboro, NC: Center for Creative Leadership.

Kanaga, K., & Kossler, M.E. (2001). *How to form a team: Five keys to high performance*. Greensboro, NC: Center for Creative Leadership.

Kanaga, K., & Prestridge, S. (2002). *How to launch a team: Start right for success*. Greensboro, NC: Center for Creative Leadership.

Klann, G. (2004). *Building your team's morale, pride, and spirit*. Greensboro, NC: Center for Creative Leadership.

Kolbert, E. (2015, Aug. 24). The weight of the world. *The New Yorker*. Retrieved from http://www.newyorker.com/magazine/2015/08/24/the-weight-of-the-world

Kossler, M. E., & Kanaga, K. (2001). *Do you really need a team?* Greensboro, NC: Center for Creative Leadership.

Lindoerfer, D. (2008). *Raising sensitive issues in a team*. Greensboro, NC: Center for Creative Leadership.

Runde, C. E., & Flanagan, T. A. (2008). *Building conflict competent teams*. San Francisco, CA: Jossey-Bass.

Sinek, S. (2014). *Leaders eat last: Why some teams pull together and others don't*. New York, NY: Penguin.

47

Time Management

Set priorities, focus on important tasks, and make time your ally in the fight for results.

There's no getting around it. Phone and email interruptions are a regular part of your day. Criswell and Martin's 2007 CCL study of 250 senior leaders reported that 52 percent of them said they are interrupted about once every 30 minutes. Another 36 percent said they are interrupted at least once every hour. Interruptions come in all shapes and sizes: phone calls, email, coworkers, direct reports, and a barrage of information that flows across your desk morning and night. In CCL's study, 65 percent of managers reported that interruptions are sometimes a problem and 21 percent considered interruptions a frequent problem.

You're set on leading your team and your projects toward specific goals with set timelines, and interruptions don't help. You're almost compelled to sift through all the information and requests that come your way. You're expected to handle multiple priorities and tasks. But you can do this. Learn how to separate the unimportant from the important. From there, you can find the focus and discipline to keep your days on track and your team and organization moving forward. If you open the door to Jack Dorsey's office, you might consider yourself among the fortunate.

Leadership in Action

Running one company is hard enough, but for Jack Dorsey, the demands on his time are doubled. As the CEO of both Square and Twitter, he has to practice time management on a whole different level in order to guide his teams and meet his goals and obligations. Because he  literally works at both companies simultaneously, he had to come up with a different system of time management that would allow him to tend to Square without taking a day off from working at Twitter, and vice versa.

In explaining his system, Dorsey points out the obvious first, saying, "The only way to do this is to be very disciplined and very practiced." To divide his labor efficiently, Dorsey gives each day of the week a "theme," which allows him to focus his efforts on a particular type of task without letting other tasks distract him. For example, on Monday, Dorsey focuses on product development. He can concentrate his team meetings for both companies on that task, which makes it easier to separate the goals of Square and Twitter without getting them confused. Furthermore, he can push back tasks from other "themes," such as marketing, confident that those tasks will get their day later in the week.

This is perhaps the most important aspect of Dorsey's method: the themed days give him permission to ignore large sectors of his companies without fretting. Because he has a whole day of the week devoted to marketing, he doesn't need to worry about Twitter's marketing distracting him from Square's product development. By successfully practicing this method, Dorsey proves that good time management can be just as much about what you are not doing at any given moment as what you are doing (McGregor, 2015; Patkar, 2014).

What High Performance Looks Like

Leaders with good time-management techniques

- set priorities and focus on what's most important

- deal appropriately with interruptions, knowing when to allow them and when to screen them out

- don't spread themselves too thin

- are excellent administrators

- focus on choices, not time

- turn away work not on their priority list

- set short- and long-term goals

- take care of routine work during periods of low energy

- take breaks from work

- break big tasks into smaller tasks

- are seen as excellent delegators and able to direct others

What's in Your Way?

When you struggle to manage your time, projects can fall behind schedule and disrupt your team's and your organization's ability to achieve the results they want. CCL's research identifies the failure to reach business objectives as a career derailer. If time flies past you, you may find yourself flying at the same level year after year in your organization. You might even fly out of your organization—either by choice or because your organization lets you go. Days filled with calls, email, staff requests, and other distractions can wreck any time-management system and distract you from concentrating on what you believe are your priorities. Review the list that follows and note the items that you believe block you from developing a sound time-management habit.

❏ You think that every task and request is urgent and important.

❏ You struggle to balance short-term objectives with long-term goals.

❏ You have a hard time saying No, even when you're already at your limit.

❏ You haven't analyzed how you use your time during the day.

❏ You work on several tasks at once (multitasking is not efficient—it just feels that way).

❏ You don't set a realistic daily objective.

❏ People become frustrated trying to get on your schedule when you block out time on your calendar for your most important work.

❏ You worry that people might think that you don't consider their time important if you don't interrupt your day to take care of their requests.

❏ You become obsessed with managing your time and give the impression you're inflexible.

❏ You continue to move your objectives to make up for lost time rather than sticking to your plan and dealing only with the most important, urgent needs.

❏ You waste time trying to find the perfect organization tool rather than modifying whatever tool or technique you have at hand.

Coach Yourself

To develop your time-management skills, create goals in the areas of personal scheduling, sticking to deadlines, prioritizing tasks, focusing on the important tasks, and delegating. These questions can help you define such focus areas:

● What stresses you at work, at home, and in your social life? How might you alleviate those stressors?

- What do you value most, and how do your values compare with your priorities?

- What is your preference for separating, dividing, or merging work with the other parts of your life?

- How accurate are you in estimating the time it takes to complete a task? How can you become more accurate?

- What kinds of work can you refuse or delegate to others?

- How do you determine the urgency and importance of a task?

- How might you resist the temptation to sidetrack yourself in email or web browsing?

Improve Now

Set the clock. Begin each day with your task list, not with your email. Choose the most urgent and important tasks from your list and set a goal to complete them by a certain date. Be realistic.

Shut your door. You may value an open-door leadership style, but choose specific times to close your door to signal that you should not be interrupted.

Prioritize your calendar. Move important tasks to your calendar and block out time to complete them. Consider color-coding your appointments—red for clients and blue for staff, for example. Mark when you're unavailable for meetings and other events. Leave some gaps in your calendar to account for unforeseen situations.

Choose when to deal with email. Choose specific periods during the day when you will review and respond to email. For example, perhaps at 9 in the morning, right after lunch, and just before the end of the day. Add that schedule to your email signature so that people know when they can expect you to respond.

Turn off your cell phone. Or set it to ring only if someone important to you calls. That might be your boss or someone else at a higher level in the organization, and it might be your spouse and your children.

Come in early. Too often today, workers at all levels feel tethered to their work 24/7/365. But you can come in a little early to set up your day and still avoid being in constant contact with the office (which can burn you out). If on the other hand your preference is to work late or work on weekends, then use that preference to reduce the tasks that await you at the office.

Map your day. Over the course of a week, keep a diary of how you spend your time each day, at work and away. To see how you can improve your time-management skills, you first have to know how much time you have to manage.

Experiment with setting priorities. Try a few methods for prioritizing and settle on the one that best suits you. People manage their time all kinds of ways. They might sort tasks between the urgent and important and the not urgent, not important, a method formalized by Stephen Covey. Or you could separate work by deadline, ease of completion, or in some other way.

Change it up. Change how you hold meetings. For example, try standing meetings. Or don't allow meetings without a clear agenda.

Manage your energy. After you map how you spend your time, compare that to the energy levels you feel over the course of the day. If you start out with high energy, tackle the more complicated work. When you are at low energy, do small tasks like responding to email.

Look closely at what's important to you. In addition to comparing your energy levels to your activity map, compare how you spend your time with your personal values and your organization's values. If you are spending a lot of time on things that you don't value, it's probably better that you delegate those things to others. Come to think of it, delegating itself is a useful time-management practice anytime.

Declutter. Organize your workspace to make it more efficient.

Arrange to work remotely. If your company supports it, see what you can do to move some of your work outside the office during regular hours. That will give you some uninterrupted time you can use to press projects forward, write an important report, and work on long-term plans.

Shift your more difficult tasks to the start of the day. If you wait to do the jobs that are hardest for you, it becomes easy to push it off until the next day. And even easier to push it again the next day.

Developmental Opportunities

- Coach a new project manager.

- Work with an accountability partner to learn, practice, and sustain time-management tactics.

- Take a project in chaos and get it back on track.

- Work with your team to create a process for tracking progress toward goals.

Activity Center

Review and download these activities you can use for your development or with your team from this book's resource page at www.ccl.org/compassbook.

Time Management: Meeting Management Coaching

Time Management: Time Management Tips

Related Competencies

Credibility and Integrity

Delegating

Leading with Purpose

Problem Solving

Urgency

Working through Others

Resources

Allen, D. (2015). *Getting things done: The art of stress-free productivity* (Rev. ed.). New York, NY: Penguin.

Cartwright, T. (2007). *Setting priorities: Personal values, organizational results*. Greensboro, NC: Center for Creative Leadership.

Covey, S. R. (2013). *The 7 habits of highly effective people: Powerful lessons in personal change*. New York, NY: Simon & Schuster.

Criswell, C. (2008). Do you have a minute? Seven strategies for limiting office interruptions. *The Journal for Quality & Participation* (31)1. Retrieved from http://asq.org/quality-participation/2008/04/human-resources/do-you-have-a-minute-seven-strategies-for-limiting-office-interruptions.html

Criswell, C., & Martin, A. (2007). *10 trends: A study of senior executives' views on the future.* (White paper). Center for Creative Leadership. Retrieved from https://www.ccl.org/articles/white-papers/10-trends-a-study-of-senior-executives-views-on-the-future/

Deal, J. J. (2013, Aug.). Always on, never done? Don't blame the smartphone. (White paper). Center for Creative Leadership. Retrieved from https://www.ccl.org/articles/white-papers/always-on-never-done/

Gurvis, J. (n.d.). *Are balanced leaders better performers?* (Podcast). Center for Creative Leadership. Retrieved from https://www.ccl.org/multimedia/podcast/are-balanced-leaders-better-performers/

Gurvis, J. (n.d.). Shifting to find equilibrium. (Podcast). Center for Creative Leadership. Retrieved from https://www.ccl.org/multimedia/podcast/shifting-to-find-equilibrium/

Gurvis, J., & Patterson, G. (2004). *Finding your balance.* Greensboro, NC: Center for Creative Leadership.

Hannum, K. M., Kossek, E. E., & Ruderman, M. N. (2011). *WorkLife Indicator: Increasing your effectiveness on and off the job.* (Facilitator's guide). Greensboro, NC: Center for Creative Leadership.

Kossek, E., Ruderman, M., Braddy, P., & Hannum, K. (2012). Work-nonwork boundary management profiles: A person-centered approach. *Journal of Vocational Behavior*, 81, 112–128.

McGregor, J. (2015, Jan. 2). How 10 CEOs work smarter, manage better and get things done faster. *The Washington Post*.

Patkar, M. (2014, Oct. 10). Give each workday a theme for productive momentum. *LifeHacker*. Retrieved from http://lifehacker.com/give-each-workday-a-theme-for-productive-momentum-1644203340

Ryan, J. R. (2014, Oct. 7). 5 moves that broke my email addiction. (Blog post). *LinkedIn*. Retrieved from https://www.linkedin.com/pulse/20141007130915-28893870-5-moves-that-broke-my-email-addiction?trk=mp-reader-card

Tracy, B. (2007). *Eat that frog! 21 great ways to stop procrastinating and get more done in less time* (2nd ed.). San Francisco, CA: Berrett-Koehler.

48

Tolerating Ambiguity

Thrive in unclear situations.

Ambiguous situations test a leader's mettle. Insufficient data, lack of direction, few rules or structure—you can treat the situation as a blank canvas, an opportunity to create, or you can falter in an uncomfortable, sometimes frightening, uncertainty. At one time, ambiguity most frequently affected leaders at the top of the organization. But in today's business environment, ambiguity is pervasive and affects leaders at all organizational levels. With the right development, you can be the leader who seizes the creative moment rather than freezes with indecision. Learn to handle ambiguity comfortably and confidently and learn to anticipate situations rather than simply react to or retreat from them. Make peace with ambiguity and gain greater control over how you handle key decisions in daily situations and over your career. Look back on dramatic events at a major US company to see how one leader engaged with ambiguity and pressed for clarity—saving one of the company's premier brands.

Leadership in Action

James Burke, chairman at Johnson & Johnson, was in a light-hearted personal meeting about physical fitness when he heard for the first time about the poisonings. At least three people had died by ingesting cyanide in Tylenol capsules. One can only imagine his reaction in that moment: aside from the obvious horror at the news, Burke now found himself in charge of a brand name in crisis, associated nationwide with sudden death.

The Tylenol brand is really the entire product. The active ingredient is acetaminophen, a generic chemical that any company has the right to produce. The public's perception of Tylenol had put it at the top of the pain-relief industry. Burke had two major jobs: investigate the poisonings to clear the company name, and do everything possible to rescue the brand.

There was so much nobody knew. Who was the perpetrator? What was the origin of the poison? At what point along the distribution chain did the poison enter the medicine? How many more bottles were tainted? One by one, Burke tackled the questions he could answer. Investigations of batch numbers, cross-referenced with the locations at which the deaths took place, made it obvious that the poisonings were not the result of a manufacturing accident, but were in fact murders committed outside the company. That left Burke with the job of cleaning up the brand name. By remaining open and honest with the press, he was able to disseminate information about the poisonings and begin the work of quelling panic in consumers.

The crime itself remains unsolved. But the poisoning crisis did not erase the Tylenol brand. Burke weathered the storm despite all he did not and could not know, and Tylenol remains a leader in its product category (Moore, 2012; Shulte 2009; Thomas 2012).

What High Performance Looks Like

Leaders who tolerate ambiguity

- thrive when there is little direction or structure
- communicate confidence and steadiness during difficult times
- forge ahead in the absence of complete data or clear objectives
- identify what they can control in chaotic or confusing situations and focus attention there
- imagine possibilities, sensing opportunity when others feel overwhelmed or hopeless
- bring clarity to murky situations
- call upon their store of experience and useful mental models to make sense of ambiguous situations
- enjoy not knowing how things will turn out
- choose paths with an unknown destination
- can learn and adjust their approach through trial and error
- acknowledge risks and accept the possibility of failure
- seek others' thoughts and experiences to better understand complex or open-ended situations
- are seen as intuitive, action-oriented, experimenters, resilient, confident, and courageous

What's in Your Way?

Many people struggle to respond productively in the face of ambiguity. That's understandable. We prefer stability to chaos. Still, performing well in ambiguous circumstances separates those people who can be counted on to lead in disruptive, confusing times from people

403

who can't. Those who can't be counted on in those times may lose the opportunity to lead. Review the following list and note the items that you believe block you from developing your comfort and focus during ambiguous times.

- ❏ You need structure, clarity, and direction to perform well.
- ❏ You expect senior leaders to provide clarity and direction.
- ❏ You haven't developed mental models that help you apply structure or process to uncertain situations.
- ❏ You're not used to making decisions without complete information.
- ❏ You're afraid to fail.
- ❏ Your organization penalizes mistakes.
- ❏ You overestimate your ability to operate in ambiguous situations.
- ❏ You're afraid to make the wrong decision based on limited data.
- ❏ You don't seek help from others.
- ❏ Other people seem to lack confidence in the direction you've set.

Coach Yourself

To develop your tolerance for ambiguity, create goals in areas that pose complicated problems that don't offer easy answers or pat responses. These questions can help you determine such focus areas.

- Can you recall a situation in which there appeared to be few rules and little direction? How did you feel and react? What was the outcome?

- Can you recall a situation in which you felt overwhelmed by complex or contradictory information and needed to make a decision? How did you feel and react? What was the outcome?

- Think of someone you know who comfortably navigates ambiguity. What behaviors do he or she engage in?

- What about ambiguity causes you the most discomfort? How might you resolve that discomfort in a productive manner?

- If you were to take decisive action in an ambiguous situation, what is the worst that might happen? How might you deal with the consequences?

Improve Now

Start and adapt. When you encounter situations that are confusing or overwhelming, sometimes it helps to jump in and start responding. Try small-scale experiments that will help you to develop clarity about the situation and confidence in dealing with it.

Focus on what is in your control. There may be many aspects of a situation that you can't control or don't fully understand. Focusing your attention on these areas can sometimes create stress and keep you from taking action. Focus instead on what you can do—just get started.

Engage other people. Overwhelming or ambiguous situations often require the combined knowledge and talent of a group. Don't try to solve ambiguous challenges alone. And don't try to address the entire situation. Give yourself permission to take it slowly for a short period of time as you sort things out.

Focus on learning. Realize that you are on a learning curve and take every opportunity to reflect on what new things you are learning.

Stay attuned to stress. Learn techniques to calm down and manage stress so that you can tackle ambiguous situations more productively.

Watch how others deal with ambiguity. Some people have more tolerance for ambiguity than others. Note the tactics they use to work out a clear direction for their work. Try some of their methods for yourself to see if they help you make progress and feel more in control of the situation.

Exploit ambiguity. Murky situations can be daunting, even paralyzing, for many people. Take charge by reframing ambiguous circumstances. Instead of allowing the lack of a clear problem or solution to inhibit you, free yourself to define the problem and the solution in some other way that you can deal with from a position of strength.

Put setbacks in perspective. Don't run away from mistakes and failures, but don't dwell on them either. Strive to get beyond the pain and disappointment and refocus on what you can learn from the experience and apply to future circumstances.

Developmental Opportunities

- Participate in the start-up of a new team.

- Take over a project that is in trouble.

- Serve on a task force to solve a major organizational problem.

- Join a project team that is experimenting with new products and services for your organization.

- Lead a team coordinating the introduction of new systems.

- Create a strategic planning group for your department.

- Work with your team to identify what it knows and doesn't know. Take time to discuss everyone's thoughts and feelings related to the things that you don't know you don't know!

Activity Center

Review and download these activities you can use for your development or with your team from this book's resource page at www.ccl.org/compassbook.

Tolerating Ambiguity: A Recipe to Manage Ambiguity
Tolerating Ambiguity: Got a Problem?

Related Competencies

Flexibility

Learning Agility

Resilience

Resourcefulness

Risk Taking

Resources

Adams, M. G. (2016). *Change your questions, change your life: 12 powerful tools for leadership, coaching, and life* (3rd ed.). Oakland, CA: Berrett-Koehler.

Calarco, A., & Gurvis, J. (2006). *Adaptability: Responding effectively to change*. Greensboro, NC: Center for Creative Leadership.

Dalton, M. A. (1998). *Becoming a more versatile learner*. Greensboro, NC: Center for Creative Leadership.

Hallenbeck, G. (2016). *Learning agility: Unlock the lessons of experience*. Greensboro, NC: Center for Creative Leadership.

Holmes, J. (2015). *Nonsense: The power of not knowing.* New York, NY: Crown Publishers.

Johansen, B. (2012). *Leaders make the future: Ten new leadership skills for an uncertain world* (2nd ed.). San Francisco, CA: Berrett-Koehler.

Moore, T. (2012, Oct. 7). The fight to save Tylenol (Fortune, 1982). *Fortune*. Retrieved from http://fortune.com/2012/10/07/the-fight-to-save-tylenol-fortune-1982/

Pasmore, W. A. (2015). *Leading continuous change: Navigating churn in the real world.* Oakland, CA: Berrett-Koehler.

Shulte, B. (2009, Nov. 24). Crisis management: Leading successfully through the storm. *US News & World Report*. Retrieved from http://www.usnews.com/news/best-leaders/articles/2009/11/24/crisis-management-leading-successfully-through-the-storm

Thomas, K. (2012, Oct. 1). James E. Burke, 87, dies; candid ex-chief of Johnson & Johnson. *The New York Times*. Retrieved from http://www.nytimes.com/2012/10/02/business/james-e-burke-ex-johnson-johnson-chief-dies-at-87.html?_r=0

49
Trust

Display confidence in others, rely on others to do what is expected, and remain consistent in what others expect from you.

Trust's power lies in mutually held, supportive relationships. Depending on the circumstances you encounter in your work, lives can literally depend on it (as in law enforcement, for example). Don't take the power of trust for granted. Make a continual investment in your relationships to help it grow, remain strong, and endure. When you do, you create a shared sense of "we're in this together, I've got your back"—and what might present as an insurmountable obstacle morphs into a daunting but engaging challenge. At this point you become a leader who will take on risk and extraordinary effort because you have something solid and reliable to count on—trust—when everything else appears fragile and uncertain. Look inside Rami Rahim's world to see how he creates and keeps trust with thousands of employees.

Leadership in Action

Every year, Glassdoor publishes a list of its highest-rated executives. Unlike other publications, which may classify excellence in terms of stock value, company growth, or revenue, Glassdoor creates its list using its thousands of employee-generated reviews of company culture and leadership. This unique method of judgment confers a special honor, since the Glassdoor model indicates a high level of trust and respect on the part of employees for their leaders. In 2016, Rami Rahim, the CEO of Juniper Networks, was recognized as Glassdoor's highest-rated CEO.

Rahim was the 32nd employee of Juniper Networks, which now employs over 9,000 people. Since being appointed CEO, he has used his familiarity with Juniper's culture to create a solid relationship with his teams. He stresses the importance of trust to his success and the success of the company. "When things are going well, we celebrate," he says. "But when things don't go as planned, we acknowledge it." It's this kind of honesty that opens the channel for the flow of trust between leaders and their teams.

Transparency, accountability, and even a measure of vulnerability are essential for Rahim's vision as a leader. It was his job to show that trust first, before he could expect it from those working for him. His reward for the trust he has placed can be found in the sense of common effort among all those working at Juniper Networks (Lovegren, 2016; McDowell, 2016).

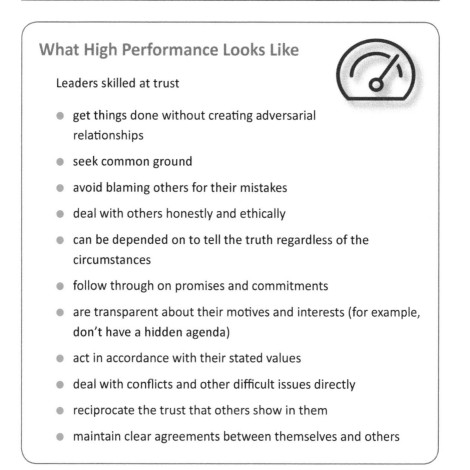

What High Performance Looks Like

Leaders skilled at trust

- get things done without creating adversarial relationships
- seek common ground
- avoid blaming others for their mistakes
- deal with others honestly and ethically
- can be depended on to tell the truth regardless of the circumstances
- follow through on promises and commitments
- are transparent about their motives and interests (for example, don't have a hidden agenda)
- act in accordance with their stated values
- deal with conflicts and other difficult issues directly
- reciprocate the trust that others show in them
- maintain clear agreements between themselves and others

What's in Your Way?

Have you ever said to someone, "I've got trust issues"? Often, that's a lighthearted, self-deprecating way of explaining an unserious social mistake. But if it's more than that, not only do your trust issues put a heavy load on you but they can weigh down your relationships with others. Sometimes, trust is difficult to establish in the first place—as can happen with a company merger. And if trust is broken, you face real limits on what you and others can accomplish together. Although your difficulties with establishing trust might stem from being let down by others, remember that trust is a two-way relationship. Review the following list and note the items that you believe are giving you difficulty in building and maintaining trust.

- ❏ You're secretive.

- ❏ You trust only yourself.

- ❏ You expect too much of others.

- ❏ You have to be in control.

- ❏ You rush into things.

- ❏ You overestimate what you're capable of delivering.

- ❏ You don't clarify mutual expectations.

- ❏ You take trust for granted.

- ❏ Others have violated your trust in them.

- ❏ You don't consistently hold yourself accountable to others.

- ❏ You tend to blame your mistakes or shortcomings on others.

- ❏ You avoid confronting difficulties in your relationships.

- ❏ You're not as forthcoming or honest with others as you could be.

Coach Yourself

To develop trust, create goals in areas that require you to put your confidence in others and vice versa. These questions can help you define such focus areas:

- What triggers distrust in you? What characteristics of others cause you to hesitate to put your trust in them? Why? Are your concerns always justified?

- When have you felt let down by others? Are there commonalities in what others did (or didn't) do? Could you have done anything to avoid the outcome?

- When have others placed significant trust in you? Why did they do so? How did it make you feel? How did you reward their trust?

- When have you felt that other people have withheld their trust from you or were reluctant to grant it? Do you know why? What could you have done to build greater trust?

- When have you missed fulfilling your commitments to others? Why? What happened? What did you do to try to restore trust?

Improve Now

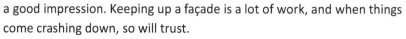

Be yourself. For others to trust you, they need first to find you credible. To some degree, we all want others to like us and think positively of our talents, but be wary of acting like someone you're not for the sake of making a good impression. Keeping up a façade is a lot of work, and when things come crashing down, so will trust.

First impressions. There is never a second chance to make a first impression. Think about how you can make a good first impression. How can you be more positive? Energetic? Motivating? Inspiring? Make note of your ideas and start putting them into practice.

Be honest. Period. When you say what you mean and others can count on knowing where you are coming from, it makes it easy to trust.

Focus on others. Observe your interactions with others over the next week—at work and at home. Note the amount of time that your interaction focuses on them and how much focuses on you. Tip the scale in their favor if it isn't already.

Practice the platinum rule. You know the golden rule: Treat others the way you want to be treated. As a leader, practice the *platinum* rule: Treat others the way they want to be treated. How are the two different? Why is the distinction important? What does practicing the platinum rule mean for your customers? How can you share the platinum rule with the people around you? How can you reinforce it?

Stay positive. No one likes to be around a negative person. Celebrate your work as an important part of your life. Be passionate about what you are doing. Think positively. Say something nice. It makes you easier to trust.

Look up, not down. Expect the best out of everyone. Your attitude will be noticed, and it will help others to think the best of themselves. Help them see the possibilities in themselves, and they will help you see all the possibilities in you as a leader.

Give people hope. Hope is the currency of leadership. Find the best in every situation and identify what people need and want. Help them see that anything is possible.

Be generous. The world is full of givers and takers. Be a giver. Share your wisdom, your resources, and your support. It will come back to you tenfold—and it becomes especially important to presence, trust, and a leadership style that others will want to follow.

Rebuild trust when it's in trouble. Find and emphasize something—anything—that allows the person with whom you're having difficulty with trust to see a link between the two of you. This forms a sense of affiliation and encourages the reestablishment of trustworthy behavior.

Be accessible and open. When you share something about yourself, let people in on the "real" you, and can laugh at yourself, you make it easy for others to trust you. If you act out of line with what you claim to believe, others notice (for example, the "team player" who is always looking out for number one). Such discrepancies can happen, and it's not necessarily intentional. Take time to honestly evaluate your values and how you act on them. Ask yourself if you're being true to those values across different situations.

Be approving and accepting. When you show that you value people and their perspectives—even if they differ from yours—you give them a reason to trust you.

Be dependable and trustworthy. When you do what you say you will do and keep your promises, people know they can count on you and you can be trusted. Write it down. Nothing seals a commitment like putting it in writing. It also, quite literally, spells out what each person in the relationship can expect from one another. Do all you can to avoid confusion and the "but I thought" statements that signal a breach of trust. If you fall short of your commitment, own up to it. Falling short on expectations can damage trust. Ignoring it, excusing it, or (perhaps worst of all) blaming it on others, destroys it.

Don't let things go unsaid. Sometimes trust is broken by the things we say to others, but often it's what's not said (especially at the beginning of a relationship) that causes the problem. If there's an uncomfortable truth that's critical for others to know in order to trust you, get it out in the open early. No truth, no trust.

Talk it up. Meet with customers and share your organization's vision and strategy. Ask for their opinions to build trust that you can depend on in the future.

Don't allow trust to erode. Trust requires ongoing investment to grow and remain strong. Lowering expectations of yourself and others, not reinforcing the basis for your commitments, and simply taking things for granted can all chip away at trust until it reaches its breaking point.

Check your capabilities. Breaches of trust can occur despite the best of intentions. Though you want others to have confidence in you and depend on you, somewhere along the line you may realize you're in over your head. Think before committing to something that might disappoint you and others because the goals turn out to be unrealistic.

Examine your motives. Genuine trust requires a commitment to someone other than yourself. Make sure you take on projects for the right reasons and don't mislead yourself with your own self-interests.

Lead by example. Build trust in your team members by showing that you trust them.

Reward others' trust in you. Reciprocity grows trust. If others take a personal risk and place their trust in you, respond in kind. As the trust flows back and forth between you, stronger bonds begin to form.

Extend trust relationships. Meet with customers, share the organization's vision and strategy, and ask for their ideas. These kinds of interactions can build trust between you that you can depend on in the future.

Developmental Opportunities

- Put yourself in a situation where you and others are responsible for drafting a formal agreement regarding what you are responsible for to each other. Examples might include forming a business contract or a team charter.

- Make an effort to rebuild a relationship and restore trust with someone with whom you've had some difficulties.

- Start with a clean slate and build a trusting relationship with someone new.

- Join with others in working through a situation where the stakes are high and there are lots of challenges to overcome. This will test, and hopefully strengthen, your trust in one another.

- Meet with someone with whom you've had difficulties in the past; ask what you could have done differently. Take good notes, give no excuses, genuinely say thank you, and then review and practice what you heard to learn to be more trustworthy.

Activity Center

Review and download these short activities you can use for your development or with your team on this book's resource page at www.ccl.org/compassbook.

Trust: 4 Ways to Trust

Trust: The Key to Good Communication

Related Competencies

Boundary Spanning

Conflict Resolution

Credibility and Integrity

Difference, Diversity, Inclusion

Interpersonal Savvy

Relationship Management

Resources

Bunker, K. A., & Wakefield, M. (2005). *Leading with authenticity in times of transition.* Greensboro, NC: Center for Creative Leadership.

Bunker, K. A., & Wakefield, M. (2010). *Leading through transitions.* (Workshop materials). San Francisco, CA: Wiley.

Evans, C. (2015). *Leadership trust: Build it, keep it.* Greensboro, NC: Center for Creative Leadership.

Lovegren, S. (2016, June 9). An employee-centric approach: Rami Rahim recognized as a 2016 Glassdoor highest rated CEO. *LinkedIn.* Retrieved from https://www.linkedin.com/pulse/employee-centric-approach-rami-rahim-recognized-2016-highest-susan

McDowell, J. (2016, June 30). Top CEOs know trust is key to employee recruitment and retention. *Recruiter.com.* Retrieved from https://www.recruiter.com/i/top-ceos-know-trust-is-key-to-employee-recruitment-and-retention/

Reina, D. S., & Reina, M. L. (1999). *Trust and betrayal in the workplace: Building effective relationships in your organization.* Oakland, CA: Berrett-Koehler.

Reina, D. S., & Reina, M. L. (2010). *Rebuilding trust in the workplace: Seven steps to renew confidence, commitment, and energy.* Oakland, CA: Berrett-Koehler.

50

Urgency

Use your bias for action to push forward, keep promises, and deliver results.

Action-oriented leaders and the results they produce are critical to any organization's performance. Look around you. How many leaders in your organization exhibit an urgency to achieve organizational results? Make a real difference in your organization's success? Deliver results consistently and on time? But don't promise results and then justify your inability to produce when you're held accountable—that has the potential to derail your career. Develop and keep a sense of urgency about the organization's work to accomplish key objectives and also dramatically affect how others regard your performance as a leader. Consider this story from the aerospace industry, where urgency acts as a force to push a business ever forward.

Leadership in Action

Lockheed Martin was already a globally recognized company, the world's largest defense contractor, when Marillyn Hewson took the helm in 2013. Obviously, as the new CEO, Hewson was expected to deliver new results and grow the firm. But when you're already at the top, how much higher can you really go? The task seems impossible, but Hewson delivered.

She started by trimming the fat: cutting out low-profit commercial services. Then, in a bold move, she purchased the helicopter manufacturer Sikorsky for $9 billion. That unexpected acquisition raised a lot of eyebrows in the aerospace industry—and it created excitement and momentum at Lockheed Martin, which is what Hewson wanted. While attention was on the firm in the wake of the purchase, Hewson teased future products, such as an antiaircraft super-laser and a jet plane three times as fast as the Concorde.

While those tactics were flashy, others were more down-to-earth. Hewson has also engaged in the most reliable method of sales: finding new markets. Since 2013, she's expanded into aircraft sales in India and Southeast Asia, more than doubling the company's market capitalization. Simple supply-and-demand stuff, but on a global scale.

Rather than sit back and enjoy the view from the top of her market, Hewson has delivered incredible results in a very short time frame. It isn't necessary to start from a position of near-maximum capacity to deliver such results, however. Hewson takes opportunities where she finds them, creates new ones where they could potentially exist, and knows when to drop unresponsive efforts in order to consolidate resources. Scale down her efforts from their larger-than-life dimensions and the fundamental good practices are revealed (*Fortune*, n.d.; Guillot, 2016; McNamara & Howard, 2016).

What High Performance Looks Like

Leaders with a developed sense of urgency

- are decisive and don't procrastinate
- take charge when trouble comes
- demonstrate an intense can-do attitude and expect everyone to do what it takes to get the job done
- clearly convey objectives, deadlines, and expectations
- align resources to accomplish key objectives
- track and monitor progress toward results
- focus on results
- are seen as authentic
- energize others
- are resourceful
- collaborate
- adapt to changing circumstances
- are methodical
- move forward in spite of ambiguity, taking on what can be done today
- promote action by encouraging people to get involved and solve problems
- understand and address challenges and obstacles
- demonstrate commitment and strength
- understand what motivates other people to perform at their best
- enjoy solving problems

What's in Your Way?

The failure to meet business objectives—the key outcome to working with urgency—separates good leadership from the rest. Even if you are great with people and loved by your superiors, peers, and direct reports, if you fail to drive results toward business objectives you are in jeopardy of falling off the career ladder. Review the following list and note the items that you believe block you from developing a feeling of urgency toward achieving results for your team and company.

- ❏ You're unsure about your role or how you can contribute to the organization's success.

- ❏ You're afraid to fail.

- ❏ You don't trust your instincts.

- ❏ You struggle to prioritize.

- ❏ You have yet to build relationships, establish credibility, or earn loyalty among your team members and with other people in the organization, especially those in senior management.

- ❏ You're not willing to push forward without full agreement from your staff.

- ❏ You've received feedback that other people see you as selfish or pursuing your own agenda.

- ❏ You're uncomfortable giving people—especially highly skilled ones—the autonomy they need to do their best work.

- ❏ You force your opinion on issues when finesse and a sharper political sense would work better.

- ❏ You underestimate the time or resources to get work done.

Coach Yourself

To develop a sense of urgency that drives results, create goals in areas that require you to coordinate action among other groups and people, call for a vision of the future, challenge you to bolster team member engagement, involve you in making changes that benefit the organization, and so on. These questions can help you define such focus areas:

- When was the last time you struggled to achieve results? What got in the way? How could you have been successful?

- When have you achieved exceptional results? What process did you use? What role did you play?

- How do you approach driving results? To what extent do you drive versus facilitate?

- Do you convey a true sense of urgency? Are you able to maintain a continuous emphasis on achieving results without coming off as pushy or impatient?

- What are your organization's cultural norms in terms of building consensus and moving quickly with decisions? How will you work with or reshape the culture and enable your drive to results?

- Do you trust your intuition when you hit a roadblock and are looking for a solution? Do you need to gain some new experiences to build depth of knowledge and confidence so that you have more potential answers at hand?

Improve Now

Assert yourself. Get directly involved in resolving problems. The best executives empower their employees, and they balance that with their ability to take control over struggling or stuck projects.

Let people know clearly and passionately where you stand. Even though it is necessary to take a genuine interest in where other people stand on issues, it is just as important that a leader let others know where he or she stands and show a passion and commitment for that position.

Make the tough calls. It takes resolve to make difficult decisions, such as laying people off or killing a long-term project that is unlikely to pay off. Those kinds of decisions often run counter to the needs of the people involved. But a leader who can drive results recognizes that those important concerns must be weighed against the broader needs of the organization.

Be flexible. You'll encounter some unexpected twists and turns, so be ready to adjust your plan. Stay creative and focused on achieving the desired results.

Define the desired outcome. Be clear about what success looks like. What will people say about your team's work? Why will its accomplishments be special? What impact will your team's work have?

Set tough but achievable goals. Work with your team to establish and hold to challenging expectations. Form a clear consensus on what is necessary to accomplish its goals.

Build relationships. Constantly pushing people as a way of delivering results isn't sustainable. If you align people around a compelling vision, you'll engage minds and hearts and have greater impact as a leader.

Solve problems collectively. Tap the wisdom of crowds when you encounter roadblocks.

Monitor and track performance. Build simple metrics to assess progress and make them a part of your regular communications.

Developmental Opportunities

- Take over a project that is in trouble.

- Fix or reform an underperforming unit or organization.

- Lead a start-up of a unit, department, or branch in a new region.

- Close a unit, program, or an organization.

- Organize an event with a short time frame, such as an annual charity campaign.

Activity Center

Review and download these activities you can use for your development or with your team from this book's resource page at www.ccl.org/compassbook.

Urgency: Direction, Alignment, Commitment
Urgency: A Checklist for Success

Related Competencies

Change Implementation
Engagement
Leading with Purpose
Resourcefulness
Vision
Working through Others

Resources

Cartwright, T. (2007). *Setting priorities: Personal values, organizational results.* Greensboro, NC: Center for Creative Leadership.

Cross, R. L., & Thomas, R. J. (2008). *Driving results through social networks: How top organizations leverage networks for performance and growth.* Hoboken, NJ: Wiley.

Fortune. Marillyn Hewson, 61. (n.d.). Author. Retrieved from http://fortune.com/most-powerful-women/marillyn-hewson-4/

Gryskiewicz, S. S., & Taylor, S. (2003). *Making creativity practical: Innovation that gets results.* Greensboro, NC: Center for Creative Leadership.

Guillot, C. (2016, July 20). How CEO Marillyn Hewson is leading Lockheed Martin to new heights. *Chief Executive.* Retrieved from http://chiefexecutive.net/ceo-marillyn-hewson-leading-lockheed-martin-new-heights/

Kotter, J. P. (2008). *A sense of urgency.* Boston, MA: Harvard Business School Publishing.

McCauley C. D., & Fick-Cooper, L. (2015). *Direction, alignment, commitment: Achieving better results through leadership.* Greensboro, NC: Center for Creative Leadership.

McNamara, A., & Howard, C. (Eds.). (2016, June 6). The world's 100 most powerful women - #24 Marillyn Hewson. *Forbes*. Retrieved from http://www.forbes.com/profile/marillyn-hewson/?list=power-women

Staver, M. (2012). *Leadership isn't for cowards: How to drive performance by challenging people and confronting problems.* Hoboken, NJ: Wiley.

51
Vision

Create and communicate a compelling picture of the future.

A compelling plan for the future. A compelling way to communicate it to your team and organization. The means to inspire others to work toward that future. Your visionary outlook makes you distinct from good, valuable managers—but a shocking number of leaders fail to create and promote a vision that engages people, according to a 2013 PricewaterhouseCoopers (PwC) survey. Without a clear sense of how their efforts contribute to the organization's future, employees lose their sense of urgency and direction.

Avoid those problems and create excitement and passion about your organization's future. But don't go it alone. Involve others in naming and charting what lies ahead for your business. Most importantly, help employees see the importance of their work in terms of creating a sustainable organization that generates good results. Once you gain comfort and skill with "the vision thing," you can communicate a sense of passion and purpose, inspiring employees, team members, and others to take action. A meaningful, ambitious vision for your organization—not a clever slogan or a clumsy mission statement—helps others see that the future the organization imagines for itself is attainable. Consider Will Allen's story of vision come to life.

Leadership in Action

Will Allen's brief professional basketball career was a long way from his beginnings as a son of small farmers who began as sharecroppers in South Carolina. But there must have been something in the soil. Something that nourished the seed for his vision of urban farms that would remake the food deserts of inner city neighborhoods and provide jobs to young people. Something that encouraged Allen to bring sustainable, affordable, healthy food to communities without much access to it. "If people can grow safe, healthy, affordable food," says Allen, "if they have access to land and clean water, this is transformative on every level in a community. I believe we cannot have healthy communities without a healthy food system" (Growing Power, n.d.). From its beginnings in 1993, Growing Power has created community networks and provided training. It now has satellite farms (including a five-story vertical farm in Milwaukee) that extend Allen's vision beyond its Milwaukee origins. Allen received a MacArthur "genius" grant in 2008, a testament to how he turned his vision into a practice for the benefit of many.

What High Performance Looks Like

Visionary leaders

- imagine the future, including radical change, and can see a world where the organization's current work gives way to new possibilities

- connect their vision to real business outcomes

- see beyond short-term commitments to a long-term, competitive, sustainable position

- draw people together to engage in the vision

- tell stories to communicate the vision meaningfully and memorably

- are comfortable with multiple communication methods, from memos to speeches to email

- stay focused on the organization's vision and keep it clear for others to follow

- model behavior that turns vision into action

- stay in touch with the evolving needs and demands of the market and look for trends and new ideas that might affect the organization

- are seen by others as insightful, intuitive, curious, inventive, focused, passionate, inspired, persuasive, inspirational, energetic, enthusiastic, and engaging

What's in Your Way?

An organization without a vision can miss opportunities to innovate, fail to meet its customers' future needs, and resort to old habits in response to new challenges. Those outcomes affect your organization's ability to meet its goals and remain competitive—organizations need a constant flow of new ideas and imagined possibilities. Without vision, it's hard to inspire people in your organization, to foster alignment among them, or to attract and hire the talented people your organization needs. Your work as a leader involves imagining the future, working with others to form a statement of that future, and communicating that vision in ways that compel people to listen and act. Review the following list and note the items that you believe block you from becoming the visionary leader you want and need to be.

- ❏ You're not interested in the future of the company.
- ❏ You accept things the way they are and don't ask why.
- ❏ You rely on other people to create a vision of the future.
- ❏ You focus on immediate objectives and results rather than a long-term vision.
- ❏ You prefer concrete ideas and projects to the exclusion of abstract thoughts and imagination.
- ❏ You focus on being a good operational manager rather than a visionary one.
- ❏ You have had few visionary role models.
- ❏ You haven't established the credibility necessary to support your vision.
- ❏ People react to your vision as if you're living in a fantasy world.
- ❏ You overlook problems with your vision.
- ❏ Your communication doesn't portray your vision in a compelling way.
- ❏ Your vision is too expensive for your organization to implement.
- ❏ You aren't up to date with customer needs, industry trends, and competitors.

Coach Yourself

To develop your ability to create and promote a vision, create goals in areas that require you to improvise, invent, question, collaborate, track relevant trends, project the organization's future, and engage customers. Look for opportunities to practice public speaking, make social media contributions, and learn other communication methods. These questions can help you define an area of focus:

- How do you imagine the world being different as a result of your organization's work?

- What excites you most about your vision? What about it do you believe will fire passion for it in others?

- What is the craziest idea you've ever had? How did other people respond to it?

- Who was the most inspiring leader you have ever worked for? What was his or her vision, and how did he or she communicate it?

- How can you align people with your vision for the organization? Can you express your vision in a way that makes it easy for people to see their place in it?

- Think about one of your ideas that your organization adopted. What was the result? What feelings do you have about that experience? How did your idea change on its way to becoming reality?

Improve Now

Write your future. Imagine yourself a few years from now. You have worked hard, and the organization has achieved all of the things it set out to do. What role did you play? What are people saying about you? What will they say next?

Map your vision. How will your story unfold? What steps will you take along the way? How will you help others? Who will help you? What obstacles will you overcome?

Use imagery. Use pictures, tell stories, and make use of impressions and metaphors to powerfully describe the situations that lie before you and your organization, and encourage others to build on your vision with their own supporting ideas.

Engage your colleagues in exploring a vision. Get together with peers and others and talk about the possibilities. Bounce ideas off each other until the right vision emerges—the one that sparks deep passion and commitment.

Tell a story. When you tell a story to illustrate your vision, people will find it easier to recall—certainly easier than reciting a vision statement. Make notes on some of the incidents you hear and see. Keep notes about how people live the vision in your organization. Then use those notes to create your story.

Perfect your "elevator speech." What compelling vision can you describe in 25 seconds, or during the time a typical elevator ride takes? Practice communicating your vision in a clear, brief way. Be prepared to talk about it everywhere—in line at the cafeteria, when you visit the customer service department, and at chance encounters walking to your car or train stop at the end of the day. Everywhere.

Learn how to use multiple forms of media. The more channels of communication you use, the better the chance people have of hearing and understanding your vision. Use the newest communication technologies, absolutely, but don't forget small tangible items such as coffee mugs, T-shirts, and luggage tags.

Connect with the people you serve. Spend time with customers and clients. Listen to what they need now and what they might want or need in the future. Collaborate with them and your colleagues to generate or pick out the good ideas, those that resonate with people and encourage them to implement those ideas.

Learn another discipline. Cross-pollination of perspectives and ideas can inspire a vision. Learn about how other people see their world and how they behave in it. What patterns might physics, biochemistry, computer science, or other disciplines suggest for your organization?

Challenge the status quo and existing assumptions. Contemporary wisdom does not often lead to bold ideas. Explore the limitations and flaws of current thinking. Expect the unexpected. Look for it.

Be everywhere your message can be. Visit different locations in your organization, whether that means a trip down to the mail room or a flight to the other side of the world. Make your presence known on your organization's intranet. Create a blog. Be the visible ambassador of your organization's vision, the champion of its success.

Spread the word. Think of the conversations you had with employees yesterday. How could you have included a mention of your organization's vision in some of them?

Developmental Opportunities

- Study the impact of emerging technologies on your unit. Develop five-year scenarios that describe the world in which your unit operates and the responses it makes to that world.

- Organize a vision-sharing event. Introduce your department and its vision to another business unit. Invite your peers to do the same.

- Volunteer to be a member of a board of directors for another organization.

- Take on a project that has gone off track and lost sight of its original objectives.

Activity Center

Review and download these activities you can use for your development or with your team from this book's resource page at www.ccl.org/compassbook.

Vision: Develop Your Personal Vision Statement
Vision: Engage Employees with the Vision
Vision: Understand and Promote Your Organization's Vision

Related Competencies

Boundary Spanning

Champion Change

Change Acceptance

Innovation

Problem Solving

Systems Thinking

Resources

Cartwright, T., & Baldwin, D. (2006). *Communicating your vision*. Greensboro, NC: Center for Creative Leadership.

Case, S. (2016). *The third wave: An entrepreneur's vision of the future*. New York, NY: Simon & Schuster.

Criswell, C., & Cartwright, T. (2010). *Creating a vision*. Greensboro, NC: Center for Creative Leadership.

Goldsmith, M., & Reiter, M. (2014). *What got you here won't get you there*. New York, NY: MJF Books.

Growing Power. (n.d.). Retrieved 7/2/2016 from http://www.growingpower .org/about/

Heath, C., & Heath, D. (2010). *Switch: How to change things when change is hard*. New York, NY: Crown Business.

Hughes, R. L., Beatty, K. C., & Dinwoodie, D. (2014). *Becoming a strategic leader: Your role in your organization's enduring success* (2nd ed.). San Francisco, CA: Jossey-Bass.

Isaacson, W. (2011). *Steve Jobs*. New York, NY: Simon and Schuster.

Palus, C. J., & Horth, D. M. (2002). *The leader's edge: Six creative competencies for navigating complex challenges.* San Francisco, CA: Wiley.

Palus, C. J., & Horth, D. M. (2010). *Visual Explorer* (Facilitator guide with image deck). Greensboro, NC: Center for Creative Leadership.

PwC. (2012). *People performance: How CFOs can build the bench strength they need today . . . and tomorrow.* (White paper). Retrieved from http://www .pwc.com/us/en/increasing-finance-function-effectiveness/assets/pwc -wharton-people-performance.pdf

Schachter, L., & Cheatham, R. (2016). *Selling vision: The x-xy-y formula for driving results by selling change*. New York, NY: McGraw-Hill Education.

Scharlatt, H. (2008). *Selling your ideas to your organization*. Greensboro, NC: Center for Creative Leadership.

52

Working through Others

Ensure that your team and its work are organized and operating efficiently.

Smoothly operating teams and organizations run efficiently, reduce frustration among members, and minimize delays when minor roadblocks appear. And that's no accident. Play a key role in supporting efficiency by understanding that the work doesn't fall to your hands alone. Working through others, while a basic function of leadership, is too often ignored or avoided—especially in fundamental matters like planning and organizing. Take the time to nail down the details, and you will help create trust and confidence among your team members and more broadly across the organization. In the story that follows, one person's heroic efforts could not be enough, and realizing that fact almost immediately saved thousands of lives.

Leadership in Action

There was nothing to prepare Dr. Jerry Brown for
what he faced in Liberia in early 2014. He had just graduated
from his medical internship and begun working at Eternal
Love Winning Africa Hospital when the first Ebola patients
began to arrive. As Casey Ross tells it in Cleveland's *The Plain
Dealer* newspaper (2015), the disease was not discussed in detail during
Brown's training, but nonetheless he was ready to operate on any number
of conditions. The real crisis was that of logistics in the face of the scale of
the outbreak.

By June 2014, patients infected with Ebola were arriving at the
hospital at a rate of five per day. Within weeks, the hospital had 80 patients
with Ebola, and all other patients had simply stopped coming to the
hospital out of fear. Fear drove a rebellion among Brown's own nursing staff,
many of whom threatened to quit or simply refused to work among the
highly contagious patients. There were no standard protocols for such an
outbreak, and there were no fully trained infectious-disease specialists in
the whole country.

Brown learned to improvise. He cleared kitchens and chapels to make
extra room for beds. He began mixing his own treatment cocktails when
the standard treatments failed, and administered the medicine directly via
IV, a procedure that at first had seemed too risky. The results were positive.
Soon there were more survivors than fatalities, and Brown was able to put
some of the cured patients to work in the hospital, writes Dr. Richard Besser
(2014). Having been exposed to the disease, these workers didn't need
clumsy gear to protect themselves.

Dr. Brown's unorthodox methods in the face of overwhelming odds
allowed his small hospital to have a significant impact on the outbreak,
curing over 200 patients.

What High Performance Looks Like

Leaders skilled at working through others

- align resources to accomplish key objectives
- clarify roles and accountabilities
- engage their team in building clear, realistic plans
- address risks and challenges in achieving objectives
- hold themselves accountable for meeting commitments
- keep everyone affected by the results well informed about projects
- are seen as organized, resourceful, committed, persistent, and energetic
- bring stakeholders together to plan
- establish important project milestones
- adhere to project schedules
- anticipate and plan for future challenges

What's in Your Way?

Leaders unable to work through others struggle to meet deadlines and fail to deliver results. Their direct reports lose confidence in the team's ability to execute, leading to disengaged, dissatisfied team members. Review the following list and note the items that you believe block you from developing the ability to work through others.

- ❏ You struggle to make the transition from individual contributor to manager.
- ❏ You underestimate the difficulty of coordinating a group's efforts.
- ❏ You don't communicate with coworkers.

- ❏ You have limited experience influencing without authority.

- ❏ You neglect your individual work responsibilities, focusing too much on managing other resources.

- ❏ Team members say they don't feel you trust them.

- ❏ You don't give your team enough leeway so that it can adapt to changing circumstances or take advantage of new opportunities.

- ❏ You focus on your own needs as opposed to the needs of your customers or other stakeholders.

- ❏ You try to control areas for which other people are responsible.

- ❏ You neglect to seek ongoing feedback about how your plan is coming along and how it's affecting other people.

- ❏ You focus on the details of the plan without reflecting on the long-term outcomes.

Coach Yourself

To develop your ability to work through others for results, create goals that demand you manage an ambiguous situation, put you in charge of turning around a failing project, or that otherwise position you to manage others toward a common goal. These questions can help you focus on such areas:

- ● Have you successfully made the transition from an individual contributor to a manager?

- ● How strong are your relationships with your direct reports?

- ● What tasks have you delegated? How well are those tasks being handled? What else can you delegate?

- ● How often do you check in with your team? Do you keep in touch only with the group? Do you only check in with individual team members? Can you check in at both levels?

- ● How do you track team progress? Do you make this information accessible to other people?

Improve Now

Promote clarity. Leaders too often fail to explain what they mean when they talk about organizational structure, financial results, their own jobs, time management, and corporate culture. Left unclear, these concepts can throw a firm into turmoil—but when given proper focus, they confer extraordinary leverage. Here's something to help: read "The Five Messages Leaders Must Manage" from the May 2006 issue of the *Harvard Business Review*. Using ideas from the article, discuss with your employees why the daily work that they do is important and how it's valuable to the organization. Plan for future discussions.

Prioritize. Identify which projects are the most important for your team to complete (this year, this quarter, or in whatever time frame is meaningful to your organization). What must your team deliver no matter what? What work can it leave for later?

Manage the work's scope. To accommodate changing situations, teams often need flexibility regarding the scope of their work. Join with your team to mark the boundaries of its work and what it needs to do to remain efficient. Act quickly to correct course if your team drifts too far off track.

Develop and maintain a sense of urgency. Show sincere and intense conviction in your words and actions. Show the care and the passion for the team and for what it has set out to achieve.

Define roles. Discuss with the team what role each member will play. You may be surprised at how team members define their roles and what expertise they believe they can bring to their work.

Identify what drives your team. Check in with team members to learn what motivates them, what they care about, and what they want to learn. Talk with them about how they can incorporate what drives them into their daily work.

Make note. Interview your manager and another leader separately. Ask them about their experiences leading others and what kind of legacy they want to leave. Think about the difference you want to make and how you can achieve that by directing others.

Define norms. Help your team reach consensus on rules and procedures and apply those norms consistently. Agreed-upon practices prevent most undesirable actions and approaches from emerging and provide guidelines for how to handle them.

Who's on first? Ensure that employees who report to you know which decisions and actions they're responsible for. If people don't understand which decisions and actions they must account for, decisions stall, overhead costs mount, and confusion sets in. Review the operational needs of your part of the business. Are you certain of who is accountable for what and when? Make a list. Get it clear in your mind.

Identify risks. A team's work, like any endeavor, is subject to Murphy's Law: "If it can go wrong, it will go wrong." Talk to your team about what could go wrong, and plan how the team might respond to those challenges.

Delegate. The assumption underneath the idea of working through others is that you can't do everything yourself. Help others help you and the team by delegating tasks—and not only the ones you don't want to do. Delegate tasks that will help team members develop individually and as a team while meeting team objectives and producing the results the organization looks for.

Developmental Opportunities

- Take a basic management or supervisory skills class.

- Manage a project.

- Coach a new project manager.

- Take a project in chaos and get it back on track.

- Organize an event with a short, defined time frame, such as an annual charity campaign.

Activity Center

Review and download these activities you can use for your development or with your team from this book's resource page at www.ccl.org/compassbook.

Working through Others: Do It Right
Working through Others: Rate Yourself

Related Competencies

Delegating
Leading with Purpose
Problem Solving
Relationship Management
Team Leadership

Resources

Beatty, K., & Smith, R. B. (2013). Developing high-impact teams to lead strategic change. In E. Salas, S. I. Tannenbaum, D. J. Cohen, & G. Latham (Eds.), *Developing and enhancing teamwork in organizations*. San Francisco, CA: Jossey-Bass.

Besser, R. (2014, Sept. 30). *Face-to-face with patients in the ebola ward*. ABC. Retrieved from http://abcnews.go.com/Health/face-face-patients-ebola-ward/story?id=25864452

Bradt, G. B., Check, J. A., & Lawler, J. A. (2016). *The new leader's 100-day action plan: How to take charge, build or merge your team, and get immediate results* (4th ed.). Hoboken, NJ: Wiley.

Browning, H. (2012). *Accountability: Taking ownership of your responsibility*. Greensboro, NC: Center for Creative Leadership.

Frankovelgia, C., & Martineau, J. W. (2006). Coaching teams. In S. Ting & P. Scisco (Eds.), *The CCL handbook of coaching: A guide for the leader coach* (pp. 379–403). San Francisco, CA: Jossey-Bass.

Gentry, W. A. (2016). *Be the boss everyone wants to work for: A guide for new leaders*. Oakland, CA: Berrett-Koehler.

Hamm, J. (2006, May). *The five messages leaders must manage*. Harvard Business Review. Retrieved from https://hbr.org/2006/05/the-five-messages-leaders-must-manage

Horstman, M. (2016). *The effective manager*. Hoboken, NJ: Wiley.

Klann, G. (2004). *Building your team's morale, pride, and spirit*. Greensboro, NC: Center for Creative Leadership.

Lindoerfer, D. (2008). *Raising sensitive issues in a team*. Greensboro, NC: Center for Creative Leadership.

Morgeson, F. P. Lindoerfer, D., & Loring, D. J. (2010). Developing team leadership capability. In C. D. McCauley, M. N. Ruderman, & E. Van Velsor (Eds.), *The Center for Creative Leadership handbook of leadership development* (3rd ed.), pp. 285–312). San Francisco, CA: Jossey-Bass.

Naudé, J., & Plessier, F. (2014). *Becoming a leader-coach: A step-by-step guide to developing your people*. Greensboro, NC: Center for Creative Leadership.

Ross, C. (2015, Oct. 23). Ebola fighter Dr. Jerry Brown tells story of courage and hope in appearance at Case Western. *The Plain Dealer*. Retrieved from http://www.cleveland.com/healthfit/index.ssf/2015/10/ebola_dr_jerry_brown_tells_sto.html

Scharlett, H., & Smith, R. (2011). *Influence: Gaining commitment, getting results* (2nd ed.). Greensboro, NC: Center for Creative Leadership.

Turregano, C. (2013). *Delegating effectively: A leader's guide to getting things done*. Greensboro, NC: Center for Creative Leadership.

Welch, J., & Welch, S. (2015). *The real life MBA: Your no-BS guide to winning the game, building a team, and growing your career*. New York, NY: HarperCollins Publishers.

Part Three
CAREER DERAILERS

How does CCL define *derailment*? First, let's talk about what derailment is not. Derailment doesn't apply to leaders who have topped out in their company's hierarchy or who elect to stay at a particular level. As a result of extensive research, CCL defines a derailed leader as one who, having reached the general manager level, is fired, demoted, or reaches a career plateau. Interestingly, organizations often see derailed managers as having high potential for advancement, based on a solid record of results. For the most part, these managers hold an established leadership position—until they derail.

In its 1989 book, *Preventing Derailment: What to Do Before It's Too Late*, CCL characterized five key factors that seriously jeopardize leadership careers:

- difficulty adapting to change (the most frequent cause of derailment)
- difficulty building and leading a team
- failure to deliver business results
- lacking a broad strategic orientation
- problems with interpersonal relationships

These five factors hold up across several derailment studies on different genders, populations, geographical areas, and cultures. The importance of any one factor over another may shift, but the five factors have remained consistent.

You can ruin your leadership position and run your career off the track in all kinds of ways. An ethical lapse, a public embarrassment that puts your company in a bad light, or a decision that jeopardizes your organization's sustainability are just a few examples. Most of this book focuses on success skills. Weakness in any one or even a few of these skills probably won't end your career, but they will keep you from advancing as far and as fast as you want. A weakness in one of the five derailment factors, however, threatens more than your advancement. If you don't recognize and correct these behaviors, you might well find yourself heading for a breakup with your organization.

Note: Lombardo, M. M., & Eichinger, R. W. (1989/2001). *Preventing derailment: What to do before it's too late*. Greensboro, NC: Center for Creative Leadership.

101

Difficulty Adapting to Change

Cannot adjust to, learn from, and embrace change as necessary for future success.

Change seems to be the only constant in today's organizational life, driven by shifts in external conditions and an organization's response to them. Because of the magnitude and frequency of the changes occurring within and affecting organizations, great value accrues to leaders who can dependably adapt to and embrace change. Leaders who resist change can stall their careers and even lose their leadership positions.

English philosopher Francis Bacon once said, "He that will not apply new remedies must expect new evils, for time is the greatest innovator" (1597/1986). You need no further evidence of Bacon's claim than to look into the last days of Blockbuster Entertainment.

Leadership Derailed

The popular wisdom about Blockbuster's downfall holds that the once ubiquitous video rental chain simply failed to compete with fledgling upstart Netflix, allowing the smaller company to sweep its market. But there's a little more nuance to it than that.

Greg Satell describes in a 2014 *Forbes* article that early in Netflix's history, its founder Reed Hastings met with John Antioco, the CEO of Blockbuster, to propose a partnership. Had Antioco accepted the proposal, the companies would have comingled their business models. But Antioco didn't recognize the nature of the competition Netflix embodied. Although Blockbuster had the advantage of instant gratification (customers could pick a movie and rent it instantly, rather than waiting for a disc to arrive by mail), Netflix had eliminated the major inconvenience of Blockbuster's model: late fees. Those fees were responsible for a huge portion of Blockbuster's profits and were also the worst part of the customer experience. By eliminating late fees, Netflix provided a preferable service.

Antioco's second mistake was in implementing adaptations incorrectly, without recognizing the context. In 2006, he eliminated late fees and implemented an online rental service using Blockbuster's library. But the short-term loss of profitability caused his investors and board of directors to revolt, and he was fired. A few years later, Blockbuster was no more.

It can't be said that Antioco "didn't know what he was doing." He had a solid reputation after massive growth for Blockbuster under his leadership. But he didn't perceive the actual problem: his company's profit margin depended upon a policy that punished customers. By the time the necessary adaptation was obvious, it was too late to implement effectively, and that delay cost Blockbuster everything.

What Potential Derailment Can Look Like

Leaders unable to accept, embrace, and champion change

- are intimidated by change or challenge
- cannot extract lessons from change or turmoil
- don't speak optimistically of change
- see challenges as problems rather than opportunities
- don't see the need to change in order to stay relevant
- aren't resilient
- don't take risks
- are unrealistic about the consequences of change
- don't believe they need to learn and grow
- believe most problems are difficult to solve
- don't learn from mistakes
- don't use feedback to adjust behavior

Why It Derails Careers

Leaders who resist change are perceived as stuck in their ways and unaware of the trends at play within the organization and the market in which it operates. Resistance to change can hamper how your direct reports and others respond to changing circumstances. Upper management may see such leaders as unready to step up to the next level of leadership—too stubborn, too fearful, perhaps even weak.

It might be difficult to get your emotional bearings as you deal with change and your development at the same time, but remain resilient and optimistic. If you falter, or worse, hide your head in the sand, you may derail because your organization recognizes that change will happen with or without your resistance—and it's easier for others to respond positively if resistant leaders are sidelined or let go. Review the following list and note the items that you recognize as contributing to your resistance to change.

- ❏ You feel little control over how your organization's adaptations to change are implemented.

- ❏ You fear failure or losing your job.

- ❏ You entrench yourself in the same approach to work as you've always used, hoping to ride out the change.

- ❏ You embrace change but haven't thought about nor developed the skills and aptitude that are needed in the post-change organization.

- ❏ You give up when the challenges brought about by change frustrate you.

- ❏ You don't heed the lessons of your past experience with changes.

- ❏ You disagree with proposed actions to change.

- ❏ You lack the resources (time, people, money) to implement ways to capitalize on the changes affecting your organization.

- ❏ You worry that people see you as a chameleon, shifting your position to meet the needs of every situation.

- ❏ You're wary of your team or organization losing momentum when it responds to change.

- ❏ You are impatient with the rate of change.

- ❏ You try to do too much too soon, failing to see the smart play or recognizing the real problem change poses.

- ❏ You underestimate the scope or complexity of change.

Avoid Derailing

Develop your capacity for accepting and adapting to change by creating goals in areas that allow you to take controlled risks, that put you into unfamiliar situations or roles, that require you to bounce back from failures, or that otherwise force you to not rely only on your traditional strengths. These questions can help you focus on such areas:

- Can you think of a time when you made a change and it worked out for you? What was the change and what happened?

- What are your personal strategies for coping with change? Which ones are healthy? Unhealthy?

- Do you have colleagues who cope well with change? What are their strategies? How does their view of change differ from yours?

- What changes in your organization have you disagreed with? Rather than resistance, are there more constructive ways to voice your disagreement?

- What are the risks of resisting change when that change is inevitable?

- What resources or support would make change more acceptable to you?

Improve Now

Other chapters in this book will help you devise strategies, tactics, and actions you can take to shore up your capacity for change. Here are those of most direct use:

3. Learning Agility
10. Change Acceptance
11. Change Implementation
26. Flexibility
38. Resilience
40. Risk Taking
43. Strategic Planning and Implementation
48. Tolerating Ambiguity

Activity Center

Review and download these activities you can use for your development or with your team from this book's resource page at www.ccl.org/compassbook.

Change Acceptance: You and Change
Change Acceptance: Your View of Change

Resources

Adams, M. G. (2016). *Change your questions, change your life: 12 powerful tools for leadership, coaching, and life* (3rd ed.). Oakland, CA: Berrett-Koehler.

Bacon, F. (1597/1986). *The essays.* (J. Pitcher, Ed.). New York, NY: Penguin Classics.

Bunker, K. A. (2008). *Responses to change: Helping people manage transition.* Greensboro, NC: Center for Creative Leadership.

Bunker, K. A., & Wakefield, M. (2005). *Leading with authenticity in times of transition.* Greensboro, NC: Center for Creative Leadership.

Bunker, K. A., & Wakefield, M. (2010). *Leading through transitions: Facilitator's guide set.* San Francisco, CA: Pfeiffer.

Heath, C., & Heath, D. (2010). *Switch: How to change things when change is hard.* New York, NY: Crown Business.

McGuire, J. B., & Rhodes, G. (2009). *Transforming your leadership culture.* San Francisco, CA: Jossey-Bass.

Pasmore, B. (2015). *Leading continuous change: Navigating churn in the real world.* Oakland, CA: Berrett-Koehler.

Rush, S. (Ed.) (2012). *The leadership in action series: On leading in times of change.* Greensboro, NC: Center for Creative Leadership.

Satell, G. (2014, Sept. 5). A look back at why Blockbuster really failed and why it didn't have to. *Forbes.* Retrieved from https://www.forbes.com/sites/gregsatell/2014/09/05/a-look-back-at-why-blockbuster-really-failed-and-why-it-didnt-have-to/#58c2a3af1d64

102

Difficulty Building and Leading Teams

Struggle to select, develop, engage, and motivate groups of people to pursue a common goal.

Teamwork may be defined as the ability of a group to work together to achieve a common goal. No one person can be successful alone. That's especially true for leaders, who by virtue of their roles take responsibility for producing results through others. No easy task. Managing teamwork is complicated. If you are unable to assemble highly efficient teams, you might develop a reputation as a poor manager of people, which will hinder your progress toward leading more senior-level teams or, in the worst case, derail your career. And though her overall career remains impressive, Carly Fiorina's tenure at the helm of Hewlett-Packard (HP) is a cautionary tale.

Leadership in Action

Before she joined the crowded Republican primary race in 2016, Carly Fiorina arrived at HP with a reputation as a "sales and marketing prodigy" with experience in the telecommunications industry. Her reputation gave the board of directors a lot of confidence, and their express purpose in hiring her was to change up the organization, which threatened to stagnate under its own size.

In a way, the board got exactly what it asked for. Fiorina embraced her role and pledged to "keep the best and reinvent the rest" (Grumbull, 2015), performing sweeping reviews and reorganizations of the company. She adjusted organizational reward systems and implemented voluntary pay cuts followed by layoffs, all while tirelessly examining the organization for inefficiency. Her most controversial move was a huge merger with Compaq, a contentious decision that divided the company's leadership nearly in half.

Fiorina's tactics were so shocking and out of step with the company's culture that she was eventually fired after a five-year tenure. In that time, HP's stock price took a steep dive, losing over half its value (Sonnenfeld, 2015). Inside the company, morale took a severe hit as well, with HP dropping from *Fortune*'s "100 Best Companies to Work for in America" after holding a high spot on the list for years.

Insiders claim Fiorina was unwilling to make compromises and showed no respect for established culture. Moreover, she consistently belittled those who disagreed with her, apparently forgetting the shared goals of her leadership team and focusing instead on "loyalty." It was this inability to find common ground and build a coherent team effort that eventually cost her the job.

What Potential Derailment Can Look Like

Leaders who have difficulty building and leading teams

- select people with good technical skills but poor ability to work with others
- don't or are unable to resolve conflict among team members
- are unable to motivate team members to do the best for the team
- don't help team members understand how their work fits into the organization's goals
- are unable to secure the resources the team needs
- have trouble creating alignment between the team and the people who depend on the team's work
- struggle to guide the team in establishing a clear mission and goals
- don't engage everyone on the team to work together to tackle challenges
- don't support team learning
- don't hold team members accountable
- find it difficult to size up strengths of individual team members and find ways to leverage those strengths for the team's benefit

Why It Derails Careers

Leaders who have difficulty building teams can fail to deliver the results they have promised. Their team members may feel undervalued, leading to dysfunction and ultimately departures from the team. Review the following list and note the items that you think prevent you from becoming a better team leader.

❑ You don't have a compelling vision for the team.

❑ You focus more on tasks than people.

❑ You don't speak up when you disagree with the team.

❑ You don't trust the people who work for you.

❑ Your team members don't trust each other.

❑ Team members are separated geographically.

❑ Your company rewards individual achievement over team achievement.

❑ You neglect your individual work responsibilities, focusing too much on managing the team's work.

❑ You spend time and resources building a team when the work could be done by just one or two people.

❑ You put too much emphasis on team members getting along and not enough emphasis on meeting team objectives or providing value to the organization.

❑ You feel you need to take control to deliver on an aggressive schedule.

❑ You spend too much time getting consensus and fail to provide strong leadership when it's needed.

Avoid Derailing

To develop your ability to build and lead a team, create goals that put you in a position to lead a work group or large project requiring teamwork. These questions can help you focus on such areas:

● Have you conveyed a compelling vision for your team? Do people know and believe in the expectations you've set?

● Have you clarified team norms—the rules about what is acceptable or unacceptable during teamwork?

- Are there specific conflicts pulling your team apart? How might you address them?
- Do you see the business advantages of collaborating as a team?
- What are the barriers to teamwork in your organization?

Improve Now

Many chapters in this book will help you devise strategies, tactics, and actions you can take to shore up your team leadership skills. Here are those of most direct use:

1. Communication
6. Boundary Spanning
12. Coach and Develop Others
14. Conflict Resolution
21. Difference, Diversity, Inclusion
28. Global Team Management
37. Relationship Management
46. Team Leadership
49. Trust
52. Working through Others

Activity Center

Review and download these activities you can use for your development or with your team from this book's resource page at www.ccl.org/compassbook.

Team Leadership: A Winning Team
Team Leadership: Rate Your Leadership
Team Leadership: Teamwork Is Fun, Too

Resources

Grumbull, M. (2015, Oct. 12). What Carly Fiorina's time as CEO says about how she might govern. *Christian Science Monitor*.

Kanaga, K., & Browning, H. (2003). *Maintaining team performance*. Greensboro, NC: Center for Creative Leadership.

Kanaga, K., & Kossler, M. E. (2001). *How to form a team: Five keys to high performance*. Greensboro, NC: Center for Creative Leadership.

Kanaga, K., & Prestridge, S. (2002). *How to launch a team: Start right for success*. Greensboro, NC: Center for Creative Leadership.

Klann, G. (2004). *Building your team's morale, pride, and spirit.* Greensboro, NC: Center for Creative Leadership.

Kossler, M. E., & Kanaga, K. (2001). *Do you really need a team?* Greensboro, NC: Center for Creative Leadership.

Lindoerfer, D. (2008). *Raising sensitive issues in a team*. Greensboro, NC: Center for Creative Leadership.

Martin, A., & Bal, V. (2007). *The state of teams.* (White paper). Center for Creative Leadership. Retrieved from https://www.ccl.org/wp-content/uploads/2015/04/StateOfTeams.pdf

Runde, C. E., & Flanagan, T. A. (2008). *Building conflict competent teams.* San Francisco, CA: Jossey-Bass.

Sinek, S. (2014). *Leaders eat last: Why some teams pull together and others don't.* New York, NY: Penguin.

Sonnenfeld, J. (2015, Sept. 20). Why I still think Fiorina was a terrible CEO. *Politico*.

103

Failure to Meet Business Objectives

Don't meet performance expectations because of a lack of follow-through on promises or being overly ambitious.

The best of intentions can fall flat when leadership fails. Leaders who are results-driven are critical to their organization's performance. Develop your ability to decisively accomplish key objectives and dramatically affect the way others view your performance as a leader—and affect your organization's bottom line. How dramatically? CCL research reveals that leaders who promise results but repeatedly fail to keep those promises can derail their careers. While they may promote themselves well, they don't have the track record to back it up. Consider the case of Elon Musk, who inspires thousands of people with his vision and his company's achievements, yet risks falling short of realizing the full potential of his promises.

Leadership in Action

He built PayPal, SpaceX, and Tesla. He wants you to buy solar shingles for your house and start selling power to the grid. He's Elon Musk, and he wants you to install a battery the size of a mattress in your kitchen wall. His ideas are exhilarating, futuristic, and optimistic, but over the past few years he's begun to run into a problem: delivery. There's a fine line to walk between grand vision and unattainable fantasy. Boldness, optimism, and ambition are great attributes in a leader, but unless they're tempered with a little realism, a leader can run real risks in terms of credibility.

Since 2015, two of Musk's SpaceX rockets have exploded, one during a test flight and one during a payload delivery to the International Space Station. This has raised doubts about the suitability of his proposals for midflight refueling, along with questions about the quality control of his firm's engineering. Alongside these setbacks, Musk makes confident but crazy-sounding claims about the potential of his automated manufacturing plants for Tesla cars. Envisioning a fully-automated factory, he hopes to eventually produce a car every 15 seconds. But with Toyota factories (some of the most efficient in the world) producing a car every 17 to 18 hours, how realistic is this claim (Rothfeder, 2017)?

Failure is natural. In business, failure is necessary as a step toward breakthrough innovations. But when failure comes at the end of a long string of big promises, it leads to disappointment, which is ultimately more damaging than the failure itself. Everyone loves to see a dreamer succeed. But if Musk continues to overpromise and underdeliver, will he be able to hang on to his chance to change the future?

What Potential Derailment Can Look Like

Leaders who fail to deliver on promises and to produce results

- are overwhelmed by complex tasks
- may have exceeded their current level of competence
- overestimate their abilities
- have difficulty meeting the expectations of their current position
- promote themselves without the results to support it
- are poor organizers
- are indecisive and procrastinate
- avoid stepping in when trouble comes
- demonstrate a laissez-faire attitude and set low expectations
- don't clearly communicate objectives, deadlines, and expectations
- don't secure and align resources to accomplish key objectives
- don't track and monitor progress toward results
- may be regarded as inauthentic and untrustworthy
- don't collaborate well
- don't empower people to get involved and solve problems
- lack resilience
- can be seen as overstressed, overconfident, perfectionists, foolish, and living in denial

Why It Derails Careers

Failure to deliver results can create a breach of trust. Leaders in danger of derailing because they don't deliver what they promise may have exceeded their current level of competence without realizing it. Even if you are great with people and loved by your superiors, peers, and direct reports, if you fail to drive results toward business objectives you are in jeopardy of falling off the career ladder. Review the following list and note the items that you believe block you from delivering on the promises you make.

- ❏ You're unsure about your role or how you can contribute.

- ❏ You're afraid to fail.

- ❏ You struggle to prioritize.

- ❏ You have yet to build relationships, establish credibility, or earn loyalty.

- ❏ You're not willing to push forward without full agreement.

- ❏ You've received feedback that you pursue your own agenda at the expense of your team's work or your organization's goals.

- ❏ You don't give people enough autonomy.

- ❏ You look for visibility and recognition over results.

- ❏ You force issues when finesse would work better.

- ❏ You procrastinate in the face of difficulty or ambiguity.

- ❏ You underestimate the time or resources to get work done.

Avoid Derailing

To develop and keep an urgency toward delivering results, create goals in areas that require you to coordinate action among other groups and people, call for a vision of the future, challenge you to bolster team member engagement, involve you in making changes that benefit the organization, and so on. These questions can help you define such focus areas:

- When was the last time you struggled to achieve results? What got in the way? How could you have been successful?

- When have you achieved exceptional results? What process did you use? What role did you play?

- How do you approach driving results? To what extent do you drive versus facilitate?

- Do you convey a true sense of urgency? Are you able to maintain a continuous emphasis on achieving results without coming off as pushy or impatient?

- What are your organization's cultural norms in regard to building consensus and making quick decisions? How will you work with or reshape the culture to produce results?

- Do you trust your intuition when you hit a roadblock and need a solution? Do you need to gain some new experiences to build depth of knowledge and confidence so that you have more potential answers at hand?

Improve Now

Other chapters in this book will help you devise strategies, tactics, and actions you can take to reinforce your intentions and deliver promised results. Here are those of most direct use:

2. Influence
18. Credibility and Integrity
22. Engagement
33. Leading with Purpose
39. Resourcefulness
50. Urgency
52. Working through Others

Activity Center

Review and download these activities you can use for your development or with your team from this book's resource page at www.ccl.org/compassbook.

Urgency: A Checklist for Success
Urgency: Direction, Alignment, Commitment
Working through Others: Do It Right
Working through Others: Rate Yourself

Resources

Cartwright, T. (2007). *Setting priorities: Personal values, organizational results.* Greensboro, NC: Center for Creative Leadership.

Cross, R. L., & Thomas, R. J. (2008). *Driving results through social networks: How top organizations leverage networks for performance and growth.* Hoboken, NJ: Wiley.

Gryskiewicz, S. S., & Taylor, S. (2003). *Making creativity practical: Innovation that gets results.* Greensboro, NC: Center for Creative Leadership.

McCauley C. D., & Fick-Cooper, L. (2015). *Direction, alignment, commitment: Achieving better results through leadership.* Greensboro, NC: Center for Creative Leadership.

Rothfeder, J. (2017, Jan. 10). Elon Musk has delivery issues. *The New Yorker*.

Staver, M. (2012). *Leadership isn't for cowards: How to drive performance by challenging people and confronting problems.* Hoboken, NJ: Wiley.

104

Lacking a Broad Strategic Orientation

Unable to navigate organizational ambiguity, politics, dilemmas, and trade-offs because of a lack of understanding of the strategic context surrounding the job.

Leading does not follow a straight or predictable path, especially in complex organizations that operate in an uncertain, global environment. When you recognize and accept the realities of whatever organization you're in, when you see how all parts of the organization work together, you'll deal more skillfully with the dilemmas of contemporary organizational life. Learn and understand the strategic context surrounding your job and your team. Think beyond the needs of your department. If you don't, the result can be drastic, such as it was in the immediate aftermath of Hurricane Katrina on August 29, 2005.

Leadership in Action

When Katrina made landfall near New Orleans, in the United States, it was already the worst natural disaster in American history. The levees holding back the storm surge broke, and 80 percent of New Orleans flooded. But those familiar with the event remember the one-two punch that resulted from FEMA's disorganized, ineffective response that made the situation even worse. How could an agency with the express purpose of responding to emergencies fail at the moment of greatest need?

Years after the disaster, federal investigations laid much of the blame at the feet of Michael Brown, who was the agency's director at the time of the event. Records of Brown's emails during the disaster indicate a complete lack of strategic orientation on his part. In fact, some of his communication with team members on the ground indicates a bizarre myopia in the face of an unprecedented disaster, focusing more on whether or not to wear a tie at a press conference than on offers of help from around the country. Under his leadership, delays in aid were frequent and logistical needs went unmet, adding to the crisis (Hsu, 2005, 2006).

Strategic orientation can be described colloquially as simply "having your head in the game." The morning after the storm, as the death toll and damage statistics were rolling in, Brown actually emailed his deputy director of public affairs: "Can I quit now?" (CNN, 2005). His attitude made him an obstacle to the relief effort, rather than the leader—and the results speak for themselves.

What Potential Derailment Can Look Like

Leaders who can't see responsibilities beyond their own contribute to silos and hinder the collaboration that organizations need to thrive. Leaders without a broad strategic orientation

- don't realize or accept that organizations are complicated

- aren't curious about their organization and neglect to learn more about key players and their perspectives

- don't acknowledge the different needs and priorities among key players and functions

- refuse to sacrifice or accept compromises in serving the organization's goals

- are stymied by tentative answers or incomplete information

- are unproductive in dealing with contradictory organizational requirements or inconsistencies

- don't understand the competing priorities in the organization

- don't see themselves as part of a system

- have trouble securing resources for their team

- risk moving beyond their current level of competence if promoted

- seem unprepared for more responsibility

- could not manage in a different department

- don't understand how other departments function in the organization

- may be seen as inexperienced, uninfluential, not insightful, overly concerned with failure, inflexible, self-centered, and poor coaches to their direct reports

Why It Derails Careers

If you struggle to envision and navigate complex organizational environments, you will find it extremely difficult to get things done, especially when competing for resources or when faced with a short deadline. Leaders more attuned to the workings and culture of the organization might well outmaneuver your play for resources. As you move higher in the organization, the ability to deal with the informal organization (the added complexity beyond the organizational chart) is as important as following the formal policies, practices, and rules. Review the following list and note the items that you believe contribute to your lack of broad strategic orientation.

- ❏ You're new to the organization.
- ❏ You have a tendency to focus on your own interests and pursue your own agenda.
- ❏ You haven't built relationships with key people from other functions.
- ❏ You lack experience in complex organizations.
- ❏ You tend to oversimplify difficult circumstances.
- ❏ You've received feedback that others see you as a people-pleaser, slick, or manipulative.
- ❏ You don't pay proper attention to the more mundane aspects of your job.
- ❏ You become caught up in the practical and tactical at the expense of the strategic.
- ❏ You favor detail over a broad view.
- ❏ You're still learning your current job (perhaps because of a rapid promotion or a transfer from another industry).
- ❏ You don't have a strong enough network in your organization to keep you up to date on what is happening beneath the surface of organizational activity.
- ❏ You don't delegate but immerse yourself too much in tasks that your direct reports are capable of handling.

Avoid Derailing

To develop a broad, strategic orientation, create goals in areas outside your specific expertise or in areas that require you to sell new ideas to your organization. These questions can help you focus on such areas:

- Whom do you need to influence to achieve the results you need?

- Who are the key players who can help you achieve your goals in this organization?

- Whom in your organization do you respect for their ability to influence and get things done? What special skills or knowledge do they demonstrate? What are their approaches?

- When was the last time you encountered a setback or frustration in your organization? How did you react? How did the situation turn out?

- Whom in your organization frustrates you the most and why? What are their goals? How can you get to know them better?

Improve Now

Other chapters in this book will help you devise strategies, tactics, and actions you can take to shore up your capacity for change. Here are those of most direct use:

Activity Center

Review and download these activities you can use for your development or with your team from this book's resource page at www.ccl.org/compassbook.

Boundary Spanning: A Plan to Span

Boundary Spanning: Powerful Questions

Strategic Planning and Implementation: Dust Off Your Strategy

Strategic Planning and Implementation: Develop Strategic-Plan Awareness

Resources

Brandon, R., & Seldman, M. (2004). *Survival of the savvy: High-integrity political tactics for career and company success.* New York, NY: Free Press.

Cartwright, T., & Baldwin, D. (2011). *Communicating your vision.* Greensboro, NC: Center for Creative Leadership.

Center for Creative Leadership. (2013). *Interpersonal savvy: Building and maintaining solid working relationships.* Greensboro, NC: Author.

CNN. (2005, Nov. 3). "Can I quit now?" FEMA chief wrote as Katrina raged. Retrieved from http://www.cnn.com/2005/US/11/03/brown.fema.emails/index.html

Criswell, C., & Cartwright, T. (2011). *Creating a vision.* Greensboro, NC: Center for Creative Leadership.

Gentry, W. A., & Leslie, J. B. (2013). *Developing political savvy.* Greensboro, NC: Center for Creative Leadership.

Gigerenzer, G. (2014). *Risk savvy: How to make good decisions.* New York, NY: Viking.

Hsu, S. S. (2005, Sept. 6). FEMA director singled out by response critics. *The Washington Post.* Retrieved from http://www.washingtonpost.com/wp-dyn/content/article/2005/09/05/AR2005090501590.html

Hsu, S. S. (2006, Feb. 12). Katrina report spreads blame. *The Washington Post.* Retrieved from http://www.washingtonpost.com/wp-dyn/content/article/2006/02/11/AR2006021101409.html

Scharlatt, H. (2008). *Selling your ideas to your organization.* Greensboro, NC: Center for Creative Leadership.

Van Velsor, E. (2013). *Broadening your organizational perspective.* Greensboro, NC: Center for Creative Leadership.

Zack, D. (2010). *Networking for people who hate networking: A field guide for introverts, the overwhelmed, and the underconnected.* Oakland, CA: Berrett-Koehler.

105

Problems with Interpersonal Relationships

Difficulty developing good working relationships with others because of a lack of understanding about what others need and how to respond appropriately.

Intelligence, acumen, and insight will take you pretty far. But without a keen sense of how to make and keep productive relationships, those things may not bring you success as a leader. You don't want to be seen as a poor team player, unable or unwilling to involve others. So rely on your strengths, and balance whatever weaknesses you have with your colleagues' reservoir of skills and experience. That's the collaborative, cooperative field of goodwill fostered by great managers and leaders. An inability to form strong interpersonal relationships, built on trust and mutual understanding, threatens that goodwill. And it can ultimately threaten a career, as it did with the CEO featured in the following story.

Leadership in Action

When Home Depot recruited Robert Nardelli as CEO in 2000, he was already recognized as a successful executive who had nearly taken the top spot at GE. It was believed that he would be able to apply his skills in a similar fashion to the hardware giant that had begun as an entrepreneurial experiment and grown to a multibillion dollar company. But only a few years later, Nardelli resigned, having created a fair amount of shake-up within Home Depot and with investors, without much to show for the disruption.

One of Nardelli's key errors was a failure to respect the Home Depot business culture, which favored a personal, service-oriented experience for customers. Nardelli alienated many on the ground level of the organization by hiring numerous part-time employees with less expertise, which damaged customer service—an obvious misunderstanding of the Home Depot brand. It seemed that Nardelli believed he could apply the same strategies he'd used to great effect within GE, without realizing that the companies were too different from one another for those strategies to work.

The situation came to a head in 2006, during a shareholders meeting in which Nardelli flatly refused to answer questions about his strategy and the company's performance. It's not clear what Nardelli hoped to accomplish with this strategy, but the result was a widespread alienation among the people Nardelli depended upon for support. By the time of Nardelli's resignation, Home Depot stock value had fallen 8 percent, which looked especially grim compared with the 180-percent growth of their top competitor, Lowe's. Although Nardelli's resignation was nominally voluntary, it's hard to imagine any other outcome (Home unimprovement, 2007).

What Potential Derailment Can Look Like

Leaders without the skill to build and maintain interpersonal relationships

- make direct reports or peers feel stupid or unintelligent
- leave trails of bruised people in pursuing their careers
- are reluctant to share decision making
- order people around rather than working to get them on board
- don't listen
- don't ask questions to learn about and understand others
- don't care much about what interests and excites other people
- tailor their communication on their own assertions without thinking of their audience's needs and motivations
- are oblivious to their impact on situations and people
- don't make the first move to engage with others
- fail to make people feel at ease in tense situations
- find it hard to build rapport with others
- lack emotional intelligence
- are seen as arrogant, shortsighted, rigid, impatient, unresponsive, antisocial, self-centered, and dismissive
- make quick judgments about others without attempting to understand their experiences
- have trouble connecting with diverse audiences
- don't build confidence in others
- suspect their colleagues aren't "up to the job"

Why It Derails Careers

If you struggle with interpersonal relationships, small misunderstandings can grow into big conflicts. Poor interpersonal relationships are a breeding ground for distrust and can undermine confidence in your leadership. If those problems persist, your organization might sideline you, or worse, dismiss you. Review the following list and note the items that you believe have the potential to derail you if you don't change how you handle interpersonal relationships.

- ❏ Your social skills are underdeveloped.
- ❏ You are impatient with people.
- ❏ Your role models lack interpersonal sensitivity.
- ❏ You prefer to talk rather than listen.
- ❏ You have received feedback that you come across as self-centered and insensitive to others' needs.
- ❏ You are quick to judge other people.
- ❏ You tend to focus on the business more than people.
- ❏ You've been told that you lack diplomacy or tact.
- ❏ You've received feedback that others see you as slick or manipulative.
- ❏ You lose touch with your core values or beliefs.
- ❏ You've been told that people see you as a chameleon, changing to meet the needs of every situation.
- ❏ Upper management sees you as too soft on people and not willing to demand excellence.
- ❏ You've been told that you come off as inauthentic—people don't trust their interactions with you and think you're "playing politics."
- ❏ You're impatient that people don't notice right away the changes you are making to your behavior.

Avoid Derailing

To fortify your current relationships and develop your ability to build new ones, create goals in areas that require you to work with groups other than your own, that push you to build a leadership network, and that otherwise contain situations in which you must get along with others and understand them to produce positive results. These questions can help you focus on such areas:

- How well do you really know the people around you?

- Do you focus on work tasks at the expense of learning about the people around you? What distracts you from focusing on the people around you?

- Do you spend enough time networking or building relationships?

- How would stronger rapport with others help you be more effective or get more done?

- How do you think other people perceive you? What feedback have you received about your interpersonal skills?

- How much are you focused on understanding and meeting the needs of others rather than only on your own interests?

Improve Now

Other chapters in this book will help you devise strategies, tactics, and actions you can take to shore up your capacity for managing productive work relationships. Here are those of most direct use:

1. Communication
2. Influence
12. Coach and Develop Others
13. Compassion and Sensitivity
14. Conflict Resolution
18. Credibility and Integrity
31. Interpersonal Savvy
37. Relationship Management
49. Trust

Activity Center

Review and download these activities you can use for your development or with your team from this book's resource page at www.ccl.org/compassbook.

Interpersonal Savvy: Choose to Be Interpersonally Savvy
Interpersonal Savvy: How They Perceive You
Relationship Management: Check Yourself
Relationship Management: Partner with Me

Resources

Booher, D. D. (2015). *What more can I say? Why communication fails and what to do about it*. New York, NY: Prentice Hall.

Cain, S. (2012). *Quiet: The power of introverts in a world that can't stop talking*. New York, NY: Crown.

Cartwright, T. (2003). *Managing conflict with peers*. Greensboro, NC: Center for Creative Leadership.

Cartwright, T. (2009). *Changing yourself and your reputation*. Greensboro, NC: Center for Creative Leadership.

Center for Creative Leadership. (n.d.). *Be grateful to lead*. (Video). Retrieved from https://vimeo.com/160131385

Center for Creative Leadership. (2013). *Interpersonal savvy: Building and maintaining solid working relationships*. Greensboro, NC: Author.

Gentry, W. (2016). *Be the boss everyone wants to work for: A guide for new leaders.* Oakland, CA: Berrett-Koehler.

Gentry, W. A., & Leslie, J. B. (2013). *Developing political savvy*. Greensboro, NC: Center for Creative Leadership.

Home unimprovement: Was Nardelli's tenure at Home Depot a blueprint for failure? (2007). *Knowledge@Wharton*. Retrieved from http://knowledge.wharton.upenn.edu/article/home-unimprovement-was-nardellis-tenure-at-home-depot-a-blueprint-for-failure/

McCauley, C. D. (2012). Reflection and integration: Supervisor-employee relationships. In L. T. de Tormes Eby, & T. D. Allen (Eds.), *Personal relationships: The effect on employee attitudes, behavior, and well-being* (pp. 95–105). New York, NY: Taylor & Francis.

Popejoy, B., & McManigle, B. J. (2002). *Managing conflict with direct reports*. Greensboro, NC: Center for Creative Leadership.

Scharlatt, H. (2016). *Resolving conflict: Ten steps for turning negatives to positives*. Greensboro, NC: Center for Creative Leadership.

Sharpe, D., & Johnson, E. (2002). *Managing conflict with your boss*. Greensboro, NC: Center for Creative Leadership.

Zack, D. (2010). *Networking for people who hate networking: A field guide for introverts, the overwhelmed, and the underconnected*. Oakland, CA: Berrett-Koehler.

Part Four
WHAT'S NEXT

By using this book you show some level of commitment to developing your leadership skills. CCL has long recognized that leaders develop through their experiences, on and off the job. But amassing myriad experiences doesn't guarantee learning. For that you need to be intentional about how you use experience to learn, be ready to learn, and have a plan with achievable goals that excite you.

Almost all organizations change over time in response to a continually shifting environment. Most likely, you will need to make some changes yourself. You must develop competency in new areas to remain valuable to your organization and to help it achieve sustainability. The competencies crucial to effective leadership are also changing. New areas of research into neuroscience, network analysis, health and wellness, and others will no doubt highlight new lessons of experience.

Leadership acumen is continuously developed over a lifetime. Start with the right information, create goals that are meaningful and challenging, and gather the support you will need to make changes to your perspective and your performance. With this strong, balanced position as your base, you will be better prepared and able to learn and to develop the skills and perspectives that will enable you to adapt to changing circumstances and to leave a legacy that others can build on.

106
Learning from Experience

Learning from experience is the number one way that leaders develop. That claim is hard to dispute. CCL has researched the "lessons of experience" and their role in leadership development since its founding in 1970. From that work, CCL has organized five categories of key developmental experiences:

- **Challenging Assignments.** A job or a task related to a job that stretches you because it is new, complex, or demanding. Examples include being responsible for turning around an operation in trouble and moving from a line to a staff position.

- **Other People.** Positive and negative role models—primarily bosses and others higher in the organization—who have strongly influenced your approach to management.

- **Hardships.** Setbacks and failures that engender a sense of loss and isolation. Examples include business mistakes, demotions and missed promotions, and personal life traumas.

- **Coursework.** Formal training and academic programs.

- **Personal Life Experiences.** Experiences that occur in your family, school, or community, and that vary in nature from difficult situations to inspirational ones.

Key Principles in the Lessons of Experience

Some people learn more from experience than others. Just because you've experienced a scenario that's rich in learning opportunities doesn't mean you're going to learn from it. Developmental experiences are only as rich as you make them. Themes that run through these five categories help focus leaders on what matters most when learning from experience.

Experience is the best teacher. We learn more about how to be an effective leader from our experiences on the job than from anywhere else. It counts for more than the guidance you get from your boss, colleagues, coaches, and others. And, as mentioned before, it counts for more than formal development, such as corporate training and academic courses. If you're committed to developing yourself as a leader, embed challenging learning experiences into your everyday work.

Not all experiences are equal. Different experiences teach different things (hence the five categories). For example, if your job is redefined to one with a bigger scope, your experience in that expanded role might teach you about handling risk and how to balance the time you spend working with the time you spend on personal, family, and community pursuits. Or if you take on a different role at the same level in your organization, you have the chance to learn how to see things from a different perspective.

Quality, quantity, and diversity of experiences enrich learning. The bigger and broader your experiences, the bigger and broader the web of lessons they offer. Experiences that push you out of your comfort zone are good opportunities for development. For example, experiences that include unfamiliar responsibilities, are high stakes, demand influence without authority, and involve working across cultures make an experience high in learning value. If you have many experiences in a certain area, you may learn the same lessons over and over, but you can also acquire a depth of learning in that area.

Your experiences are yours alone. Although you might share an experience with others, (working on a team that's developing a new product line, for example), what you draw from that experience is influenced by your perspective, your role, your openness to learning, and other factors. Certainly, your experiences can't be reduced to any other person's experiences. But at the same time —

The value of experience is universal. CCL's research shows that the learning potential of experience is constant for all kinds of people—across gender, ethnicity, and culture. The power of learning from experience transcends demographic groups and lines on the map. It's a fundamental quality of how we learn. Learning from experience is for anybody and everybody.

Misunderstanding Lessons of Experience

Just as there are patterns to our developmental experiences, there are also misunderstandings that can hinder your learning from experiences. Try hard to set these preconceptions aside and open yourself to all of the developmental potential of experience.

Your resume is a complete record of your leadership experiences. Even though much leadership development derives from work experiences, there are uncountable opportunities to learn from your experiences outside the workplace. It is often the case that nonwork settings yield lessons that you can adapt to the work challenges you encounter.

Learning on the job is mostly about learning to do your job more effectively. Different on-the-job experiences teach different things. They don't just teach you about how to work better. CCL research shows that the lessons learned from experience can potentially fall into three different "worlds": the world of work, the world of people, and the world of self. While the lessons in these worlds emerge and are applied differently, they don't always translate directly to work performance. Nevertheless, they ground you in understanding, self-awareness, and in other fundamental ways that enhance the lessons available from your experiences and that you can apply in a variety of circumstances.

Learning from experience is an event. Learning from experience is an ongoing process. You haven't really learned a lesson until you apply it. Absent application, a lesson's value lies unrealized. And because applying a lesson is itself a new experience, the potential to learn never ends. There's always something that might be revealed or looked at in a different light.

Readiness

You may sincerely want to develop your leadership acumen, but if you approach potential learning experiences without clear expectations, goals, or a plan to put what you learn into practice, then you may not be ready for the lessons embedded in those experiences. Increase the learning potential of experience by clarifying expectations and by understanding and increasing your motivation to learn.

Think about What You Need to Learn

Spend some time thinking about your development needs, both for your immediate circumstances and for your long-term career goals. Think hard about connecting your personal leadership development goals to your organization's strategic goals. Take time to consider your level of enthusiasm for taking on a developmental experience. Reflect on the following questions to connect your development to organizational goals, to measure your enthusiasm, and to understand your motivation to learn:

- Do you struggle with motivating your employees?
- Do you want better communication between yourself and your staff?
- Do you have trouble delegating?
- Does your manager discount your ideas?
- Have you received feedback from others that contradicts the way you see yourself?
- Has a performance review indicated a serious weakness?
- Are you looking to advance in your current organization?
- Do you want to move to another company in a different industry?
- Have you been thinking about setting up your own business?
- Do you think about leaving the corporate world and contributing your talents to a nonprofit organization?
- Do you want to move from the nonprofit world to the corporate arena?
- What skills will you need for the future you have in mind for yourself?
  - Will you need to be very accomplished in selling yourself and your ideas?
  - Will you need to be able to elicit the highest contribution of other people?
  - Will you need to quickly establish rapport and trust with people you work with but never see in person?
  - Will you need to hone your ability to prioritize tasks and projects?

Motivate Yourself to Learn

One way you can increase your enthusiasm for tackling developmental experiences is to reflect on the benefits. Think about how such experiences connect with your career interests, professional concerns, and personal growth. Consider your personal values and how they play out in your work life and your personal life. Check the items below that reflect what motivates you to develop (or add your own statements to this list).

- ❏ I value development.
- ❏ I want to maximize my potential as a leader.
- ❏ I have ambitions to rise in my organization and to succeed in my career.
- ❏ I want to learn new techniques for presenting my ideas to upper management.
- ❏ I can benefit from learning how others have communicated and led major organizational initiatives.
- ❏ I want to know how I can leverage my individual strengths to be more effective in my job.
- ❏ I need time to focus on myself, my personal growth, and my career goals.
- ❏ New experiences will make me more marketable inside and outside of my organization.
- ❏ I could use more effective strategies for motivating my employees.
- ❏ I want to learn how to influence others and to lead in situations where I don't have authority.
- ❏ I could use more effective strategies for dealing with my boss.

Another strategy to developing readiness to learn and develop is for you to consider the implications of not participating. CCL research shows that leaders who resist making changes or ignore development needs risk derailing their careers. Consider the following questions to shore up your motivation to learn:

- Am I relying on my track record for promotion?

- Do I depend too much on my strongest skills?

- Does the feedback I've received about my leadership skills match the way I see myself?

- Can I build an effective team and lead it to its goal?

- If I continue with the same management tactics I use now, will my team continue to perform well?

- Can I work effectively within my organization without learning to understand diverse viewpoints, personalities, and communication styles?

- Can I afford not to develop a broader understanding of my organization's strategy?

- Can I succeed by relegating interpersonal skills to a lower priority than technical skills?

Assessment, Challenge, and Support

During the course of your career, you will have many different kinds of developmental experiences. All of those experiences follow a common path—they are avenues toward personal and professional growth. CCL believes there are three key elements that drive leadership development: assessment, challenge, and support. Assessment is information, presented formally or informally, that tells you where you are now; what are your current strengths, what development needs are important in your current situation, and what is your current level of effectiveness. Challenge refers to elements of an experience that are new and that may call for skills and perspectives not currently available to you, or it can refer to elements in an experience that create imbalance for you and provide an opportunity to question established ways of thinking and acting. Support includes elements of an experience that enhance self-confidence and reassure you about your strengths, current skills, and established ways of thinking and acting.

On Your Way

Learning from experience is your best chance for developing the skills you need to promote direction, alignment, and commitment in your team and among employees and groups across your organization. In the best circumstances, you want to have a variety of experiences to gain a broad and deep source of skill and knowledge. That way, you are prepared to lead in any situation—even a situation you've never experienced before.

Learning from experience doesn't happen without your attention and action. Think about the kinds of experiences you need to develop the skills that will sustain your career and your organization. Seek out those experiences. And make yourself ready to learn. Pay attention to what motivates you to learn, and use your motivation to make the most of learning opportunities. When you're faced with difficult circumstances, use your motivation to transform difficulty into lessons. And then apply those lessons to new situations you encounter.

Think carefully about the three elements that comprise learning: assessment, challenge, and support. Make sure to include all of them in preparing yourself for development. Know where you stand and what you need, find experiences that offer the potential for learning how to do what you need or that bolster your current skills, and seek others for support and encouragement—and feedback—as you develop yourself into the leader you want to be.

Resources

Browning, H., & Van Velsor, E. (1999). *Three keys to development: Defining and meeting your leadership challenges.* Greensboro, NC: Center for Creative Leadership.

Hallenbeck, G. (2016). *Learning agility: Unlock the lessons of experience.* Greensboro, NC: Center for Creative Leadership.

Hallenbeck, G., & CCL Associates. (2017). *Lead 4 success: Learn the essentials of true leadership.* Greensboro, NC: Center for Creative Leadership.

McCauley, C. D., DeRue, D. S., Yost, P. R., & Taylor, S. (Eds.). (2014). *Experience-driven leader development: Models, tools, best practices, and advice for on-the-job development.* San Francisco, CA: Wiley.

McCauley, C. D., & McCall, M. W. (2014). *Using experience to develop leadership talent: How organizations leverage on-the-job development.* San Francisco, CA: Jossey-Bass.

Ruderman, M. N., & Ohlott, P. J. (2000). *Learning from life: Turning life's lessons into leadership experience.* Greensboro, NC: Center for Creative Leadership.

Scisco, P., McCauley, C. D., Leslie, J. B., & Elsey, R. (2013). *Change now! Five steps to better leadership.* Greensboro, NC: Center for Creative Leadership.

107

How to Set Development Goals

Effective goal-setting includes these elements: clarity, challenge, commitment, feedback, and complexity (Locke & Latham, 1990). Your goals should be clearly stated so you can measure your progress toward achieving them, be difficult enough that they stretch your abilities and promote learning, inspire commitment so that you stick to them, include ways to get feedback on your progress, and be complex but achievable with support and resources.

CCL's five-step, developmental-focused, goal-setting method adheres closely to these five components. The method is a result of CCL research into this simple question: Why do people get stuck when they try to make a change in habits of behavior and thinking? The quick and easy answer, while accurate, isn't very satisfying: change is hard. But it's possible. Review your life and see the many instances of learning and development described by goals: an advanced degree, proficiency in a second language, running a marathon. You can probably remember how frustrated you felt during the initial stages of development and how elated you felt every time you reached a milestone. Those experiences are hallmarks of the learning process.

Don't look at goals as check boxes or hoped-for results. They are part of the process of development. It's a process that focuses your attention on the kinds of change that excite you, that reveals what kinds of obstacles you might face, that spells out what you will do when achieving your goals turns difficult, that musters the support you need to get through the inevitable letdowns, and that gives you a way to celebrate your progress so that you feel energized to keep going. Elements that comprise successful goal-setting and development are:

- Focus on one area of change.

- Set goals that work for you.

- Craft your plan.

- Overcome obstacles.

- Stay on course.

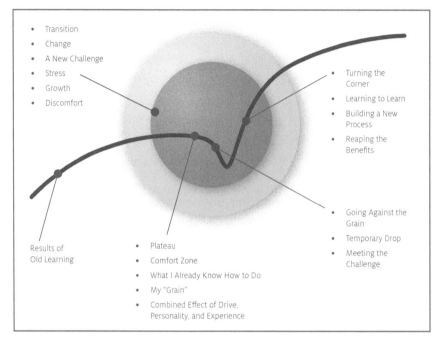

- Transition
- Change
- A New Challenge
- Stress
- Growth
- Discomfort

- Turning the Corner
- Learning to Learn
- Building a New Process
- Reaping the Benefits

- Going Against the Grain
- Temporary Drop
- Meeting the Challenge

Results of Old Learning

- Plateau
- Comfort Zone
- What I Already Know How to Do
- My "Grain"
- Combined Effect of Drive, Personality, and Experience

Learning almost always causes a drop in performance before improvements become noticeable.

Focus on One Area of Change

The competencies you want to develop fall within broad areas. To "focus on an area" means that in creating your development plan, you should pay attention to what matters most and to what you can do differently, what you can do better, and even what you should stop doing. To keep these qualities in mind while setting goals, think about these three things when you pick an area for change:

- Focus on a change that energizes you.

- Focus on a change that creates positive outcomes.

- Focus on a change that is at the right level of difficulty—not so easy that it's not a challenge, and not so difficult that you can't develop the competency you need.

It's not always easy to pick just one area of focus. What you want to change and how you want to change depend a lot on your point of view. Perhaps the area you want to focus on is to be more effective in your role. Other areas of focus could include achieving your career aspirations, developing and living up to your reputation as a leader, or moving from skilled to highly skilled in a technical area. By creating a list of focus areas, you increase your access to development goals that you can set for yourself. The point is that you can't set effective goals at the level of a focus area. You have to dive into that area to create specific goals for change—and before you do that, you have to focus on one area of change.

Set Goals That Work for You

We often use goals to focus time and energy. We use goals to achieve what we want to do and what we are asked to do. The right set of goals drive you forward, but goals without purpose are like tires spinning in mud—a lot of action, but you're not making any progress. Get your development goals rolling by creating actions and measures that help you grow as a leader and that map your progress.

The first thing to know about goals is that there are three kinds:

- Goals that change how you act. These are *behavioral* goals.

- Goals that improve a skill. These are *competency* goals.

- Goals that meet a target. These are *outcome* goals.

Your challenge is to figure out the right combination of goals for the results you want. This book includes many different competencies. Developing any of them can call for any of these three kinds of goals (don't assume that you should set only competency goals). To achieve competency, you might have to change some of your behaviors. And you might learn what you need to achieve competency by reaching specific outcomes.

Setting a behavioral goal. Set a behavioral goal when people tell you that you are acting in a way that undermines your ability to lead. Set a behavioral goal if you avoid taking some action or another because it makes you uncomfortable or because you don't make time. Behavioral goals are readily noticed, so set one if you want others to know that you are committed to being a better leader. Qualities of an effective behavioral goal are:

- others can see you working toward the goal
- you know the times and places where you will act differently

Setting a competency goal. Set a competency goal when you need to develop in an area beyond a single behavior, such as strategic thinking, delegation, or managing conflict. Competency goals are useful for preparing yourself to take on increased responsibility or a more complex job. You can also use a competency goal if your organization has a competency model that lays out what its leaders need to know and what they need to be capable of doing, and you want to connect your goals to that model. Qualities of an effective competency goal are:

- a competency label that describes and focuses the competency; for example, "shorten response time to customers" rather than "provide better customer service"
- performance results that say why you want to develop the competency; for example, "to increase repeat business" is a result of improved responsiveness to customers

Setting an outcome goal. Create an outcome goal when you can identify specific activities that will jump-start the change you want to make in your selected area of development. Use one when you can create discrete actions that lead to the achievement you want to reach. You might also use an outcome goal if measurable goals are important for you and your organization and will motivate you. Qualities of an effective outcome goal are:

- specific accomplishments or achievements; for example "train for and complete my city's marathon race" rather than "participate in athletic activities"
- a time frame; for example, "during the next six months" rather than "spend more time on athletic pursuits"

Craft Your Plan

Once you have set out your goals, it's time to write a plan that will help you achieve them. As you draft your plan, think who, what, when, where, and how. You will use your ideas about the following four critical elements of development planning to make a solid plan:

- tactics
- resources
- tracking
- celebrating

Tactics describe actions you will take. Name the specific things you will do to change a behavior, acquire a competency, or accomplish an outcome.

- **What** are you going to do?
- **When** will you do it?

Match your tactics to the type of goal you're setting. A behavioral goal such as "check in daily with two people working on projects I supervise" suggests a tactic such as "Post a list of project members on my wall with the question 'Who will I talk to today?' in bold letters at the top." A competency goal might employ a tactic such as reviewing other people's ideas about the skill by reading books or talking with people who have mastered the competency. An ambitious outcome goal might call for a tactic such as breaking that goal into discrete steps to make it manageable.

Resources describe time, money, and people. If you lack support in place, reaching your goals becomes too difficult.

- **What** will you invest?
- **What** resources are available to you?
- **What** do you need from others?

Tracking means regularly checking your progress. It's important to know whether you're on track for meeting your goals and how far you have to go to achieve them.

- **How** will you check how you're doing?
- **When** will you check?

Celebrating refers to how you acknowledge your progress and reward yourself for it. Celebrating each step along the way toward your goal can help you stay energized and engaged with your development. It gives you a chance to reflect on what you've learned.

- **What** kind of reward is meaningful to you?

- **How** will you reward yourself when you achieve milestones and goals?

- **Who** will you celebrate with?

Overcome Obstacles

You will encounter barriers while working toward your goals. Obstacles can knock you off track and frustrate your efforts to change. However, if you know what those barriers are, then you can plan how you will deal with them so you can keep moving forward. Though you can't anticipate every roadblock, you can prepare for the most common obstacles you're likely to face. From the previous three steps in CCL's goal-setting process you've already learned how to avoid some of them. You chose where to focus your attention. You wrote clear, energized, and achievable goals. You developed tactics to help you change. Inaction in any of those areas can stymie your development. Other common obstacles to be aware of include:

- not enough time to spend on your development

- people who react negatively to the changes you make

- fear that can accompany change

Figuring out how to fit new commitments into a busy life is challenging. If time is a potential obstacle to reaching your goals, consider these four strategies:

- Estimate—if you have underestimated the time it is taking to reach your goal, ask others who have achieved the goal how long it took for them. If your estimate varies a lot from theirs, rethink the time you will spend working on your development.

- Prioritize—review your schedule and mark your essential commitments. Defer, delegate, or delete the rest. Achieving your goals is an essential commitment, so create time for your goals in your daily schedule.

- Negotiate—new commitments can affect the people around you. Talk to them about how to minimize that impact and listen to what they—your staff, your peers, your family, and others—have to say about how your changes affect them.

- Plan—don't work on all your goals at once. Sequence and stage them to create more focus and to set priorities. You might want to start with your most important goal. If that's an ambitious goal, break it down into manageable pieces that take less time to achieve.

People will react to your changes. Don't ignore the impact of your changes on them and how they respond. Other people aren't likely to sabotage your development, but they might inadvertently stifle your efforts when they react to them. Here are some things to do about that:

- Share—tell others why you are pursuing your goals. Help them to understand your perspective, motivations, and intentions. You might also get their cooperation and support in the bargain.

- Sell—when you succeed, so do others. That may not be obvious to other people, so help them see how they benefit from the changes you're making. Perhaps your growth will gain them recognition, give them new experiences, or help their careers. Be realistic. Things will be different—no getting around that. But your development doesn't have to be a negative influence on others.

- Enlist allies—gather a support network in order to demonstrate why your goals are important and why other people should cooperate with you. Enlist your boss, your direct reports, your peers, and people outside of your organization.

Fear can disrupt your development. Fear can be the most difficult obstacle you'll face. But it doesn't have to stop you in your tracks. You can make fear work for you, but you have to get to know it first.

- Practice—you don't have to practice your new behavior or skill where the whole organization is watching. You can practice the changes you're making in many low-risk places. For example, many roles in volunteer organizations offer practice opportunities without putting your career at risk. Agree to be a choir director. Organize a book or a movie club. Use the lessons that you learn from low-risk experiences on challenging work situations.

- Reminders—show your commitment. Make yourself personal and unique reminders to bring your focus back to your goals. Don't bury your reminders on your to-do list. Put them where you, and others, will see them. If your reminders create curiosity and conversation about your goals, then you can use that interest to recruit more allies.

- Watch the downsides—pursuing a goal has benefits and can have effects that might make you hesitate. For example, if you want to become better at delegating, think about the downsides of that skill that bother you. Delegating means turning over some control. Are you comfortable with that? What if the results don't meet your standards? Decide ahead of time how you will deal with negative emotions that might arise as you work toward a goal.

- Find a guide—look for someone to share lessons from his or her own experience in the area you're focused on. Pick a person you trust to give you alternative perspectives about achieving your goals. Use those perspectives to push back fear about trying new things.

- Be confident—at this point in your career, you've enjoyed some successes. Don't forget that just because you're trying something new. After all, your success isn't entirely based on luck. Review your track record. Use your own history for the courage to change.

As you meet obstacles, think about how you can adapt your development plan so that you stay on track. Make allowances for setbacks, but don't let them define your progress.

Stay on Course

You know what changes you want to make and what goals you want to achieve. You know why you want to achieve them and how. And you have ideas about how to deal with obstacles along the way. Other priorities might tempt you and demand your attention. Stay focused on accomplishing your goals. Here are some ideas and tips that will help:

- Regularly revisit your development plan.

- Keep your goals in the forefront of your mind.

- Make your development part of your daily routine.

- Record your daily reflections—in a journal, in an audio recording, on your phone, on a video.

- Write down what you're doing to realize your goals.

- Pay attention to how other people react to what you say and do as you try out new behaviors and skills.

- Ask others for feedback.

- Learn from failure. Write down what went wrong and what you learned from that.

- Ask people interested in your success for suggestions about how you can adjust your plan.

- If a tactic isn't working, don't abandon your goal. Come up with other tactics.

- Make sure your timeline for development is reasonable. If your deadlines are tripping you up, make your timeline more realistic. But keep it challenging.

- If a goal seems overwhelming, break it down into smaller, more manageable steps.

- Are you losing energy? Slow down a little. Take a break. Development isn't a race.

- Periodically review your goals to ensure their relevancy.

Change happens when you decide what to do and act. Keep your eyes on the finish line. Pay attention to the impact your development is having on others. Deal with the obstacles that come your way. Adapt and adjust to keep yourself moving forward.

Get started!

Resources

Browning, H., & Van Velsor, E. (1999). *Three keys to development: Defining and meeting your leadership challenges*. Greensboro, NC: Center for Creative Leadership.

Chappelow, C., & Leslie, J. B. (2004). *Keeping your career on track: Twenty success strategies*. Greensboro, NC: Center for Creative Leadership.

Dalton, M. A. (1998). *Becoming a more versatile learner*. Greensboro, NC: Center for Creative Leadership.

Giles, S. (2016, March 15). The most important leadership competencies, according to leaders around the world. *Harvard Business Review.* Retrieved from https://hbr.org/2016/03/the-most-important-leadership-competencies-according-to-leaders-around-the-world

Hallenbeck, G., & CCL Associates. (2017). *Lead 4 success: Learn the essentials of true leadership*. Greensboro, NC: Center for Creative Leadership.

King, S. N., & Altman, D. G. (2011). *Discovering the leader in you*. (Workbook). San Francisco, CA: Jossey-Bass.

King, S. N., Altman, D. G., & Lee, R. J. (2011). *Discovering the leader in you* (Rev. ed.). San Francisco, CA: Jossey-Bass.

Locke, E. A., & Latham, G. P. (1990). *A theory of goal setting and task performance*. Englewood Cliffs, NJ: Prentice Hall.

Martineau, J., & Johnson, E. (1999). *Preparing for development: Making the most of formal leadership programs.* Greensboro, NC: Center for Creative Leadership.

McCauley, C. D. (2006). *Developmental assignments: Creating learning experiences without changing jobs*. Greensboro, NC: Center for Creative Leadership.

Mount, P., & Tardanico, S. (2014). *Beating the impostor syndrome*. Greensboro, NC: Center for Creative Leadership.

Scisco, P., McCauley, C. D., Leslie, J. B., & Elsey, R. (2013). *Change now! Five steps to better leadership*. Greensboro, NC: Center for Creative Leadership.

108
Future Competencies

Change is the one constant. Trends active now will affect organizations of the future. And that implies that the context in which leaders develop their skills, and the skills themselves, will also be affected. Expect competencies to be reconfigured in response to changing contexts. Differences in their granularity and in the scope and depth of their practice will reconfigure leaders' perspectives on many current competencies.

Consider the kinds of changes already afoot. In technology, artificial intelligence is moving beyond robotics on factory floors to algorithms that augment and in some cases replace human decision making altogether. Human augmentation itself is rapidly developing—already visible in wearable technology that provides input of all kinds, from health data to geographic location services to heads-up displays (once relegated to complex machines such as fighter jets). Advanced safety features on cars, such as lane and parking assists and auto-braking are becoming the norm. And the Internet of Things is taking shape all around us, linking feedback data from many sources to organizational systems.

Demographics are already forcing change in many organizations and in how leaders work with multiple generations and diverse differences among their employees. More women are rising to senior positions. The gig economy supports a mobile, untethered, unaffiliated workforce where competencies such as trust and delegation take on new aspects. Globalization and its accompanying population migrations continue to affect the very environment in which organizations operate. And though not all of these changes directly affect leaders and leader development, they add increasing layers of complexity onto the world in which leaders work.

Changes to organizational environments are being matched by growing attention to and appreciation of the inner life of leaders. New associations have arisen between leader development and brain science and to the cross-pollination of cultural practices that promise to make real differences to leader performance. From that perspective, which CCL calls *holistic leadership*, the principles of leader development appear incomplete. The traditional focus on observable actions (which will remain vital to leader performance) ignores automatic cognitive processes and influences of which leaders are largely unaware (Ruderman, Clerkin, & Connolly, 2014). Practices once foreign to commercial enterprises, such as mindfulness and meditation, are gaining favor as neuroscience provides evidence of their positive effect on productivity, stress, focus, and other concerns. Beyond a shift in behavior lie new ways of thinking. Leaders who become aware of and can take cognitive control of their inner wiring can respond to circumstances and to other people in positive, productive ways that might otherwise be short-circuited by automatic reactions.

The World to Be

CCL remains vigilant to these and other trends, marking several that seem destined to influence leadership and leader development—including the kinds of competencies that may be required for top performance in the future. In 2007 and again in 2016, CCL reviewed its then-current database of 360-assessment responses to ask the bosses and coworkers of tens of thousands of leaders three key questions:

- What leadership skills and perspectives are critical for success?
- How strong is the leadership bench in these critical skills and perspectives?
- And what potential pitfalls lie ahead for these leaders?

They told us that *leading employees, strategic perspective, decisiveness, composure, change management,* and *building relationships* were the most critical skills in order for the organizations to survive and thrive. Interestingly, both studies, though ten years apart, revealed almost the same results (*composure* dropped out of the top six, replaced by *being a quick study*). CCL also asked about the skills most needed to ensure career success. In both studies, *managing change, learning agility, interpersonal relationships*, and *collaboration* led the list of critical skills.

In general the studies show how these skills are shaping organizational change today and in the future. New generational preferences, new forms of technology-supported collaboration, globalization, flatter organizational structures, more open organizational boundaries, rapid advances in knowledge of all kinds, and the use of big data analytics to shift the landscape within which leaders (and others) exercise influence are all affecting the competencies leaders will need. And in today's hyperfast world of constant complex change, some competencies will rise to greater prominence, as Bill Pasmore and Sylvester Taylor describe in a 2017 article:

Discovery-based learning. Continuous learning will remain critical in a fast-paced, innovation-driven, and continually changing future. The type of learning that will be required is not just learning from books or even experience, but combines *learning agility* with learning from experiments.

Collaborative strategic decision making. *Decision making, collaboration,* and *strategic thinking* are important contemporary competencies. Parts of each merge to meet the challenge of leading in flatter organizational structures, amid cultures of equality and teamwork among knowledgeable contributors in and outside the organization, and new generations' unwillingness to put up with positional power over knowledge-based power. Leaders who are most comfortable with control-oriented leadership in the guise of collaborative leadership will lose much of their effectiveness in future organizations.

Shaping work for meaning. Millennials, today's largest generational group, look for challenging assignments and opportunities for learning and development. Most people of that generation don't want to flee large bureaucratic organizations to join start-ups; most would prefer to continue to work where they are but won't if opportunities to learn, grow, and advance seem limited or a long way off (Deal & Levenson, 2016). Leaders who want to be successful in the future will have to figure out how to increase the meaningful challenges available in organizations so that they aren't reserved for "high potentials" but available to all.

Active, open networking. Future organizations will rely heavily on networks of temporary contributors from outside the organization much more than organizations do today. Knowing how to create and leverage open networks will be a key differentiator between successful leaders of the past and those of the future. That means, among other things, knowing when people outside of the organization can add value, having skill in virtual collaboration, and influencing outside contributors.

In some of its other work, CCL identifies other current trends that may affect how leaders develop and what they will need to develop to be successful in the future. For example:

- use of the ready-made as assists to learning and development, including templates and just-in-time instructions that disrupt the culture of experts

- microlearning opportunities that feature individualized content that's customized for use in specific situations

- social media's influence on organizational transparency, partnerships, and collaborative networks

- analytics and data visualization that makes complex information more accessible and understandable

- the increase in numbers of women in leadership roles, which may affect beliefs about leadership and performance

- the management of temporary workers and teams charged with short-term assignments

CCL isn't the only organization looking toward the future of leadership competency and performance. Bob Johansen's *Leaders Make the Future: Ten New Leadership Skills for an Uncertain World* (2012) drew on his work at the Institute of the Future to describe ten leadership skills that he argues will take on greater importance in the future:

1. maker instinct: ability to exploit your inner drive to build and grow things, as well as connect with others in the making

2. clarity: ability to see through messes and contradictions to a future that others cannot yet see (what CCL calls *Vision*)

3. dilemma flipping: ability to turn dilemmas—which, unlike problems, cannot be solved—into advantages and opportunities

4. immersive learning ability: ability to immerse yourself in unfamiliar environments, to learn from them in a first-person way (what CCL calls *Learning Agility*)

5. bio-empathy: ability to see things from nature's point of view; to understand, respect, and learn from its patterns

6. constructive depolarizing: ability to calm tense situations where differences dominate and communication breaks down (related to what CCL calls *Boundary Spanning*)

7. quiet transparency: ability to be open and authentic about what matters—without being overly self-promoting (related to what CCL calls *Credibility and Integrity*)

8. rapid prototyping: ability to create quick early versions of innovations with the expectation that later success will require early failures (related to what CCL calls *Innovation* and *Risk Taking*)

9. smart-mob organizing: ability to create, engage with, and nurture purposeful business or social change networks

10. commons creating: ability to seed, nurture, and grow shared assets that can benefit all players—and allow competition at a higher level (related to what CCL calls *External Partnership Management*)

Like the work from CCL and Johansen, a 2017 Deloitte report credits the continued rapid rise of technology as a factor that may determine future leader competencies and that calls for developing new mindsets and "new rules for people, work, and organizations" (p. 1). According to that report, there is a gap separating technological sophistication and performance. The difference between the rate of technological developments and the rate of human adaptation to the new environment shaped by that technology is growing wider, and business has not kept pace with the accelerated rate of that change. In meeting that challenge, organizational agility becomes increasingly important, and the report notes the movement from hierarchical structures to networked teams as signs that organizations are working to become more agile. They are seeking younger and more diverse leaders—which makes the challenge of accelerating leader development and ideas about difference, diversity, and inclusion ever more critical.

In light of these rapid changes, according to the report, leader competencies will likely change to suit future organizational environments, and leaders are likely to practice skills, attitudes, and mindsets in different ways. For example, competencies covered in *Compass* might conceivably shift (although it's not a certainty) in these directions:

- Leaders may experience *Negotiation* as an expansion from a skill for building consensus to a skill that manages different cultures and populations toward achieving a common goal (what Bob Johansen calls *commons creating*).

- *Systems Thinking* may become an engagement not just with an organization's systems but with external systems with which his or her organization interfaces and is interdependent. Consider further a potential shift to what might be called *network thinking*, which combines systems thinking and insight and skillful application of deep, broad networks of connections that create and bolster better communication, collaboration, and cooperation.

- *Resilience* (bouncing back from obstructions) may adopt aspects of *antifragility*, which involves not just bouncing back but bouncing forward to a new, stronger state.

- *Collaboration* may continue to grow in significance as fewer and fewer borders and boundaries separate organizations from their partners and competitors, and leaders find themselves operating in ad hoc groupings that may or may not rise to the level of formal partnerships.

- *Feedback* may conceivably broaden its scope as new technologies create a stream of data to help leaders modify their actions; for example, adding biofeedback to what they are learning from the developmental and performance feedback they give and receive.

Stephen Hawking once asked, drawing from Sir Arthur Eddington's "arrow of time," why is it that we can remember the past but not the future? But memory isn't necessary to understand that the surest thing about the future is that it will be different from the present. No amount of speculation will give us perfect vision of the world to come. But leaders can prepare for what circumstances will plausibly occur. They can prepare by remaining watchful and curious. They can look not just to the fringes of their industries but to the fringes of adjoining industries (think about leaders in the automotive industry remaining vigilant about the conversations and trends in the biomedical field). And they can bring in some of what they see to their own organizations to create what Stan Gryskiewicz calls "positive turbulence" (1999), which can potentially generate innovative responses.

Moreover, leaders can extend their understanding of current competencies to embrace a broader field of action:

- collaboration in virtual environments

- strategic thinking at all organizational levels

- delegation in an environment of temporary workers and autonomous robot labor

- ethics in a world where decisions are reached with algorithms rather than human reasoning

- the idea of organization itself in a sharing economy (Uber and Airbnb are two well-known examples of organizing the sharing economy)

Thinking in bigger ways is at the heart of what Nick Petrie calls "vertical development." Competency-based training is horizontal development—development of skills and the accumulation of knowledge. Admittedly, that's a simplistic definition that brings to mind filling an empty glass with water. Vertical development isn't exclusive to horizontal development, as competencies operate in areas of knowledge (learning agility works within vertical development, not outside of it, for example). Vertical development isn't about more skills but about greater cognitive abilities—which leaders derive through competent practice of important skills. Effective leaders will develop a "bigger mind" to stay effective as the future unfolds in unexpected ways (2014).

You may be familiar with the French phrase, *plus* ça *change, plus c'est la même chose*—which in English usually appears as "the more things change, the more they stay the same." No matter how clouded our sight into the future, we might have to update our idioms once we get there.

Resources

Deal, J. J., & Levenson, A. (2016). *What millennials want from work: How to maximize engagement in today's workforce.* New York, NY: McGraw-Hill.

Deloitte Development. (2017). *Rewriting the rules for the digital age: 2017 Deloitte global human capital trends.* (Report). New York, NY: Deloitte University Press.

Gryskiewicz, S. S. (1999). *Positive turbulence: Developing climates for creativity, innovation, and renewal.* San Francisco, CA: Jossey-Bass.

Johansen, B. (2012). *Leaders make the future: Ten new leadership skills for an uncertain world* (2nd ed.). San Francisco, CA: Berrett-Koehler.

Pasmore, B., & Taylor, S. (2017, Jan. 19). Core competencies remain critical to success. *Workforce.com*. Retrieved from http://www.workforce .com/2017/01/19/core-competencies-remain-critical-success/

Petrie, N. (2014). *Future trends in leadership development.* (White paper). Center for Creative Leadership. Retrieved from http://www.ccl.org/wp-content/uploads/2015/04/futureTrends.pdf

Ruderman, M. N., Clerkin, C., & Connolly, C. (2014) *Leadership development beyond competencies: Moving to a holistic approach.* (White paper). Center for Creative Leadership. Retrieved from https://www.ccl.org/articles/ white-papers/leadership-development-beyond-competencies-moving-to-a -holistic-approach/

Center for
Creative
Leadership·

ABOUT THE CENTER FOR CREATIVE LEADERSHIP

The Center for Creative Leadership (CCL) is a top-ranked, global provider of leadership development. By leveraging the power of leadership to drive results that matter most to clients, CCL transforms individual leaders, teams, organizations, and society. Its array of cutting-edge solutions is steeped in extensive research and experience gained from working with hundreds of thousands of leaders at all levels. Ranked among the world's top providers of executive education by the *Financial Times* and *Bloomberg BusinessWeek*, CCL has US offices in Greensboro, NC; Colorado Springs, CO; and San Diego, CA. Outside the United States, CCL operates worldwide from offices in Brussels, Belgium; Moscow, Russia; Addis Ababa, Ethiopia; Johannesburg, South Africa; Singapore; Gurgaon, India; and Shanghai, China.

CCL PRESS IDEAS INTO ACTION SERIES

The Ideas into Action Series of books draws on the practical knowledge that the Center for Creative Leadership continues to develop in its work with leaders at all levels and in all types of organizations. The series' purpose is to provide leaders with specific advice on how to complete a developmental task or solve a leadership challenge. Books in the series (more than 60 at present) cover a wide range of topics, including feedback, coaching, team leadership, conflict, influence, resilience, learning from experience, and others.

Ordering Information

To get more information, to order books in the Ideas into Action Series, or to find out about bulk-order discounts, please contact us by phone at 336-545-2810 or visit our online bookstore at http://solutions.ccl.org/books/ccl -press-publications/ideas-into-action-guidebook-series.

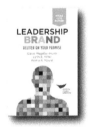

INDEX

humility, executive image building and, 200

humor, executive image building and, 199

Hurricane Katrina, 461–462

Hurricane Sandy, 10

I

"Ignorance is the Enemy Within" (Walker), 110

imagery

    for communication, 257

    promotion through, 354

    vision creation and, 430

imagination, innovation and, 254

imaging, in organizational culture, 274

immigration, flexibility about, 222

impact, competencies of, 41

improvisation, executive image building and, 200

impulse control, interpersonal skills and, 265

inclusion, development of, 177–182

    problem solving and, 308

inclusive language, communication and use of, 13

Industrial Light And Magic, 170

influence skills

    barriers to, 19–20

    change acceptance and, 89

    as core competency, 7–8, 17–23

    development of, 22

    interpersonal skills and, 266

    self-coaching in, 20–21

infographics, self-awareness, 34

information gathering

    business development and, 65

    strategic planning and, 366

initiative

    barriers to, 247–248

    leadership and, 245–251

innovation, 253–259

    barriers to, 255–256

    future leadership development and, 499

    problem solving and, 308

    risk taking and, 339

in-person meetings, 97

inspiration, balance and sources of, 47

Institute of the Future, 498–499

integrity

    development of, 151–157

    future leadership development and, 499

    interpersonal skills and, 265–267

interdependencies, creation of, 358

Interface company, 280

international professional development, 182

    global perspectives, 229–235

International Space Station, 238, 456

interpersonal skills

    barriers to development of, 263–264

    change management and, 95–96

    compassion and sensitivity and, 109–111, 113–114

    development of, 261–267, 433–439

    difference, diversity and inclusion and, 177

    problems with, 467–472

    relationship management and, 312–317

    team building and, 389

    tolerance for ambiguity and, 405

    trust and, 409–416

    trust skills and, 413

    vision creation and, 430

introductions, relationship management and, 316

invitations, boundary spanning and, 55

Iran, EU military agreement with, 230

Irvine, Ian, 26

J

"Jane The Concussion Slayer," 320

job descriptions, 129

Jobvite, 109

Johannsen, Bob, 498–500

joint ventures, 208

journaling

    decision making and, 164

    organizational skills and, 300

Juniper Networks, 410

K

Kahn, Salman, 304

Kahn Academy, 303–304

Kaiser Permanente, 178

S

MOVE FROM ASSESSMENT TO ACTION FASTER THAN EVER.

CCL COMPASS™

CCL's exclusive, on-demand digital tool provides you with a quick visual reference of your assessment data, as well as customized real-time development tips and strategies to support your growth goals.

Available for use with CCL's Benchmarks® for Managers™ and Skillscope.

Explore all the options CCL Compass has to offer at www.ccl.org/compass

One new platform. A multitude of benefits.

Speed:	Clarity:	Convenience:	Effectiveness:
Go immediately from receiving an assessment feedback report to putting a plan into action.	Understand assessment data and streamline the goal planning process.	Get on-demand, relevant answers to your leadership development questions.	Improve motivation and outcomes from your work as a leader or executive coach.

CCL ASSESSMENTS

Benchmarks® Suite

CCL pioneered the use of assessments and feedback in leadership development decades ago. Since then, CCL has earned the trust of thousands of organizations worldwide for our assessments and feedback. Providing an array of proven and simple to self-administer tools, CCL supports all your assessment initiatives with our dedicated staff, cutting edge research, and development expertise.

Millions of leaders.

Thousands of organizations.

Hundreds of countries.

One source for leadership assessments.

Center for Creative Leadership®

All CCL assessments are supported by our knowledgeable product specialists. If you need assistance defining objectives, selecting an assessment, training facilitators, administering and interpreting data or development planning, email info@ccl.org or call +1 800 780 1031.

Get certified with CCL's

360° Assessment
Certification Workshop.

Power Up 360 Potential

360-degree assessments are widely used for leadership and talent development.

Employers, coaches, and consultants can help talent at all levels:

Identify skill caps and create development plans.

Recognize strengths and ways to leverage them.

Prepare for next steps and new opportunities.

What do participants learn?

1. Reading and interpreting reports.

2. Facilitating a feedback session.

3. Connecting feedback to goal setting.

4. Customizing assessments based on competencies and organizational needs.

5. Administering assessments the CCL way.

www.ccl.org/acw | info@ccl.org | +1 336 545 2810

CPSIA information can be obtained
at www.ICGtesting.com
Printed in the USA
FSHW01n1405200918

9 781604 916515